THE PHANTOM OF THE OPEN

Scott Murray writes for the *Guardian*, *FourFourTwo* and *America Online*. He has also written for the *Observer*, *GQ*, *Men's Health*, *Sport* and *Shortlist*. He is the author of *Day of the Match: A History of Football in 365 Days* and *Football for Dummies*.

Simon Farnaby has starred in the films *Your Highness*, *Burke and Hare* and *Bunny and the Bull*, on which he also wrote. He has also starred in the television shows *The Mighty Boosh*, *Jam and Jerusalem*, *Spoons*, *Angelo's*, *Blunder* and the incomparable *Horrible Histories*.

The pair also co-wrote E4's *Golf War*, the great lost sitcom of the fairways and airwaves.

THE PHANTOM
OF THE OPEN

Maurice Flitcroft,
The World's Worst Golfer

Scott Murray & Simon Farnaby

YELLOW JERSEY PRESS
LONDON

Published by Yellow Jersey Press 2010

2 4 6 8 10 9 7 5 3 1

First published in Great Britain in 2010 by
Yellow Jersey Press
Random House, 20 Vauxhall Bridge Road,
London SW1V 2SA

www.rbooks.co.uk

Addresses for companies within The Random House Group Limited
can be found at: www.randomhouse.co.uk/offices.htm

The Random House Group Limited Reg. No. 954009

A CIP catalogue record for this book
is available from the British Library

ISBN 9780224083164

The Random House Group Limited supports The Forest Stewardship
Council (FSC), the leading international forest certification organisation.
All our titles that are printed on Greenpeace approved FSC certified
paper carry the FSC logo. Our paper procurement policy can be
found at www.rbooks.co.uk/environment

Mixed Sources
Product group from well-managed
forests and other controlled sources
www.fsc.org   Cert no. TT-COC-2139
© 1996 Forest Stewardship Council
FSC

Typeset by Palimpsest Book Production Limited
Falkirk, Stirlingshire

Printed and bound in Great Britain by
Clays Ltd, St Ives plc

For
Alexander Murray and Margaret Murray
and
Jeff Farnaby and Barbara Farnaby

Contents

Introduction: The Warm Up

'WE DON'T get very many visitors here,' announces Trevor Kirkwood, as he wheels around the avenues of Barrow-in-Furness, Cumbria's number-one industrial port. 'People don't pass through it on their way to somewhere else either. We call it the insular peninsula, the longest cul-de-sac in Europe. It's said that Barrow's not quite the end of the world . . . but you can see it from here.'

Well, we can *sort* of see it: we're in the back of Trevor's van, rattling around alongside detritus from his print and photo stall in Barrow's indoor market: pieces of a broken photocopier, some *Buffy the Vampire Slayer* posters, a signed photo of The Jam, a box of XXXL replica rugby league shirts. Trevor has kindly agreed to show us Barrow's sights. Or, more specifically, the one-time stomping grounds of his old friend, the late, great Maurice Flitcroft: the man who shot a failure-redefining 121 in the greatest golf championship of them all, the man who would go down in history as the Phantom of the Open.

Trevor has been friends since school – four decades past – with Maurice's twin sons, the impressively monickered James Harlequin Flitcroft and Gene Van Flitcroft. Abandoned as a baby and brought up in a children's home near the Flitcroft family terrace, the resulting stigma in the less-enlightened Sixties led young Trevor to be shunned by most of the local kids and parents alike. Maurice, however, invited Trevor in to play with his sons. A glass of squash, a biscuit and a spot on the carpet in front of the TV was always on offer *chez* Flitcroft.

'Maurice didn't care that I was different; he always had time for me,' remembers Trevor. 'In some ways he was the dad I never had.' The moving eulogy is tempered only by the discomfort of our touring vehicle. The heater isn't working, a major flaw while driving through this chilly appendage to the Lake District. It is freezing and soaking, and no wonder: the Barrow peninsula pokes out into the Irish Sea from the most remote point on England's far north-west coast, miles from Carlisle, inaccessible to Blackpool, and ostracised from the tourist traps of the Lake District.

We chug through rainy red-brick terraced streets, then past grimy blackened tenements. All the while, a miserable grey sky grumbles aggressively overhead, almost as though it's about to accuse someone of spilling its pint. We drive down Laurence Avenue, passing the tiny gun-metal-grey council house where Maurice lived all his life with his loyal wife Jean and the twins. We visit the meagre strips of boggy waste-land where Maurice spent hours practising his short game. And we swing through the rusty shipyard where

2

he toiled as a crane operator, his old workplace now dwarfed by titanic iron hangars hiding nuclear submarines from prying eyes in the spurious interests of national security.

'When you left school in Maurice's time it was either the shipyard or the shipyard,' explains Trevor. 'The place needed twenty thousand men to work it. So if you were a lad from Barrow this is where you went. They called them shipyard fodder.' The last place, then, where you'd expect to discover a future champion of the Open. And, alas, it still is. But by God, Maurice Flitcroft tried his damnedest to put Barrow on the golfing map.

He was a working-class man from Barrow who tried as hard as he could to avoid becoming 'shipyard fodder'. Harbouring artistic ambitions since childhood, he tried his hand at painting, songwriting and poetry. He even toured for a summer in a high-diving comedy troupe in the Sixties. But he was always drawn, ineluctably, back to the shipyard. Until, that is, he was bitten by the golfing bug in 1974. The experience would change his life.

Within two years, he had chanced his way into the Open and carded the worst-ever round in the tournament's 116-year history, his score of 121 a depth unlikely to be plumbed ever again. In retrospect, it wasn't too much of a surprise: he had never before played a full round of golf in his life. The press had a field day, and golf reporters nationwide revelled in the oddity.

But the Royal & Ancient Golf Club of St Andrews,

the game's governing body and the organisers of the Open Championship, took a much dimmer view of Maurice's antics. Humiliated by a mere hacker bodyswerving his way past the entry regulations and into their prestigious tournament, the R&A did everything in their power to make sure Maurice would never make a monkey of them again.

Never one to shy away from a fight, Maurice responded to the R&A's punches with a couple of jabs of his own, and for the next decade-and-a-half the two traded blows. R&A secretary Keith Mackenzie escalated the row into a personal vendetta, while Maurice deliberately turned it into a farcical game of cat-and-mouse. Determining to secure a place in the Open by any means possible, he cast himself as David taking on the R&A's Goliath. Observers might paint him as a modern-day Don Quixote, a deluded fool, tilting his nine-iron at the sacred windmills of the R&A.

Maurice's battle would not be limited to the golf course, often spilling over into the mean streets of Barrow. 'People would throw stuff at him and call him names when he went to practise in his check trousers, diamond jumper and his bobble hat,' says Trevor. 'People just didn't behave like that in Barrow. He totally divided the town. Half of them thought he was a pillock, but the other half, including me, loved him for showing you could do something different with your life.'

Maurice's sons, James and Gene, would be blessed with this approach to life, too, taking the scenic route whenever possible. James claims to have won the 1984 Malibu World Disco Dancing Championship, only to have the title wrested from his grasp after some off-floor politicking involving an unnamed coke-addled record producer, several ladies of the night, and a six-foot-two dancer called Venal John. ('Why was he called Venal John?' we asked him. The reply was straight to the point: 'Cos he were, y'know, venal.') His pseudonym for this escapade was Paris Ventura. Meanwhile Gene – a dancer too, trading under the brand Troy Atlantis – had the added distinction of having caddied for 1971 and 1972 British Open champion Lee Trevino at the 1990 Open at St Andrews.

But, alas, Paris and Troy's glamorous escapades have long since been replaced by James and Gene's episodic bursts of booze-fuelled bleak farce. Their *Saturday Night Fever* mojo long gone by the turn of the millennium, the Flitcroft juniors were awarded the UK's very first ASBI [anti-social behaviour injunction] after sword-fighting each other in their back garden. The pair starred in an episode of Channel Five's Jerry Springer-lite show *Trisha* entitled 'I hate my twin!', James detailing how he had slept with nearly 400 women and once had his leg broken by his golf-club-wielding brother. ('He were too quick for me, he used to be a boxer,' he said with a smile, a strange sibling pride oozing from every pore.) And both men spent the 1990s and 2000s systematically picking up bans from just about every pub in Barrow and the town's immediate surrounds, as a result of their wholesale commitment to creative drinking.

Trevor drops us off at our hotel, and informs us that the twins have agreed to an evening out with us to talk about their dad – as long as we buy the drinks, which is fair enough. Maurice died in 2007, so all that is left are the memories of his sons and a few friends – principally Trevor and his partner Karen Storr, a Cumbrian artist who in 2007 staged a stunning photographic exhibition, *At Home with the Flitcrofts*, which essayed the idiosyncratic lives of Maurice, James and Gene. Maurice was so fond of Karen that, days before he died, he entrusted to her his prized possession – a faded 400-page manuscript. It was his memoir, initially handwritten and typed up onto foolscap by his late wife Jean, variously entitled *The Phantom of the Open*, *The Golfer Who Tried*, *Golfer Extraordinary* and *The Artful Golfer*. In a collective act of criminal literary neglect, the publishing world inexplicably turned down this sprawling epic when it was touted around in the early 1990s. Maurice's words have therefore never seen the light of day – until now, with James, Gene and Karen granting us exclusively the right to quote from the manuscript, so this unique story may be told.

'My dad should have a statue erected to him,' says Gene, midway through what becomes a Homeric evening of booze-fuelled debauch. He's tottering unsurely on his feet outside Barrow's busy Duke of Edinburgh hotel bar, which is relatively new and hasn't got round to banning him yet. He's gesticulating wildly at a bronze tribute to the town's other much-loved and much-missed sporting son, the late footballer

Emlyn Hughes. 'I mean, what did he ever do?' wonders Gene as he flicks his cigarette towards the two-time European-Cup-winning captain of Liverpool, England and *A Question of Sport*.

The main event of the evening is a Northern Soul night Trevor has helped organise at a local cricket club. Our presence there lasts around two seconds, if that, with Gene instantly dispatched back through the door. 'That were quick, even for him,' notes Trevor with a resigned sigh, one eyebrow raised. After a long search, we eventually find a pub willing to allow the twins to remain on the premises. It is in an area of town known to locals as the Gaza Strip. 'The Flitcroft brothers are in the house!' announces the DJ. It's a seemingly surreal touch, but these lads are notorious. Within seconds, they are surrounded by – there is no other way of putting this – a bevy of buxom beauties, who all want to see the pair's best moves. James and Gene glide across the dancefloor, light on their toes despite their advancing years. After his dismissal from the cricket club, it is the second time tonight Gene's feet don't appear to have touched the carpet.

Towards the end of the evening, Gene goes AWOL. A few frantic phone calls are made, before Trevor finally locates our fallen soldier. He's been taken home by kindly and long-suffering police officers after being found wandering aimlessly around the street.

'He's absolutely fine,' reports Trevor. 'This much I know because he's claiming to have slept with one of the policewomen.'

The morning after, with heavy heads but lighter

hearts, Trevor takes us on another whistle-stop tour of Maurice-in-Furness, around a few old haunts we'd failed to take in the previous afternoon. There's a rugby league ground where Maurice would clatter long irons between the posts and occasionally get into fights. There's an old abbey ruin, the National Trust's least-popular property in the country, and perfect for working on his driving. And then there's Sandy Gap on Walney Island.

Walney is a 14x1-mile behemoth plonked in the sea alongside Barrow. A middle-class enclave, it is home to Vickerstown, built in the early 1900s by local shipyard magnates Vickers to house their workers, and the Furness Golf Club, the area's most windswept and interesting course. Maurice was never allowed on to play, not that he could afford it. Instead, he headed for the vast dunes of Sandy Gap. As do we, tumbling out of Trevor's van into a full-force gale.

'The least-visited seaside resort in the British Isles!' offers Trevor with a proud grin just about visible as the rain lashes his wide moustachioed face.

'This is a *resort*?'

We stop to take some seaside snaps. Sandy Gap is a place so windy we have to lean on each other to keep the camera steady, a human tripod. So it was over this barren vista, a good one-hour walk from his home, where the tide comes in so quickly you literally have to run to get away from it, that Maurice practised his long game?

'Oh yeah, he had no other option,' chirps Trevor, ignoring the sideways, coat-penetrating rain. 'It was the only place where he could guarantee he wouldn't hit anyone. He would spend hours here in all weathers. He nearly drowned a few times, but he were bloody good out of bunkers!'

Which, of course, he wasn't. There's a pretty strong argument to be made, as we shall see, that Maurice Flitcroft was the world's worst golfer. But there's a counterclaim, too: OK, he didn't exactly boast the golfing ability of a Golden Bear or Tiger, but painting him as a cartoon oaf, a personification of hopelessness, is an outrageous slight on a wildly creative and talented man. Either way, though, debating Maurice's sporting skillset spectacularly misses the point. What was important was that Maurice tried. And, by God, did he try.

Out

WHITE COURSE   **FORMBY GOLF CLUB**   PAR 72

(Standard Scratch Score 72)

Player _Maurice G. Flitcroft_   Competition _1976 Open Qualifier_

Handicap _n/a_   Date _2nd July 1976_

Marker's Score	Hole	Length in Metres	Length in Yards	Score	Strokes Rec'd	Par	Won + Lost - Halved 0 Points	Marker's Score	Hole	Length in Metres	Length in Yards	Score	Strokes Rec'd	Par	Won + Lost - Halved 0 Points
	1	370	405	7	12	4			10	469	513		4	5	
	2	348	381	5	7	4			11	355	388		11	4	
	3	466	510	6	3	5			12	372	407		5	4	
	4	286	313	6	14	4			13	349	382		15	4	
	5	148	162	6	17	3			14	384	420		9	4	
	6	370	405	6	6	4			15	369	403		2	4	
	7	453	495	12?	1	5			16	113	124		18	3	
	8	316	346	6	10	4			17	432	472		8	4	
	9	166	182	7	16	3			18	358	392		13	4	
Out		2923	3199	61		36		In		3201	3501			36	
								Out		2925	3199			36	
								Total		6127	6700			72	

Holes won _____

Holes lost _____   Handicap [ ]

Result _____   Nett [ ]

Players's Signature _____   Marker's Signature _____

PLEASE REPLACE DIVOTS

Hole 1: Mean streets and hard-earned treats

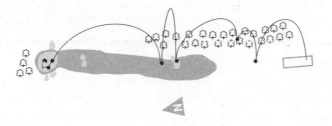

MAURICE TIED his shoelaces as best he could and pulled his socks up to his knees. They were far too big for him, he thought. In fact, everything was too big for him. His shorts settled near his ankles, his tie almost dragged apologetically along the floor, and the rim of his cap fell well below his eyes unless pulled back every few seconds. It wasn't ideal but it would have to do. This was young Maurice Flitcroft's first day at school, and nothing would stop him enjoying it.

Maurice Gerald Flitcroft was born on 23 November 1929 at 67 Robert Street, West Gorton, Manchester. His mother's name was Olive Mabel. His father Herbert was a bus driver. He was the middle child of five brothers, and they all lived together in a quiet, cobble-stoned street lined with identical redbrick terraced houses distinguishable only by the occupant's choice of curtains.

He was a tiny baby, and as he grew – slowly, and in an almost haphazard angular fashion, all elbows and knees – it quickly became clear the description 'wiry' would forever be used to describe him. Even through his adult years he would maintain this diminutive figure, only ever reaching a waist size of 26 inches. (His son Gene would reminisce in 2009 that 'he was a huge man, my dad, six foot two he was, hands like shovels', but pride distorts; Maurice was five foot seven in his golf shoes.) But what he lacked in stature he made up for with energy. 'Me mother used to call me Hoppy as a small kid, Hoppy Johnny she'd call me,' he told Dick Nelson of American network WGVU-TV-35 in 1988, 'cos I was always hopping and skipping around the place like a rabbit.' Given Maurice's future sporting misadventures, old Mrs F's bunny comparison was eerily prescient.

Like all rabbits, Maurice never felt comfortable with city life and craved open spaces where he could gambol and frolic. One such area was a small croft near the family home, about an acre in size, which would become the stage for his first brush with the law – a taster of what would become a regular occurrence in his life.

Maurice claims not to have known that the croft was, in fact, private land, but one summer's night in 1933, this fact was made plain to him in no uncertain terms. That evening, during a peaceful game of 'pitch and toss' with other children on the croft, the area was stormed by police. Maurice, below average in dimension, slipped through a gap in a neighbour's fence and hid in the backyard. Others weren't so lucky. 'Struggles took place and arrests were made,' he recalled. 'It was exciting and amusing, although why the police would make such a to-do about what seemed to be a rather dull game I've no idea.' It was the first time Flitcroft found himself chased from a grassy area by men in uniform while wondering exactly what he had done wrong and what their effing problem was; it would be by no means his last.

Maurice's father, Herbert Flitcroft, was an honest and hard-working man. He kept pigeons in the yard, and enjoyed reading, listening to plays, opera and the news on the wireless, and swimming. The family would enjoy occasional trips to the cinema and regular walks through the Belle Vue Zoological Gardens. The walks were some of Maurice's most treasured memories from his early childhood. He would replay them in his mind with great fondness, especially as they would soon become faded, like a silent film reel, by the outbreak of war. Decades later, as the cherished moments became ever more distant, he would describe the scenes in the gardens as 'being very much like the painting *Sunday afternoon on the Île de la Grande Jatte* by the French Impressionist Georges Seurat'. For a working-class man with no classical education, Maurice's knowledge of art and literature was impressive, every inch the Barrow bohemian.

'Oh he always had his head in some book or other,'

said his son Gene. 'He especially loved art and pictures and that.'

In summer, the family would enjoy trips to the countryside where they would engage in epic games of 'armies' with other children. These games would start off friendly but become more serious and life-like, resulting in the very real threat of extreme physical violence by one little soldier to another. Yet no matter how heated these battles became, a temporary ceasefire would be declared when Mrs Flitcroft turned up with ice creams. As Maurice noted, 'One cannot enjoy the full flavour of a red, green or yellow cone-shaped lollipop while being so energetically engaged in mock mortal combat.'

Maurice realised early on that bigger children were wont to regard him as easy pickings because of his size. Lacking physical strength, he'd need to acquire super-human mental skills if he was to survive the mean streets of Manchester. And he got the chance to test these powers before he'd even started school.

Returning home from the local shop one day, having taken his usual short-cut down an alleyway, he was confronted by a boy of eight, twice his age and size, and was asked rather impolitely to relinquish his handful of sweeties. The more the thief pushed and cajoled Maurice to open his hand, the tighter his grip became. As the bully began to attack him physically, with a few thumps in the solar plexus, Maurice simply closed his eyes and stood there, taking the punishment in silence. He hoped to bamboozle 'the Juvenile Highwayman', as Maurice called the bully in his memoir. If he stood his ground, maybe the tyrant would get tired and go away, a junior version of the rope-a-dope technique, made famous by Muhammad Ali in the Rumble in the Jungle.

But unlike George Foreman, Maurice's attacker didn't tire. Instead he began to enjoy himself, hoofing and flinging the poor little mite around the back streets like an old sock. At one point, the bully wedged young Maurice's head in a drain and pressed on his face with the sole of his shoe while concurrently trying to prise open his fist. Maurice took the punishment in silence, theorising that any cries of pain were unlikely to encourage the Highwayman to eschew a belief system that saw the meting out of torture rewarded with tasty sweeties. Eventually, his stoicism was rewarded when one of his brothers turned up and chased the bully away. A beaten and bruised Maurice shared his well-protected spoils with his saviour: three white mice and a couple of midget gems. Not much of a celebratory feast, but it was a defining moment in young Maurice's personal development, an act of defiance that provided him with the confidence to begin school without fear, having stood up to the Dick Turpin of the alleys.

And so Maurice tucked his shirt into his voluminous shorts, adjusted his cap and tie, and pulled his socks up one last time before leaving home for his first day at school. He waited for his older brother Roy to leave the house and followed him out shortly afterwards. Maintaining a respectful distance behind Roy, he reached the school some twenty minutes later.

As there appeared to be no spare seat for Maurice, he took up a position on a small bench at the back of the class and waited patiently for the learning to begin.

Ten minutes later, a kerfuffle was heard at the door and the headmaster made a rare appearance. Seeing the rest of the class stand to rigid attention Maurice followed suit. 'Is there a Maurice Flitcroft in the room?' asked the head, who to the school debutant appeared to be about 25 foot tall. Maurice declined to answer. The tone of the headmaster's voice engendered a feeling within him that, should he own up, the resulting events would not be to his liking, nor cause any pleasurable physical or mental sensation. 'Roy! Have you seen your brother this morning?'

'No, sir,' Maurice's elder brother replied shakily. Maurice held firm. Perhaps this will play out all right after all, he thought.

'Mrs Flitcroft, please step inside,' asked the head-master. To his surprise, Maurice saw his distraught mum enter the room. 'Do you see Maurice in here, Mrs Flitcroft?' Olive frantically scanned the children to no avail. Then, sensing a better perspective was required, she knelt down and scanned the gaps between the grubby knees. Suddenly, and much to her relief, she spotted a familiar nose and mouth beneath an over-sized cloth cap, much like the one her husband Herbert owned.

'Ah, there he is! Sorry about this!' she exclaimed as she zig-zagged her way to the back of the class and swept Maurice into her grateful arms. She paused to apologise to the headmaster on her way out. He in turn furrowed his brow into a frown, but couldn't keep up the pretence, almost immediately letting a smile play across his face as he shook the tiny hand in mock formality.

'Very nice to meet you, young Maurice,' he said. 'I just hope you have the same enthusiasm for learning once you reach the legal age to attend school. See you next year!' And with that, Olive Flitcroft whisked the errant interloper back home for a stern telling off, and some egg mixed with bread in a cup.

'I just couldn't wait to start,' recalled Maurice some seventy years later. 'Mother had to come and pick me up several times after that. I had a thirst for knowledge.' When he was finally allowed to stay in school the following year, Maurice found it a doddle. 'I took to it like a duck takes to the water,' he claimed with typical modesty.

But the halcyon days of Manchester were short lived. One day, his father cut his thumb on some chipped crockery. Though Herbert thought nothing of it at the time, the wound soon became septic, hospitalising him for two months. In the days before penicillin was freely available, the lay-off meant that he lost his job on the buses. When he eventually recovered, he spread his net wide in the search for work. Eventually the family settled in the Lancastrian town of Barrow-in-Furness, with Herbert finding employment in the shipyards. Maurice himself was forced to start a new school, which meant subjecting himself to the human hacky sack treatment all over again.

Hole 2: The gap between hope and reality

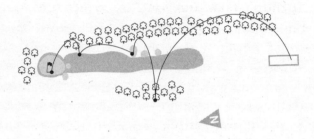

MAURICE HAD barely turned seven years old, but his face was settling into a distinctive old-fashioned form. It was already beginning to resemble the one that would be carried years later on photographs by nerve-racked R&A officials the length and breadth of the country. A long narrow nose separated two large bulging eyes, which protruded from sunken eye sockets. His mouth was a tiny pillar box, set back deep into his chops, making it difficult for a casual observer of his face to discern the presence of any teeth. (In later years, Maurice would have nearly every molar smashed out in a diving accident. Often he wouldn't bother wearing the false set he was given to replace them, because he thought he 'pretty much looked the same' with them in or out.) But his most

striking feature were his ears, which protruded farci-
cally from the side of his head like two halves of a
cheap radar dish, presumably positioned by some
mischievous gene to detect the nearest trouble and
instruct the brain to head straight for it.

With the family Flitcroft now denizens of Barrow,
Maurice was packed off to Rawlinson Street Junior
School. It didn't take him long to attract the attention of bullies and other assorted little eejits, all of
whom would be wont to tease him with the usual
height slurs, now accompanied by ear-referencing
monickers showcasing varied levels of wit and imagination: the Goblin, Wingnut and the common-or-
garden Big Ears were three of the most popular. It
was again time for young Maurice to take a stand –
but unlike on the back streets of Manchester, this time,
the human punchbag would swing back.

As the bell sounded to end playtime one morning,
and the children queued up to be allowed back into
the school hut, a large boy regarded widely as 'the
cock of the class' made the mistake of pushing
'Wingnut' out of the line. Maurice stumbled slightly,
but ignored him, rejoining the line at the back,
refusing to rise to the bait. The Cock, not used to
being ignored by jug-eared squirts, followed Maurice
to the rear and shoved him out of line again. It was
a none-too-subtle attempt to attract the attention of
the teacher and get 'Luggy' into trouble. A gauntlet
having been thrown down twice, it was time for the
little man to step up to the plate and let The Cock
know who and what he was messing with: 'I responded

by turning and slapping him hard in the face and inviting him to meet me after school behind the Waterloo Hotel across the road.'

During the afternoon, the entire school crackled with expectation of the impending fight. At the allotted time, behind the Waterloo Hotel, Wingnut and The Cock squared up to each other in front of a large crowd of baying spectators. They were disappointed at first: Maurice's rope-a-dope technique may have been vaguely effective for self-preservation, but it was no crowd-pleaser. Finally, sensing the need to do something to lift the atmosphere, Maurice began to strike out, haphazardly at first as he had his eyes closed, but he soon enough located his target. To Maurice's delight the crowd loved his offensive efforts, cheering on the little man for all they were worth. But whipping the audience up into such a fervour would seek to bring about the final bell sooner than expected. 'Things were just starting to warm up nicely,' reported Maurice, 'when the roar of the crowd – goading, encouraging, inciting – attracted the attention of the hotel's landlady who, brandishing a broom, told us to break it up and go home, or else. Well, children were more respectful in those days than they are now, so we did as we were told.' Still, for Maurice, the job was done. The nicknames stuck, but were now tempered with affection. And The Cock never bothered him again.

Independence of mind came naturally to Maurice, but its supplementary fearlessness was occasionally less beneficial to his well-being. Maurice was proving himself an indomitable soul, which would explain a litany of medical catastrophes, including broken noses, burst eardrums and broken arms. If there was a tree that seemed unclimbable, Maurice would scale it – and then fall out of it. If there was a canal notorious for danger, Maurice would dive headlong into it – and burst his head open like a bag of crisps.

All challenges, physical or mental, were met head on. Before he could face plummeting head-first into canals, Maurice was forced to conquer a deep-seated fear of water. The sight of a mere puddle would send him into shivers, and he'd regularly have to sit out of swimming class at school. So, as a determined eight-year-old, he set about ridding himself of his phobia. 'I overcame this fear quite simply by lying in a bath of tap water, taking a deep breath, holding it and ducking my head under,' he explained, describing how he would force himself to hold his head in the tub for a few extra seconds every night, only emerging when total panic had set in.

After a few weeks, he got a little braver. 'I soon progressed to opening my eyes underwater,' he recalled, 'which is why the water must be clear, not soapy, as soapy water will make your eyes sting and smart and perhaps discourage you from continuing with the exercise.' His description had segued from personal account into positivity seminar for the benefit of aquaphobes worldwide. Maurice considered the episode as pivotal in his development as a human being, and he was sure children or even adults could benefit from literally diving headlong into his water-conquering technique. 'A word of warning,' he added. 'Be sure that you are well clear of the taps when using this method, to avoid hitting your head on them when you raise it out of the water.'

It was a lesson clearly learned the hard way. But Maurice didn't stop there. Now he'd beaten his fear of what he melodramatically referred to as 'The Blue Watery Vagueness', the child could not rest. 'The next step for me was to become a competent diver. This in the course of time I did – but not in the bath.' In years to come he would value water-based leisure pastimes second only to golf. 'Swimming, like golf, is something you can do on your own. You don't need to be a member of a team to enjoy it.' And, of course, solo pursuits allow participants to judge how good they've been based on arbitrary criteria set down in their own head.

Maurice began to flourish intellectually towards the end of primary school. His reading soon graduated from the whizzo works of D.C. Thomson – the *Dandy*, *Wizard* and the *Beano* – to the more cerebral output of William Shakespeare, Charles Dickens and Renaissance author and poet Giovanni Boccaccio. Every inch the prodigy – he was only *ten years old* – Maurice would read and re-read these works again and again, along with the western novels of Zane Grey and the spine-tingling thrillers of Sax Rohmer, the creator of Fu Manchu. He listed among his favourites the mysteries of Edgar Wallace, *The Three Muskateers* by Alexandre Dumas, the foreign legion tales of P.C. Wren and *The Coral Island* by R.M. Ballantyne. For the pre-teenage son of a shipyard worker in late-1930s Barrow, this was exotic fare and marked Maurice down as something different. It is safe to say that The Cock's reading list would not have contained any doomed romantic legends penned in fourteenth-century Italy.

Here was a well-read boy, although he preferred to read for pleasure rather than academic success. 'If I was interested in a subject I would listen and pay attention; if I wasn't interested I would pass the time drawing caricatures of other pupils and teachers, who I considered worthy and suitable subjects for my artistic intentions.' Maurice further demonstrated his independence when he decided, against the advice of his teachers, to sit his eleven-plus exam. While his teachers (and even his parents) didn't think Maurice would make the grade, he felt he belonged with the cream of Barrow's youth at Alfred Barrow Grammar School for boys. In truth, he was mainly attracted not to the quality of teaching on offer, but rather to the extensive playing fields over which he could give his spindly legs free rein. He could also picture himself cutting a dash in the school's fancy cap and blazer. Whatever the allure, to everyone's astonishment, Maurice passed the exam with flying colours.

This triumph would, sadly, be short-lived: Maurice soon had to uproot his life again with the outbreak of the Second World War on 3 September 1939. Barrow was the home of the naval construction arm of Vickers-Armstrong Ltd, one of the most renowned warship manufacturers in the world. The town therefore was brought to the attention of a Mr Adolf Hitler and his Luftwaffe squadrons. After Maurice's home was bombed out – the family survived by taking shelter under the stairs – it was felt that the children should be evacuated to a safe haven.

To this end, Maurice would spend the next four years in the Lake District town of Kendal, his guardian a Mrs Langhorn. It was to prove an eventful period, which began with the forced acquisition of yet another unfortunate nickname from his new classmates at Kendal Grammar School. Popular at the time was a poster warning of the dangers of unexploded bombs. In it, a cheeky cartoon personification of a torpedo – Firebomb Fritz, with his bomb-shaped nose, landmine eyes and wings for ears – wagged his finger as a warning not to come near him. His new school friends noted a startling similarity between Maurice and the impish anthropomorphised incendiary, and so during his stay in the Lakes he would forever be known as Firebomb Fritz, Fritz or simply The Firebomb. Maurice would, during his golfing career, garner many nicknames, such as The Open Joker, The R&A Rabbit and The Phantom of the Open. It is something of a shame that nobody picked up on The Firebomb, fizzing over the hallowed turf of the R&A as he would later do, undetected, unexploded, before detonating a hysterical frenzy of shanks and snap-hooks, shrapnels of embarrassment whizzing through the clubhouse at St Andrews, eventually razing the reputations of golf's top administrators to rubble.

Soon after arriving in Kendal, Maurice joined the

Boy Scouts and found once again that he had a flair
for pretty much whatever he turned his hand to. With
an annual parade only days away, the drum major in
the Scouts' marching band, responsible for flinging a
heavy mace into the air, making it perform elaborate
twirls and revolutions, was taken ill. The Scoutmaster,
an experienced mace thrower, was prepared to step
in himself, but Maurice begged to be given an opportunity. Despite initial misgivings, Maurice's persistence
– he considered it 'a challenge not to be ignored' –
ensured he was entrusted with this most vital of tasks.

Taking a mace home, he practised day and night
in order to replicate the feats usually performed by
the stricken drum major. Soon realising that Mrs
Langhorn's front room was too small and generally
ill-equipped for hurling a four-foot mace – a point
made with some directness by his guardian as she
swept up two broken china cups – Maurice took to
the local playing fields to hone his skills. The difficulty of top-quality mace-throwing soon became
apparent. 'Performing this feat standing still was one
thing. Doing it whilst marching was something else!'
And all this while surrounded by 'a veritable confusion of drummers and flautists'.

Despite all the hours of practice, Maurice had a
back-up plan should he find himself accidentally
knocking another child's teeth out with a 48-inch metal
pole. In such circumstances, he'd simply recite the
Scout Law – to 'smile and whistle under all difficulties' – and exhale a cheery trill through a fixed rictus.
But he needn't have been concerned. The march was

a triumph. In fact, after a couple of early nervous fumbles, he soon got so confident that he performed the most difficult sections of his throwing act 'whenever and wherever the spectators that lined the route were most numerous'. He also notes with great pride that 'in the days that followed, I learned that my showmanship was the talk of the town, which I must say I found very gratifying. But being of a modest nature, I didn't let it go to my head.' It was further evidence of Maurice's innate showmanship. Perhaps more crucially, it was his first taste of fame. Certainly the episode has some parallels with his later pursuit of golfing excellence – the hours spent brushing up his talent on school playing fields, by way of example – although his adroit twirling of a mace was never quite matched by his handling of a golf club.

It was also during his Kendal sabbatical that Maurice began his fateful love affair with the world of sport. Rarely was there a discipline in which, according to his own record, he failed to show a remarkable talent as soon as he stepped onto the field of play. Cricket? 'I showed a natural ability for it. I finished the season with the best bowling average.' Track and field? 'I acquitted myself spectacularly at all of them and even won a couple come Sports Day.'

He gave himself a particularly hearty slap on the back for his rugby skills. 'What I lacked in knowledge and experience, I more than made up for in enthusiasm.' He recalls how in the very first game he played, he did his usual trick of switching off whenever a teacher was explaining the rules to a game: 'I would often stare into the distance with a faraway expression on my face. Daydreaming, my teachers called it.' Consequently when the game started, the daydreamer was somewhat stunned to see bodies everywhere, arms and limbs flying all over the place, contorted in unspeakable angles and trapped under sweaty writhing piles of flesh and bone. Despite his confusion, he decided to join in with gusto. Upon seeing the ball pop out of a thing called a 'scrummage', he sensed his moment to make an impression and pounced on the oval object 'with a reckless disregard for my life and limb. But as I did so another player with even less regard for my personal well-being kneed me in the back of the head – a sickening blow.' Being knocked unconscious during his first game didn't dampen his enthusiasm for the sport, however. Soon enough, just as he had done with cricket, he joined the school team, citing his 'speed and all-round ability to gain advantages' as the two main quivers in his bow.

Another sport at which Maurice excelled was cross-country running. Before one particular race, he was so confident of victory that, as the field lined up, he asked the other competitors if they wanted his autograph now or after he'd won the race. Sadly, his cockiness backfired when, mid-joke, the race started. 'I'd only just finished laughing at my quip when to my surprise I found myself at the back of the field,' he moaned. Despite his bad start, Maurice soon found himself up with the leaders, though the effort left him 'in a state of distress'. Halfway through he was joined

by his new best friend, Geoffrey Todd, pedalling alongside on his bicycle shouting words of encouragement.
The sentiment was not totally appreciated. 'It was all
very well for him to say, sitting comfortably on his
bike,' grumbled the runner, who fired a few choice,
if breathless, words back at his pal. Even so, the
support propelled Maurice along, and when he
crossed the finish line with no one in sight, he cele-
brated like all champions should, running around
in small circles, arms aloft, screaming. Unfortunately,
Maurice was then informed that he had finished in
second place, the winner having finished some fifteen
minutes previously. 'I often wondered if I'd have
finished first had I'd started at the front and not the
back,' recounted the deflated runner-up. It is unlikely
that the entire field took a quarter of an hour to cross
the start line – this wasn't the New York Marathon –
but the episode did at least illustrate Maurice's
burgeoning confidence, a prerequisite in all top-level
sports stars.

Maurice may have possessed athletic ability, but he
never knew it was possible to make a career out of
sport. 'In those days, sport was something you did
for recreation and not something you did in order to
make a living,' he remembered, before adding with
a soupçon of regret: 'I was told this quite often.'
Maurice knew any success in the future would depend
on his academic career. But the young fellow was
beginning to become distracted by even loftier goals.

One day, Geoff Todd told Maurice that he had something incredible to show him after school. It would

be a life-changing event. Geoff took him back to his house and pulled a thick black vinyl disc from a sleeve, then placed it on a turntable. Frank Sinatra's croon crackled from the speaker as the record span at seventy-eight revolutions per minute. It was revolving at a similar rate to Maurice's head. He was transported to a place high up in the clouds, from where some argue he would never return. 'My first ambition in life was to become a singer and dancer, like Frankie. He was "the end", to use a popular expression of the time.'

If the *X-Factor* had been up and running in the 1940s, on the one television channel transmitted by the British Broadcasting Corporation from Alexandra Palace, there is a fair bet Maurice would have turned up to perform at the auditions. Whether he would have made it to the live shows, or even boot camp, is another matter. If reports of his air-curdling, tone-deaf attempts at emulating Frankie in school assemblies are to be believed, he would only have made it onto screen as a deluded and comically bad auditionee. In fact, it is not a facile comparison to wonder if Maurice Flitcroft was the golfing equivalent of an *X-Factor* wannabe. After all, he too practised at home alone, a golf club his hairbrush, the playing fields his bedroom mirror, only to head out into the real world and realise he was not quite as up to speed as he thought he was, R&A secretary Keith Mackenzie the sneering and judgemental Simon Cowell of his nightmares.

Even so, when it came to singing, Maurice quickly

realised he didn't quite have what it took for world domination, and turned his attentions towards painting and drawing instead. In fact, he displayed genuine artistic aptitude with brush and pen. He particularly liked the cartoons of Leslie Illingworth and David Langdon, satirists who frequented the Sunday papers of the time. Maurice would toy with the idea of becoming either a cartoonist or a portrait artist for decades to come.

Even before he reached working age, Maurice was oscillating wildly between career paths. But he did make one decision which he was to stick to in later life, namely that money would never be his driving concern. 'I might not make a fortune,' he promised himself, 'but being happy in my mind is a preferable state to being ma-terially successful but not necessarily happy.'

When the war ended, Maurice was sad to leave Mrs Langhorn, Geoff, and all his other school friends. They, too, particularly Geoff, were sad to lose their Firebomb Fritz. It wasn't that he didn't want to go home; he'd simply got used to the beautiful scenery around Kendal. The rolling hills, grassy meadows and old grey-stone buildings beat the redbrick industrial landscape of Barrow any day. Also, many crucial formative episodes had been played out in this Westmorland wonderland. But it was home time, and besides, he'd have his brothers waiting there, even though he knew he'd 'have to fight with them for a place next to the fire come winter, as usual'.

Two years after returning to Barrow, Maurice left school with very few qualifications under his belt. It would be a source of great regret later in life, and could have all been so different if he hadn't missed the final, crucial weeks of revision because of a needless incident involving a gatepost and a tree.

Walking home from school one evening with a group of friends, Maurice spotted an entrance gate with a spectacular large oak tree next to it. The tree's lower branches lingered tantalisingly over the gate, providing instant access to the skies. The sight was too much for Maurice, 'an irresistible temptation' to scuttle up high. Clambering onto the gatepost, and urged on by his companions, he made a few trial attempts at hurling himself off, just enough to ascertain that a leap with great purpose would enable him to seize one of the branches and swing high above the ground for all to see. The feat would be worthy of a tumultuous round of applause. After some deep breaths, he made the great, heroic leap.

'All would have been well if my hands had been bigger, or the branch in question been thinner,' Maurice recalled. But the span of his hands were too small, the branch far too thick, and The Firebomb crashed to the ground. His initial assessment was that he'd sustained minimal damage. Then he realised he couldn't feel his right hand. Meanwhile his friends were shrieking and pointing in the vague direction of some horror beneath him, coincidentally where his right hand would have been had he been able to feel it. Nervously casting his gaze downwards, he discovered that his forearm 'was not in its correct position in relation to the rest of the arm'.

It took weeks of surgery and physiotherapy before Maurice could use his writing arm again. He missed so much classwork, when he entered his final exam he heard his French language teacher ask someone: 'Who the hell is he?' The results came in, and under the circumstances were grimly predictable: he'd failed almost everything bar literature and art. The grades were simply not good enough to secure a place in further education. He had dreamed of going to university, throwing himself into lectures and libraries, and slaking his thirst for knowledge. He always knew it was something of a pipe dream, but up until now it had at least in theory been attainable. No longer. Creative and instinctively intellectual, a bohemian in a time before 'simple folk' like him even knew what a bohemian was, Maurice was cast out into the world aged sixteen with a bleak future ahead of him. If only he hadn't been so tempted by that gap between the gatepost and the branch. A gap between hope and reality. A gap he would attempt to breach for the rest of his life.

Hole 3: Drills, thrills and mandrills

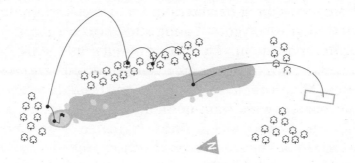

A T THE tender age of sixteen, Maurice was stunned to find himself striding through the wrought-iron gates of Vickers Shipyard, a cloth cap perched on his scalp and a lunchbox swinging by his side, just like his father and older brothers before him. How had this happened? Here was a boy who had wowed crowds with his pugilism and gymnastic mace-throwing. He had been a pivotal player in every school sports team. His paintings were heavily influenced by rose-period Picasso. He wrote and drew Establishment-baiting political cartoons. He had even tamed an Element in The Blue Watery Vagueness. And yet, for all these achievements, here he was with the rest of his classmates, stranded in the Ordnance Department, Machines, No2 Bay, Vickers Shipyard,

Barrow-in-Furness – otherwise known as the Gun Shop.

The first thing Maurice noticed was the excruciating noise: 'The tortured scream of metal, protesting at being turned and planed, milled and bored by huge machines, steel monsters which chewed the raw metal in their massive jaws and spat out gleaming objects that were to form parts of some other kind of machine, engine or weapon.' T.S. Eliot himself could scarcely have described the awesome horror of industry any better. Maurice's wage for grafting through a fifty-hour, six-day week was one pound and five shillings.

As might be expected, within a matter of weeks of turning up in the Gun Shop, Maurice claimed to have seized the mantle of 'Best Machinist' from older youths who had been working there for several years. Instructively, this title seemed much more important to Maurice than anyone else in the factory, and few bothered to argue the toss with him. It was almost as though he had announced the award himself. But natural competitiveness could only sustain Maurice for so long. Once the novelty of a new job wore off, he found the work mind-numbingly tedious. He started smoking roll-ups 'just to have something to look forward to'.

Maurice looked to dancing at the Public Hall on Saturday nights for salvation. Now an independent young buck about town, Maurice was free to start courting. The talk between he and his work pals would be of nothing but ways and means to pull a girl, and the possibilities Saturday night had in store. But

Saturday night did not always deliver. 'It held out a promise which it didn't always fulfil,' he admitted, 'but nevertheless, ever the optimist, I still looked forward to it every week.' He put his inability to hustle the ladies down to an embarrassing lack of rhythm, freely admitting his dancing was so bad that, on the rare occasion a girl did accept his invitation to cut some rug, the best he could hope for was 'a smooth, happy and incident-free progression around the dancefloor'. More often than not, Maurice's attempt at a soft-shoe shuffle would send both himself and his prospective paramour tumbling into a crumpled heap. Eventually tiring of such ballroom balls-ups, he spent most evenings as a wallflower.

The terrible wages and long hours soon took their toll on the young man. He would often get home at night, take a light nap before going out, only to fall into a deep sleep and wake up just before it was time to start work again. It was no life, and so he quit, taking a holiday to visit his Aunt Edith in Manchester where he would revisit the happy days of his childhood, and the zoological gardens at Belle Vue. It was here that Maurice encountered yet another bully who would blight his existence, albeit one who took a very different shape to the 'Juvenile Highwayman' and 'The Cock' of his childhood.

Deep within the Belle Vue Gardens was the zoo. It was necessary to pay to get in, but Maurice, with little money in his pocket, would sneak through the woods on the north side of the zoo, where he could easily peer through some railings into the monkey house. There he would sit for hours watching the chimps wheel and clamber about. However, it was not the chimps who held the chief fascination for Maurice, but another primate who had a cage all to himself: the mandrill. 'I found him fascinating, not because of its size, power, grace and beauty, but because of its demeanour. I was amused by the way it strutted unselfconsciously displaying its brightly coloured red-and-blue bottom.' Maurice would self-deprecatingly tell his friends that the mandrill would probably be more assured on the dancefloor at the Public Hall than him.

After a few visits to stare transfixed at the mandrill, Maurice – with the detailed eye of a robber cataloguing the habitual movements of bank employees – noticed that the monkey-house attendant would leave a bag of prunes just outside the main gate after feeding time. One day, when the attendant had turned his back, Maurice took a handful of prunes and attempted to make friends with the multi-coloured primate. He held a prune in the palm of his outstretched hand. The mandrill observed it for a second, before violently snatching the dried-fruit piece, nearly breaking Maurice's arm with the swipe. Maurice let out a yell but, undeterred, tried again. Again the mandrill snatched with some vigour, causing Maurice to emit a small yelp.

It is important to highlight the danger involved in such games. For those struggling to recall, mandrills are those large plate-faced baboons with the outrageous red, white and blue muzzles that were a staple of wildlife documentaries in the 1980s, but like multi-coloured cocktails suddenly went inexplicably out of fashion. They would be seen in packs on the plains of Africa, grooming each other and occasionally yawning to expose jagged rows of ferocious teeth, David Attenborough or some other similarly hushed narrator explaining how the charming colours of their faces and backsides belied a terrifying temper, and that they are, in fact, regarded as the most belligerent of primates. However, with two ungrateful swipes of its hand, this particular mandrill had made an enemy of the most belligerent of Homo erectus, Maurice Gerald Flitcroft. It had made a grave error of judgement. So affronted was Maurice by the creature's nonchalant rudeness, he hatched a plan to take revenge the very next day: 'I was determined to teach this fierce creature a lesson, and give it a taste of its own medicine.'

Maurice returned twenty-four hours later and repeated the trick. He grabbed a handful of prunes from the attendant's bucket, and crept towards the greedy mandrill. The monkey, perhaps anticipating the joyous sugar rush that comes with the consumption of dried fruit, let its eyes light up when it saw Maurice hoving into view. It skipped towards the bars of its cage and waited impatiently to receive his treats. Maurice held out a prune. The beast swiped at it in the same pig-ignorant manner of the day before. Maurice held out his hand for a second time – but when the mandrill made a snatch for the prune, Maurice dropped the fruit and grabbed its arm with both hands. 'The fearsome creature went wild,'

Maurice later recalled. 'It was screaming with rage, rattling the bars and baring his huge canines.' Part one of the lesson now complete, Maurice proceeded to part two: a playful slap on the wrist, similar to the sort a mother would administer a wayward but confused toddler. Satisfied that the beast had learned his lesson, Maurice finally let go of the mandrill's arm. The primate scuttled to the back of the cage, while its tutor in etiquette swaggered off through the woods. The next day, Maurice visited again, and again offered a prune on the platform of his outstretched palm. This time, no snatching took place. The baboon showed incredible courtesy, picking the prunes from Maurice's hand with a great gentleness, Maurice noting how the mandrill's hands were 'surprisingly gentle and warm and human to the touch'.

The episode begs several questions. What kind of man takes umbrage with the manners of a wild animal? What kind of man vows to teach a baboon a lesson? And what kind of man would be brave enough – or irresponsible enough – to seize the arm of one of the most dangerous animals on earth and slap its wrist? The answer to all is Maurice Flitcroft, and it is a telling one, shining a light on his later golfing exploits. Somewhere out there had been a wild beast with impeccable table manners that could have advised the R&A not to start a fight with Maurice, no matter how much the odds seemed to be in their favour.

On his return from Manchester to Barrow, Maurice worked for a time at a peat company on the edge of nearby Morecambe Bay, regularly turning over freshly cut bricks of fuel to aid their drying. He found the task so repetitive that one morning, instead of getting up and going to work, he simply turned himself over and went back to sleep. Worried that his father would hit the roof upon coming home from his nightshift at Vickers, Maurice only allowed himself some very shallow breaths when he heard the front door click. But his dad was sympathetic. He knew there was no money in labouring for the peat firm, which was notorious for low wages and long hours. He left Maurice to his dreams for the rest of the day, put in a quiet word at the shipyard, and soon enough had managed to get his son more work at Vickers. This second stint at the yard was to prove more exciting for Maurice, as he was employed as a driver on the electric 'bogies' which zipped around the yard fetching and carrying material and equipment. Sure enough, Maurice soon became the finest driver of the electric bogie that the yard had ever known. The self-appointed winner of the 'Best Bogie Driver' award was back on top where he belonged. Little did he know the resonance those words would hold for him.

He might have been the best driver of bogies, but that didn't necessarily make Maurice the greatest instructor. Given the task of teaching a new girl, Patricia Rose, how to operate the electric trucks, Maurice allowed the lesson to descend into slapstick chaos. Handing over the controls to Patricia and half-hanging from the side of the bogie as she drove for the very first time, he was forced to leap off when the

learner violently steered right to avoid crashing into
a wall. Maurice advised Patricia, in industrial termin-
ology and with some volume, to turn back left a bit,
as she had over-compensated her steering. It was to
no avail. 'It was as if she was possessed by demons,
because with a wild expression on her face she was
frozen at the controls while the bogie, its steering
locked, continued in a circle. All would have been well
had not a steam locomotive chosen that particular
moment to puff pompously out of the Engine Shop.
"Stop! Take your foot off the pedal!" I yelled. But as
learner drivers are apt to do, Pat hesitated a moment
too long and the bogie ran smack into the side of the
engine.'

Thankfully, nobody was hurt, though Patricia's ego
was slightly bruised. The situation wasn't helped by
Maurice's bellowed cackles and rasping guffaws. It
was clear the two hadn't hit it off immediately.
Unfortunately for Maurice, his elder brother Roy had
been introduced to Pat at a dance, and the two soon
became an item. Their relationship flummoxed
Maurice. 'Why he should choose this particular girl
was beyond me, and I told him so. But to Roy she
was Betty Grable, Dottie Lamour and Lana Turner
rolled into one.' Roy and Pat soon became engaged,
and within three years were married. Maurice was
forced to bite his tongue. 'We would often strike sparks
off each other,' he would explain, 'but being of a
tolerant and understanding nature I excused her.'
Maurice's irritation was exacerbated when he developed a mild, unrequited crush on Pat's younger sister

Jean, though when she soon married and moved away from Barrow, he put it behind him quickly.

In any case, Maurice would have other, more serious, battles to fight before romance could play a part in his life. One fine winter morning in early 1948, Maurice received a letter instructing him to report to training barracks in Lancaster on Saturday 2 February. He was to begin his National Service. Maurice left home with great fanfare and with the advice of his father ringing in his ears: 'Take an interest in sport and keep out of trouble.'

Maurice succeeded in heeding the first part of that advice with ease. He would be a sharp-shooting rifleman, a valued member of the swimming and diving teams, and – as any mandrill would be able to testify – a competent welterweight boxer. The second part of his father's counsel, however, was never going to be easy to adhere to. Not long after joining the Army, Maurice and a few other lads had their weekend leave stopped, as punishment for the state of their untidy barracks. They all went home anyway. On the Saturday morning, back in Barrow, Maurice was dragged out of bed by a local policeman, who advised him to get back to Lancaster quicksmart.

Being wet behind the ears, he and his fellow miscreants were let off with a caution. However, the lesson wouldn't be learned. After completing training, Maurice joined the 2nd Battalion South Lancashire Regiment, stationed in the Free Territory of Trieste in northern Italy, and within a matter of weeks, he was in deep trouble again. This time he would find himself standing before the Commanding Officer of his battalion on charges of mutiny.

Maurice had been sent there by the sergeant of the 3rd Platoon 'C' company, with the recommendation that he be court-martialled, the most extreme course of disciplinary action that can be meted out to a serviceman. What occurred in that room would become one of Maurice's favourite anecdotes, described in detail in his memoir and verified by Gene and James. In a whirl of energy, Maurice would regularly perform it as a mini-play to a captive audience of his wife and sons and whoever happened to be visiting, playing all the parts himself.

INT. DISCIPLINARY COMMITTEE ROOM. BRITISH ARMY BARRACKS. LAZZARETTO – FREE TERRITORY OF TRIESTE.

COMMANDING OFFICER: Let us start with asking how the soldier's dorm was destroyed in the first place. Some sort of fight broke out involving yourself. Is this correct?

MAURICE: I wouldn't say that was a fight, sir. More an impromptu boxing match of the bare-knuckle variety.

CO: Let us not talk semantics, Flitcroft. How did it come about?

MAURICE: This chap John Wigmore, a coal miner from Wigan, was, for reasons unknown to me at that time, spoiling for a fight.

CO: And how did you ascertain this goal of his?

MAURICE: Because he was making derogatory remarks about grammar schools and the people who attended them – knowing full well I myself went to grammar school and did not like to hear them cursed.

CO: Grammar-school boy, eh?

MAURICE: Yes, sir.

CO: You do surprise me.

MAURICE: Thank you, sir.

CO: Then what happened?

MAURICE: I made my displeasure known by placing one hand onto his face and pushing him off his chair, sir. This I accomplished with great speed, before he knew what was happening at all.

CO: And I take it this inflamed the situation?

MAURICE: It did, yes, sir.

CO [shaking his head, making a note]: *What next?*

MAURICE: Mr Wigmore then challenged me to a fight, sir, which I duly accepted on condition that it be fought with gloves on, inside a boxing ring, Queensberry Rules. But he would have none of that. 'What's wrong with here?' he demanded. To which I replied: 'OK.'

CO: Hm. And where was 'here'?

MAURICE: Between a row of beds in the barracks dorm, sir. Not, in my opinion, the best spot to engage in a bout of fisticuffs. There was a stove in front of us, not to mention a pile of logs that were stacked next to it.

CO: Logs? Logs? Why are you talking to me about logs, Flitcroft?

MAURICE: They were to play an important role in the part-destruction of the dorm, sir. For when we started to throw punches in earnest, every time I stepped backwards to avoid one of my adversary's wild charges, I would step upon a log and be sent crashing around the place into all manner of furniture. The logs eventually proved more menacing than the punches that were being aimed at me. Soon there were logs everywhere, causing onlookers to slip. Other fights broke out because of the chaos brought on by the rolling logs, sir. So frustrated were our efforts to stand up properly and fight, myself and Wigmore shook hands and called it a day. But by then the whole platoon were at each other like mad dogs.

CO: Mad dogs on logs? I've never heard anything so ridiculous in my life. Like some cartoon strip.

MAURICE: I couldn't agree more, sir.

CO: Really. Now to how the mutiny came about. I will call upon Platoon Sergeant Arthur Leyton to make his case.

PLATOON SERGEANT: The men had succeeded in repairing the dormitory by the Friday, but had not yet washed it down to my satisfaction. As it was a Friday, the men were parading before they received their pay packets as usual. There was some delay in the payments being made and some of the men, including Mr Flitcroft, made remarks to the effect that they were not best pleased to be kept standing.

MAURICE: Aye, for two hours. All we wanted to do was sit down, is that such a crime?

CO: Quiet, Flitcroft!

PS: You can see the trouble he can cause, Company Commander.

MAURICE: Ah, I don't agree with—

CO: Quiet, Flitcroft! Get on with it, Platoon Sergeant.

PS: To counteract what I perceived to be a breach of discipline, once the men had collected their pay packets I ordered them not to alight to the mess bar to buy cigarettes and alcohol as is their habit, but to conduct a comprehensive wash-down of the barrack dorm and present their kit, neatly laid out on their beds with them-selves stood to attention beside them. I added that the order applied to EVERYONE who didn't have a good reason to be absent, for example those on guard duty. Those who were absent should leave a note on their bed stating their good reason.

CO: And what happened when you arrived for the inspection?

PS: The barracks had been washed down to my satisfaction, sir, and they had laid their kit neatly on their beds as I had instructed. But the entire company was absent and they had each laid a note on the end of their bed, sir.

CO: All absent? Where were they? Not all on guard duty, surely.

PS: As I read the absent notes I discovered that none of them were on guard duty, sir.

CO: None of them? And what reason did they give?

PS [presenting a piece of paper and preparing to read from it]: *I shall read one of them, sir, written by Mr Flitcroft, which represents well enough the other notes also. 'Dear Platoon Sergeant, apologies for my absence but I have good reason. I have retired to the mess for the purchasing of cigarettes, alcohol, chocolate and other delights for my personal enjoyment. Ta ta, toodle pip and cheerio, yours, Maurice G. Flitcroft.'*

CO: And each letter said the same thing?

PS: Yes, sir.

CO: And Flitcroft, you orchestrated this protest?

MAURICE [pointing to Platoon Sergeant]: *He said 'unless you had good reason', and I think letting off some steam on a Friday night was good reason enough.*

CO: And you encouraged the others to write similar notes?

MAURICE: Once I planted the seed of the idea, they found the escapade too humorous to resist, sir. It was a good piece of team-building, actually. Even John Wigmore thought it were funny and we buried the hatchet. But yes, I take full responsibility for the idea.

PS: Sir, this mutiny will not stand. I recommend you issue a court martial on the grounds of gross insubordination.

MAURICE: Oh take yourself off!

PS: I beg your pardon!

CO: Quiet, Flitcroft! Guards, take this man away!
MAURICE [insisting on the last word]: *It were only a joke!*
[Exeunt]

Despite being bang to rights, Maurice was let off lightly with a four-day prison spell followed by ten days' confinement to barracks. His Commanding Officer told him privately that he accepted that it was a joke, an ill-advised one maybe, but certainly nothing that amounted to a serious mutiny. Even the Provost Sergeant, as he condemned Maurice to his tiny, dark cell, quipped: 'See you in four days; don't be leaving any notes on your bunk.' Meanwhile, having taken full responsibility for the prank, Maurice was hailed a hero by the rest of his platoon. As he whiled away the hours in confinement, he mused at how sticking it to The Man seemed to be a sure-fire way to court popularity with the masses. That was one lesson he certainly was going to heed.

Hole 4: The Girl in the Green Blouse

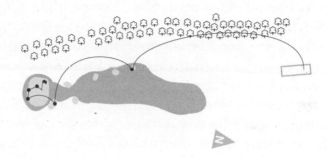

M AURICE TREATED the remaining months of National Service in Trieste as an elongated spa holiday. His station of Lazzaretto had been a former sanatorium, bounded on three sides by the Adriatic Sea, and on a fourth by Trieste's verdant vales and their health-giving properties. When not seeing to his regular duties as a sign-writer – the most artistic job the Army had to offer Private Picasso – he spent most of his time diving into the emerald Adriatic from the nearby quayside for a long swim. For once, keeping out of trouble was a doddle. 'Although Trieste was a likely hotspot at that time, it was peaceful while I was there,' he recalled, before adding magnanimously, 'although I take no credit for that.'

Maurice was cashiered from the Army in early 1950.

Adjusting to life back on Civvy Street wasn't easy. He had enjoyed the camaraderie of the other soldiers; only a few months earlier he had been a 'political prisoner', treated to a hero's welcome on his release, a prototype Nelson Mandela. Now, within a week of his return, he found himself working alone on a dairy farm on the outskirts of Barrow, steam-cleaning milk churns for a pittance.

Finding the work mundane and brain-mashing, Maurice once again put the feelers out for a job at Vickers Shipyard. Soon enough, he was back there, working in the sheet-metal department, building ventilation shafts for luxury liners, the *Orion, Orcades* and the *Oronsay*. Once again blessed with a few pennies in his pocket, he started going out of a Saturday night with a few old chums. One of these, a man call Eddy Bruce, would guide Maurice's career in a new and very different direction – albeit one which utilised some of the 'skills' he had learned during his time in Trieste.

While Maurice had been living the life aquatic by the Adriatic, his pal Eddy had taken up stunt and comedy high diving. While it's hard to imagine now, in the 1950s nearly every British seaside town had a large outdoor pool or lido with banked seating where teams of divers, water-gymnasts and comedy performers would don ersatz yellow swimming caps and splash, swirl and belly-flop for the entertainment of thousands. Eddy worked for The Stan Bonds Troupe, one of the most prestigious in the country, and remembered that Maurice had been a keen

swimmer in his youth. Never one to undersell himself,
Maurice informed Eddy that he had been practising
diving in the Army and had reached 'international
standard'. Eddy urged him to apply in writing to Stan
Bonds himself.

Maurice announced himself to Bonds as 'probably
the most entertaining diver in the country, and
certainly the best'. He received an immediate reply.
Bonds was impressed by Maurice's confidence but
couldn't send him, sight unseen, on tour around the
country with Eddy and the rest of his top-flight divers.
He was, however, willing to give him a trial at the
Troupe's summer-long residency at Rhyl, North
Wales. 'If you're as good as you say you are, you can
start right away,' promised Bonds. Maurice experienced a momentary thundering panic, having slightly
exaggerated his abilities. This manifested itself as a
pain in his cranium, the like of which he'd never felt
before. It soon subsided and Maurice put the attack
to the back of his mind – but it wouldn't be the last
time this mysterious malaise would leap upon him in
times of grave concern.

Maurice gave himself a pep talk. OK, so he wasn't
quite 'international standard', but he was able to hit
the water pointing in the right direction (downwards)
roughly eighty per cent of the time, and could even
execute a couple of pikes and tucks. That wasn't bad,
way more than most swimmers or beach-bums could
manage. And besides, seven pounds a week was not
to be sniffed at, so he didn't worry about the subterfuge
too much. With the start of rehearsals in Rhyl still a

couple of weeks away, Maurice knew he could squeeze in at least one practice session to sharpen his skills. This he did at the open-air pool on the Barrow resort of Walney Island. It didn't quite go to plan.

While limbering up, Maurice's eye was caught by an attractive female swimming lengths of the pool. He stretched and posed, showing off his tight sinewy muscles as best he could, eventually eliciting an approving nod from his prey. Having captured her attention, Maurice then nodded towards the top diving-board, some fifteen metres up, a confident grin spreading across his cheeky face. The message was clear: check this out. The object of Maurice's ardour accordingly stopped and began to tread water. Her message was similarly clear: let's see what you've got, then, sonny. Fully limbered, Maurice began climbing the stairs to the mighty top board. In doing so, he attracted the attention of other swimmers and attendants, and a small crowd gathered to watch his efforts. He ran through the options in his head, selecting the 'pike dive' from his repertoire. He took one last deep breath, and sprung off the board to gasps from the onlookers.

'I performed the dive so well,' he recalled, 'I cut through the water like an arrow and hit the bottom of the pool – which wasn't altogether surprising as I later found out it was only six feet deep.' The lady Maurice had been flirting with rushed to help him, and he even tried to secure her name, but the blood was pouring from his forehead, rather scuppering any romantic notions. 'I had sustained a deep cut to my head just above the right eye that I needed to go to hospital to have stitched.' It was not ideal preparation for a summer of professional diving. Still, when he finally joined the Troupe, he realised that he needn't have worried about his diving skills being tested at all. 'Not every member of the team was expected to perform like an Olympic gold medallist,' he noted. 'The show called as much for nerve as it did acrobatic ability.' And Maurice had plenty of nerve.

As well as being expected to perform pike and swallow manoeuvres in the synchronised diving show, Maurice was cast in the part of 'Lightning' in the comedy set. His initial delight at being offered this part subsided when his fellow, more experienced, divers all laughed, slapped him on the back and wished him good luck with knowing smiles – then disappeared completely when he started to read the script.

The comedy segment ran thus: at the beginning of the second half of the show, an announcement would be made over the loudspeaker. It would be claimed that, during the first half of the performance, the highest diving-board had been damaged and would therefore be out of use. The crowd would boo and hiss. The announcer would then claim that, hold on, all was not lost! A team of builders from the local area had offered to fix the board there and then, allowing the fun to continue. Cue huge cheers from the crowd as 'the builders' enter the arena.

First to enter would be Foreman, all bluster and

bravado, whistling for his team to follow him towards the board. A second man, Worker, would then rush into view carrying a plank of wood and a saw. Both men then stop, tap imaginary wristwatches, and gesticulate in mock incredulity: the third member of the team is late again. 'That's why we call him Lightning!' they cry, to hoots from the crowd. Enter Maurice, as Lightning, rushing around the pool carrying a bucket. As he nears the two men, Worker would spin around to greet him, only to clout him upside the skull with his plank, sending him crashing into the swimming pool. Lightning would emerge from the briny with his bucket stuck on his head. If they hadn't guessed already, the crowd now knew these were not real builders. Equally, by this time, Maurice would have worked out why the other divers had wished him such hearty good luck.

The three builders would then try to climb the ladder to the top board all at the same time. This would take a while, with the man highest up constantly being clumsily yanked back to the ground in the mad scramble, and having to start all over again. These were comedy basics, for sure, but the public lapped it up. Once all three were atop the high board, the act was brought to a riotous climax. Worker would lay down his plank in such a way that the far end protruded some three feet over the edge of the board. Maurice's Lightning was then handed the saw, and dispatched out to crouch on the end of the overhanging plank. By now, the crowd were usually up on their feet, desperate to see how and why the hapless builder was going to end up in the water.

The 'how' soon became apparent, as Lightning began to saw the plank at the side nearest the diving-board, therefore condemning himself with every scrape to a fast descent towards the Blue Watery Vagueness below. The 'why' is best not dwelt upon, though neither would anyone much care as Lightning repeatedly asked the crowd if he should keep sawing. The reply was a fevered affirmative. And so the plank of wood bowed to the inevitable, a great sickening crack reverberating around the stadium. The effect was in Maurice's words 'sometimes calamitous but always visually comical'.

It is not difficult to see how progress in health and safety legislation throughout the years has led to the banning of routines such as these. On his very first outing as Lightning at Rhyl, Maurice hit the Vagueness of the pool flat on his back, causing the wind to be knocked straight out of his lungs. As he sank beneath the surface, he momentarily questioned whether it had been worth the hassle of holding his breath in the bath to conquer his fear all those years ago. 'I was concerned to find myself spitting blood afterwards and a visit to the doctor confirmed I had ruptured a blood vessel,' ran the none-too-cheery reminiscence of his debut as a comedy performer.

But Maurice was not going to give up. Having to miss the next three shows gave him enough time to design a damage-limitation technique for future plank-sawing adventures. 'I decided that instead of attempting to enter the water feet first, I would attempt to enter head first. It didn't guarantee that I would never have another accident but it did give me more confidence and control.' Soon Maurice was back on the plank. After several injury-free performances, his theory seemed to be holding water, as it were. But soon another danger announced itself. Maurice would term it 'the wind factor' – which caused his body to be blown into twisted positions, occasionally causing his knees to meet his head at high velocity. One such scrape with a stiff breeze resulted in a split to his right cheek and a heavily bruised eye.

The wind also affected the plank, especially when they ran out of specially weighted ones and had to use old pieces of floorboard donated by nearby theatres or travelling circuses. Despite Maurice's best efforts to prep the wood by making small incisions before the show, the plank would invariably splinter and enter the water at random places in space and time. This meant that twice a day, every day, seven days a week, Maurice would play a game of Russian roulette with a potentially lethal piece of sawn-off wood. On one such occasion, the plank – having buckled to send Maurice deep into the pool, but not snapped off – dangled tantalisingly off the edge of the board for a couple of seconds. It eventually fell off just as Maurice floated back to the surface, heading downwards into his mouth like an unwanted slice of wood pie. 'That one required stitches too,' said Maurice, 'and made eating anything other than ice cream and jelly very difficult.'

As well as the other divers, a team of female synchro-nised swimmers were also stationed with the troupe. While Maurice admitted they were physically endearing, none of them touched his heart or mind, and so he vowed to keep himself to himself. Besides, he didn't want to be tied down. However, yet another accident would inadvertently lead to a change in this philosophy.

One Saturday morning the team assembled at the pool as always, and awaited their pay packets. As they were running late, a couple of the divers took to prac-tising on a trampoline at the side of the pool. Maurice had never been on such a device before, but charac-teristically fancied himself as a natural and so clambered on, allowing himself to be coached from the sidelines by the two experts. On receiving encour-agement from his mentors, he decided to surprise them with a forward somersault. He'd seen them perform it a hundred times, and it didn't look so diffi-cult. Anyway, how dangerous can springing around on a taut piece of material be, especially compared with sawing oneself off a diving-board in the sky? And so, having announced his intentions to protestations of 'Jesus Christ, no, Maurice!' from his helpless teachers, Maurice took one giant bounce, tucked his knees into his chin and rolled for dear life.

'Unfortunately,' Maurice recalled, 'I put too much effort into it and accidentally executed one-and-a-half somersaults instead of one. I hit the end of the steel frame with a crunching blow on the chin. So crunching, it caused my upper and lower front teeth to grind together, breaking off the enamel and exposing the nerves.'

Times like these suggested Maurice desperately needed a guardian angel, someone who would grab him by the lapels and scream: 'You have never been on a trampoline before! You will not attempt anything more than a jaunty bounce, never mind a somersault, under such circumstances! Otherwise you will shear all the teeth out of your stupid head, you daft bugger!' Alas, such angels do not exist outside Frank Capra movies and, in any case, even if they did, they would be told to 'take themselves off' by their charge. For Maurice it had looked easy, and no amount of persuasion would have convinced him otherwise. A man immersed in pioneer spirit, he simply had to find out for himself. 'Some time during the administration of first aid, I passed out,' was his final word on his career atop the trampoline.

Stan Bonds must have been a very patient man, because the resulting injury caused another lay-off, this time for two weeks. The break afforded Maurice time to rest his aching body in beachfront cafeterias, where he listened to the latest pop platters by Frank Sinatra, Dick Haymes and Brenda Lee. It was in one such café, late at night, when everyone else was at the pub drinking – 'I was never a big drinker, preferring the easy charm of the café environment,' explained our cosmopolitan hero – that he noticed he was not alone. There, across the Formica tables and sticky tomato-shaped ketchup bottles, he spotted a young lady in a green blouse whom he found most endearing.

He was self-conscious at first about his chin-strap, which was secured with a bandage tied atop his head in the style of a Bash Street Kid suffering from toothache. He was also concerned that she should notice the large bowl of jelly and ice cream in front of him, a meal that had more or less become his staple diet since joining the diving troupe, thanks to his catalogue of unfortunate mouth injuries. But he noted a warmth and even a hint of amusement in her eyes. They weren't the only things about her that he was attracted to: 'I couldn't help but notice she had magnificent breasts which stretched the material of her light green blouse taut and threatened to burst the buttons which held the front of it together. Politeness dictated that I look away, but their attraction proved irresistible and I found myself looking more than once.'

To his surprise, The Girl in the Green Blouse got to her feet and came over to sit next to him. Maurice was lost for words until she asked what had happened to his chin. From there the chat followed free and easy, and he was pleased to discover that far from being a liability, the chin strap was an ideal ice-breaker. It had given him the perfect start to a conversation that flowed through the evening as painlessly as the jelly past his broken teeth. They must have been quite a sight to passers-by, as Maurice rolled up his trousers to display scars, and hopped upon tables to act out his various acts of derring-do upon the boards.

As they strolled along the promenade through the perfect moonlight, Maurice discovered that The Girl in the Green Blouse's name was Sally, and she usually worked in the café but had popped in on her way back from the cinema for a refreshing milkshake. They eventually reached the end of Rhyl's deserted pier, where they discovered an enormous wicker chair seemingly placed for the purposes of bringing together young lovers. 'We talked and laughed and kissed and cuddled,' remembered Maurice with obvious fondness. 'I couldn't think of a lovelier way to spend the evening.' They arranged to meet again the very next day, and the day after that too. Yes, she had magnificent breasts, but more importantly The Girl in the Green Blouse had touched Young Maurice's heart. He was in love for the first time.

But alas, when fortune smiled on Maurice Flitcroft, its foe calamity was not far behind, brandishing a cudgel. That night would be the last time the moon or stars would be visible that summer. 'For the next six weeks, I don't remember a day going by when it didn't rain at some point. On one occasion we performed in a shower so heavy we could barely see the other side of the pool, let alone the handful of spectators.'

Audiences dwindled and the run was cancelled. Maurice was forced to return home. He would never again take a moonlit walk with Sally, The Girl in the Green Blouse with the Magnificent Breasts, their affair over before it had really begun. And he would miss the occasional roar of the crowd when, as Lightning, his comedy act was at its zenith. But Maurice wouldn't be Maurice if he hadn't spotted a chink of bright light at the end of an otherwise dank, damp tunnel. 'In a way I looked forward to going home,' he sighed, 'for at least I didn't have to saw myself off a plank twice a day, seven days a week.'

Hole 5: Swannee whistles and sleeping on thistles

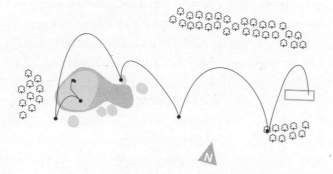

O N HIS return to Barrow, Maurice was reunited with Eddy Bruce, who had been touring the country with The Stan Bonds Troupe while Maurice was serving his apprenticeship in Rhyl. The two swapped stories and tips picked up during a summer spent clowning around in water. The two men vowed to return to the pools the following year, but in the meantime they both needed work. They joined what was then known as 'the gold rush', a response to the flood of job opportunities on offer at a previously un-heralded village in the north-west called Seascale. A huge nuclear processing plant was being built there – Windscale, later known as Sellafield – and the payment on offer was way beyond that available in Barrow's shipyards. If you were prepared to become a 'ghoster', which involved completing a day shift followed by a night shift followed by another day shift, you could make a pretty penny. Maurice tried it once or twice, but always returned home 'in a state of bug-eyed befuddlement', and soon pared back his shifts.

During fagbreaks while helping to build Windscale, Maurice and Eddy cooked up a plan: they didn't need diving impresario Stan Bonds any more. They would strike out on their own as a diving, juggling and tumbling act: Fumble & Tumble. And so, in the summer of 1954, the pair attempted to secure bookings in resorts across the nation, undercutting Bonds considerably. Sadly for Fumble & Tumble, the act failed to attract a single major booking, all pool and theatre owners preferring to stay with their established revues. Maurice and Eddy did get a one-off gig at a lido in Barrow, though, and it went down well, especially the stunt where Maurice was tied up in a coal sack and shoved into the drink. The Houdini-style trick was a brave one, though as far as Maurice was concerned, ripping his way out of a pre-prepared sack was a walk in the park compared to being routinely smacked in the face by a splintered plank of wood.

Despite Fumble & Tumble's signal lack of success on the showbiz circuit, Stan Bonds was prepared to forgive Maurice and Eddy, asking them both to stop attempting to nick his business and rejoin his troupe for the summer months. They refused. Maurice demanded a ridiculous pay rise, which was not met. In any case, he'd taken a wholly irrational dislike to the powder-blue crimplene suit Bonds wore, considering the outfit gauche: aesthetics were important to him. He could afford the grand gesture, as a friend of Eddy's had put them in touch with another travelling troupe: a comedy, dancing and diving revue called Grin & Splash. Jobs were offered – and because the show was indoors, the work was full time, all year round! Ghosting at Windscale was consigned to the past.

The 'grin' part of the show would be provided by comedian Tom Moss, the 'splash' aspect fielded by Maurice, Eddy and three other divers, known collectively and delightfully as the Water Maniacs. Entertainment in between was provided by The Marie de Vere Lovelies, a group of trilling female singers Maurice found pleasing on both ear and eye, and a European-style dancing, balancing and tumbling act called The Three Karloffs. 'They weren't Russian, as their name suggests,' said Maurice, 'but were as British as roast beef and Yorkshire pudding, bowler hats, pin stripes and the Union Jack.' He was subconsciously taking notes: one could pass oneself off as coming from anywhere in the world, if one simply said so and brazened it out. It was a confidence trick he would utilise more than once later in life to win a place in the Open.

Grin & Splash was a huge success and toured Empire theatres from West Hartlepool to Shepherd's Bush, and Hippodromes from Manchester to Lewisham. It is hard to imagine a diving show inside a theatre now, but back in the 1950s it was commonplace. Every day, Maurice and Eddy helped to erect a huge 15-foot-square wrought-iron indoor tank, complete with glass front so the audience could see what was going on in the water. During the perform- ance, they had to assist the main diving act Betty Slade (eight-times winner of the European diving champion- ship), then perform their Water Maniacs act. Then after the show they had to take the whole caboodle down. It was tiring work. Maurice enjoyed performing with these masters of the trade, but hated dealing with the huge tank. 'That tank was a dark cloud that loomed every morning when I woke up,' he grumbled.

One evening, Maurice joined a scouting mission to see a rival diving act, The Trio Morlanos. Expecting to see three Italian stallions somersaulting into water tanks with continental élan, Maurice was stunned to spot a familiar face amid the fake tans and jet-black bouffants. It was none other than his old Kendal school chum, the man who introduced him to Ol' Blue Eyes, Geoffrey Todd! 'I could hardly believe it but there it was,' recollected Maurice with fondness. 'It surprised me, because although he was a good athlete like me, he wasn't a good swimmer at school. What a remarkable coincidence, though, that two strangers should become friends because of war, go our separate ways, then discover we followed similar paths in show business.' The two old pals went out for a drink that night, the evening ending with the pair singing Frank Sinatra songs, Maurice slightly out of key, just like the old days.

Maurice's other friend in the wonderful world of showbiz had a shock in store for him. Tiring of falling over and getting soaking wet just to earn a crust, Eddy decided to stop acting the giddy goat, announcing plans to emigrate to Canada with his family. Maurice found the news hard to deal with. The pair were at the top of their game, touring the country, making a few quid, and generally having the time of their lives. Now, in one fell swoop, it was over. Eddy was gone. Maurice had lost a companion, a business partner and a confidant.

'I never saw Eddy again,' he said. 'He was a good friend and a good diver. Of course, I put a brave face on it and wished him luck. Though why anyone would want to go and live in Canada I've still got no idea.'

Maurice was relieved to find Grin & Splash still wanted to keep him on as a Water Maniac, but it was never quite the same again. He stuck it out for over a year, seeing support acts come and go, and even a change of name to Whirls, Splashes & Girls after the introduction of an ice-skating segment to the show. Poor Maurice, it hardly needs to be said, was the man who had to cart the sheets of ice from the freezer truck.

Once a source of pleasure, his job was becoming a drag. Enjoying it less and less by the day, some of his colleagues were now beginning to cause the familiar 'heat' to rise within him. His closest workmate, a diver who shared the job of erecting and dismantling the tank, was Bob Martin, who Maurice described as 'a likeable chap but one who has an inferiority complex

underneath a superiority complex'. This would manifest itself in Bob trying to gain authority and social
kudos by calling Maurice impolite names in the
company of one or more of the Marie de Vere Lovelies.
Maurice would reply with his own brand of venom,
and the pair would spar like rutting stags. Usually,
the exchanges would 'slowly become heated', whereupon a stage manager would step in to douse the fire.
Inevitably, though, one night, while waiting behind
the curtain during a performance, tempers snapped.

'I don't remember exactly how it started,' said
Maurice, 'but I do recall Bob threatening to knock
me through the diving tank. Well, that did it! I
exploded into action, sprang forward and landed two
left-handers in the direction of his head, but Bob
jumped back like a scalded cat and they missed, which
was just as well as they packed dynamite.'

Maurice and Bob were only prevented from killing
each other when the curtain flew up and they were
exposed to the full glare of the crowd. Maurice,
thinking on his feet, built the brouhaha into the start
of the diving routine. Bob picked up on the impro-
visation and the two avoided a confrontation with the
stage director, who had every right to wonder why
his performers were improvising a throttling scene
when they should have been opening the Water
Maniacs segment. Soon after the altercation, the pair
were separated to avoid further on-stage spats,
although they would later become firm friends. A new
man was introduced to dilute everyone's suffering, in
the shape of renowned swimmer Johnny McGrath,

but alas he too ended up going toe to toe with Maurice. 'I think it's only fair to say that I got along with Johnny no better or worse than I did with Bob,' recalled Maurice, 'and just as I came to blows with Bob, so I did with Johnny.'

The unpleasantness between the two erupted one night in the prop room, when Johnny accused Maurice of mislaying a box of bolts for the tank. Maurice countered that he hadn't touched the box, and that the fault must be with someone else. Johnny then made a grave error. He called Maurice a liar. His honour and dignity challenged, Maurice ordered Johnny to take back the outrageous slur, else he would receive a sock on the nose in no time at all. Johnny responded by threatening to get Maurice fired if he did. It was the wrong tactic, fatally misjudging Maurice's value structure, which put personal dignity way beyond mere employment. Johnny was issued with one last chance to rescind the 'liar' slander. When Johnny taunted that he wouldn't dare, once again it was on.

'The fight that followed was reminiscent of a scene from a wild-west film,' says Maurice. Taking place as it did in the prop room of a major theatre during a comedy revue, the variety of weaponry lent the rumble a farcical air, with rubber hammers, outsized shoes and collapsible chairs flying left and right. It was only a wonder the affair was not soundtracked by cymbals and swannee whistles. The fight drew quite a crowd as it reached its climax. 'Even old Bob Martin came to watch the spectacle,' remembered Maurice. 'He told me later it was the best fight he'd ever seen.'

This time the two protagonists didn't become friends post-fight, and Johnny – a 'name' performer with more clout than Maurice – followed through with his threat to get Maurice the sack. Two weeks later, after dismantling the huge tank one last time, Maurice received a letter from Tom Moss telling him his services were no longer required; his contract had been terminated. There was one last sting in the tail. On inspecting his final pay slip, Maurice realised he'd been paid only until the day before his sacking. He'd worked one extra day for free. The heat rose once more. Maurice located Moss and enquired politely where his money was. Moss, who by now had Maurice pegged down as a troublemaker, gave him short shrift, telling him to leave the theatre as he had no right to be there any longer. Maurice cut loose. In a rant delivered approximately one centimetre from Moss's nose, Maurice told the comic-impresario 'exactly what I thought of him, and the manner in which I was given the sack. He didn't like it one bit, but having already given me the boot, there was nothing he could do.'

Maurice felt conflicting emotions as he boarded the next train back to Barrow. On the one hand, he had left with his dignity intact: neither Johnny McGrath nor Tom Moss had taken *that* away from him. And he had, once again, stuck it to The Man, something that was vitally important to him. But on the other hand, he was a day's wages down on the deal. He didn't have a job. And, most tragically of all, his hopes of making it in show business were numbered.

He might have started one or two fistfights, but he'd always given one hundred per cent devotion to work that was often back-breaking. Were the delicious goals of fame and fortune simply unattainable for the likes of him? Did honesty, always telling it like it is, really not pay? These were complicated moral questions. Maurice was not sure he had all the answers. One thing seemed certain, though: he would surely never again set foot on a stage, or hear the thrilling laughter and tears of a huge crowd. The dream was over.

Broken and beaten, Maurice arrived back home and regrouped. He could go back to Vickers, where he was all but guaranteed some sort of employment, but boredom always seemed to track him down there. Instead, he decided to take a laissez-faire approach to career development. What will be will be, he announced to the world. It was a novel approach to take in the mid-1950s, when men were expected to take a job with a firm and stay there for life, but then Maurice was always ahead of his time – if never quite connected to the everyday world. Throughout the rest of the 1950s and most of the 1960s, Maurice embarked on a decade-long employment odyssey that would take him halfway round the world – and straight back again.

He calculated that 'the most efficient way to see most of the world would be to get a job on a boat'. First he joined the Merchant Navy, but soon lost the gig after his ship left dock – and him behind – in Gibraltar. He had been taking an unannounced 'nice refreshing dip' in the sea, and was 'carried away out of sight by the cool waters'. He joined a luxury liner as a fireman, but was 'sacked after a fight with a colleague over a bag of chips'. This was followed by a stint on a passenger ferry as a boilerman, but that was abruptly 'ended by a bout of acute sea-sickness'.

Deciding the seafaring life was not for him, Maurice returned to dry land, and to home. He spent time as a shunter for British Rail, only to leave the train company 'after relations with the management became strained'. He went back to Vickers to become foreman's clerk in the general engineering shop, but decided to leave when 'relations with the foreman became strained'. A period as a gopher on a building site ended after 'relations with some of the bricklayers became strained'. A pattern – none too difficult to discern – was beginning to emerge.

He was a warehouseman at an overall manufacturers, a machine operator at a woollen mill, a lorry driver for a glue firm, a car washer and polisher, and a door-to-door shoe-polish salesman. Drama was always around the next corner, though; if he wasn't 'fired', 'sacked' or 'let go', 'relations became strained' before he 'walked out'. He did enjoy his time as an ice-cream man, but 'that job really only lasted for the summer months, and there are not many of those in Barrow'. After a while, prospective employers began to eye Maurice's curriculum vitae with some suspicion. 'Surprisingly for me,' he said, 'the pattern of my employment was regarded by employers as a sign of instability rather than enterprise.'

Tired of job-hopping in Barrow – especially as he'd eventually ended up back at the Vickers Shipyard again, on the tower cranes – he was buoyed by an article in the *Sunday Pictorial*, which told of rich pickings available in the London building trade. Maurice handed in his notice and packed his bags for the golden streets of the capital – but just before he departed, his plans were nearly thwarted by an unexpected visitor.

'The day before I was set to move to London,' he recalled, 'I received a call from a police sergeant with an order for my arrest and committal to prison.' It was not the best start to his new life of prosperity. The charges arose from a sum of unpaid income tax which the Inland Revenue claimed was owed to them from wages earned during his time with Grin & Splash, and had long been defaulted on. Maurice vigorously disputed the amount, claiming it didn't take into account his expenses. The Inland Revenue eventually settled on the sum of £20 – about three weeks' wages – which Maurice planned to pay off with his London booty. Sadly, this intention hadn't been communicated with the necessary clarity, if at all, and with several official demands ignored, the police had been sent round to take action.

Informed that a twenty-eight-day spell in the jug was facing him, Maurice felt the heat rising again, one degree in Fahrenheit for each day he faced inside. A full and frank exchange of views ensued. The policeman gently put his hand on Maurice's shoulder to usher him to the car. It would later be the firmly held view of Maurice's brother Stanley that, had he not arrived at that very moment to cool down the situation, Maurice would have thrown one of his uppercuts at the policeman there and then. Stanley offered to pay the £20 for Maurice, and a spell inside was averted.

An ecstatic Maurice thanked his brother heartily, and offered to pay him back with interest on his return from the Aladdin's cave of London. He had heard so much about the riches on offer and the abundance of work opportunities. Having acquired so many skills on his job odyssey, finding lucrative employment was surely going to be a breeze. Plus, he sensed his luck was turning: he'd just narrowly escaped his second stint in a prison cell, and one that would have been a sight longer and more unpleasant than his four-day break in a military clink. Things were surely on the up!

Six weeks into his London adventure, Maurice was sleeping in a field.

His descent into vagrancy was entirely unforeseen, as life in the capital had started well enough. Almost immediately upon arrival in the big smoke, he secured a job on a building site in Brixton. He had found digs locally thanks to an old theatrical contact, and money was coming in. It wasn't quite the riches the *Sunday Pictorial* had described – about £8 a week, not much more than the tower cranes back in Barrow – but it was a promising start nonetheless. Sadly, the building work was soon complete, and Maurice had to find alternative employment, which he did as a car washer and polisher in Kingsbury. This, however, was in north-west London, miles from his base in Brixton, south of the Thames. The daily commute was hideous, sometimes taking the best part of an hour each way. The wages were also substantially lower, which meant Maurice was barely breaking even once he had factored in the cost of his digs, travel and rolling tobacco. Drastic measures were required. So he left his lodgings and embarked on life as a hobo. 'I spent a couple of nights on Euston station, one night in a waiting room at Waterloo, a night in a thistle-covered field, and one night in the back of a car parked outside the garage where I worked.' Exactly where one finds a field, never mind one strewn with thistles, in the middle of London is a secret Maurice would take to the grave.

Not a fan of alfresco living, Maurice decided it was time to return home. He had been defeated again, just as he had been by Grin & Splash. In fact, this time it had been a total rout. Maurice's life was in turmoil, his efforts to become someone – something, anything – had come to naught. This was the nadir. But as Maurice himself said, 'Sometimes things need to get worse before they get better.' London had, therefore, served its purpose. Ever the optimist, Maurice told himself that this was a pivotal moment. So it went that his night in a field, the hedge his only friend, represented the ashes from which Maurice's phoenix arose. Years into the future, many would wonder at the thickness of the man's skin when the R&A victimised him, when the press mocked him, and when residents of Barrow young and old pelted him with clumps of mud for playing golf in loud checked trousers on public land. But when you once slept in a field on a mattress of thistles, the chill night air your quilt, a molehill your pillow, everything else is just a minor irritation.

The only way was up – and Maurice was finally about to enjoy some wonderful luck. It was his first good fortune in a very long time, and it would be life-changing. Firmly ensconced back in the bosom of Barrow, he visited his brother Roy and his wife Pat one summer evening in 1961. It was a beautiful balmy eve, the atmosphere so mellow that Maurice had not fired a single barbed aside in the direction of Pat, whom he had sparred with ever since that fateful day on the electric bogie at Vickers. Maurice would count himself lucky that he was in a charming mood that evening – because Pat's radiant younger sister Jean just happened to pop round to visit also. While relations between Maurice and Pat were, by his own admission, 'sparky', a different type of spark was generated by Jean. The vague crush he had had on her back in the day, for so long dormant, awoke with a passion. He had known Jean since Roy and Pat got married back in 1951, but their lives had taken very different tracks. She had married and moved away; he had pursued a career in comedy high diving. But now she was divorced and back in Barrow with her two sons, Philip and Michael. Maurice had returned, too, with his tail between his legs. They both had a yearning for stability. 'During the course of the evening something just clicked,' recalled Maurice. 'Or, to put it another way, we found each other.'

The romance blossomed and the pair were eventually married on 23 March 1963. All of a sudden, Maurice's years of being footloose and fancy-free were behind him. And when Jean gave birth to twin boys, he welcomed the extra responsibility with open arms. He took to fatherhood 'with the ease and assurity of an eagle taking wing'. They named the boys Gene Van Flitcroft and James Harlequin Flitcroft. Gene was named after Jean, and one of Maurice's heroes, Vincent Van Gogh. James' unusual middle name had been inspired by one of Maurice's favourite Picasso paintings. A few eyebrows were raised at the christening when the names were read out, but Maurice was already used to standing out from the crowd. Jean, meanwhile, was only too happy to indulge her husband's more bohemian leanings. 'Marriage changed the pattern of my life,' reflected Maurice, adding ominously, 'except where jobs were concerned, of course.'

A brief period of normality came when he was employed by Barrow Corporation Transport as a bus driver and conductor. As was the custom at the time, each bus would be run by a partnership. One would drive while the other sold tickets, then the two would swap roles. Duos had to work as a team, otherwise the whole operation would end up in chaos. As his employment history suggested, it took Maurice some time to find a partner he was happy with. But find one he did at the fifth attempt – and he would make a friend for life.

'My first impression of Maurice was that he looked like the film star Alan Ladd,' recalls Dennis Crabtree. 'He had charisma and looked like he could handle himself. He was only small like Ladd, but he had a powerful voice as well, very clear.' Dennis remembers his time on the buses with affection. 'Maurice was good to work with. The sort of fellow you'd look forward to working with because you had a laugh. He was very humorous, in my opinion.'

For his part, Maurice found Dennis 'a kind, fresh-faced young man. We got along very well together. In fact, it was after we split up that I got the sack.'

The official reason given for Maurice's dismissal was 'failing to stop to pick up an intended passenger'. However, he was bewildered by the charge, as he had never knowingly missed a single person waiting at a bus stop. 'There had to be some dark arts afoot,' he decided. It wasn't long before he put his finger on the likely culprit – a former conductor who, a couple of years previously, had found himself embroiled in a spat with Maurice, and had since been promoted into management at Barrow Corporation Transport.

Maurice had been on his way to work one winter's morning at the woollen mill – he was then a machine operator. Riding on the top deck of the bus, he noticed a young woman choking on cigarette smoke from the other passengers. Ever the champion of the underdog, Maurice leant over and opened a window to allow the smoke out and alleviate the young lady's discomfort.

He was thanked for his efforts by the lady – but the chill which then engulfed the top deck sent certain passengers into a flat spin. A frenzy of protest erupted.

'Shut that bloody window!' yelled a puffing smoker.

'I'm letting some fresh air in so that we might breathe a bit better,' replied an indignant Flitcroft.

The shouting soon attracted the attention of the conductor, who clambered upstairs to see what the commotion was. Maurice explained that the top deck was too smoky, and so he'd opened the window to help those in discomfort. This explanation fell on deaf ears, and the conductor closed the window. Maurice opened the window. The conductor vigorously closed it. Maurice vigorously opened it again.

'That window stays shut, or else!'

'That window stays open!'

'Right, that's it, give me your name and address,' demanded the conductor, getting his notebook ready.

'What I'll give you is a punch on the jaw,' Maurice replied calmly.

'No you bloody won't.'

'Yes I bloody will.'

'No you won't.'

The heat was rising. But Maurice could see his stop approaching. Fearing that this circular conversation may go on all day, and desirous of bringing the matter to a speedy conclusion, he delivered a short sharp right to the jaw of the conductor as promised. It caused the clippy to, as Maurice put it, 'go down like a footballer in the area looking for a penalty'. Maurice then opened the window one final time, as several worried passengers furiously extinguished their cigarettes and swiftly opened their nearest windows, for fear of similar retribution from this fresh-air vigilante. Maurice bade the slightly shocked young lady farewell, stepped off the bus, and strode through the gates of the woollen mill. In his wake scuttled the now-recovered and freshly fuming bus conductor, who tried to follow his assailant through the gates but was stopped by two burly security guards and sent packing. This denouement further sweetened Maurice's sense of righteous victory. A satisfied smile played over his face, the cat who got the cream.

Things soured a week later when he received a summons to appear before the local magistrates to answer a charge of causing a disturbance on a public vehicle. Maurice pleaded that the window was surely designed to be opened. If it wasn't, then a ban on smoking on public transport would make travelling more pleasant. (Once again, Maurice was decades ahead of the curve.) As so often happened, his seemingly rational pleas fell on deaf ears. Maurice was found guilty and fined £2. He had wondered if this episode would come back to haunt him when he applied for a job on the buses. It took a while, but the ghost caught up with him in the end. It is certain, though, that for a time, some buses in Barrow were the best ventilated in the land.

The safety net, as always, was Vickers Shipyard. Maurice soon found himself working the tower cranes once again. But this time things would be different. With a wife and children to support, he promised to stay put in the job. It looked like Maurice's creative pretensions might never be fulfilled – though that didn't mean he was going to stop dreaming.

Hole 6: Renaissance man – from da Vinci to Vickers

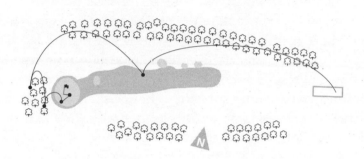

FROM 1968 until he discovered golf in 1974, Maurice was employed as a crane driver at Vickers Shipyard. It gave him and his family some much needed stability after a period of great flux, and meant that they didn't have to worry while the boys grew up. It was an idyllic time for the Flitcrofts.

'We never wanted for anything as kids,' says James. 'If we wanted a football, Dad would get us a football. Boots, he'd get us boots. Cricket pads, whatever. They spoiled us rotten, our mum and dad.'

The crane in which Maurice spent the majority of those six years was situated in Bay 4. It had simple controls: forwards, backwards, up and down. Swinging gently in the air was a giant hook on which containers would be carried to and from docking ships. It was a

job that allowed the driver to indulge in occasional bouts
of idleness when there were no ships or containers to
deal with. Maurice made sure he spent this time wisely.

For starters, he decided to make his cabin a bit more
homely. On a walk to stretch his legs one breaktime, he
found some old teak floorboards in a disused foundry.
He cleaned them up and decked his cabin walls with
them, a very chic look in the early 1970s. His workmates
laughed at him as he hauled the wood up the ladder,
but they were the first to admit his cabin, now resembling a cross between a gleaming poop deck and a
Scandinavian sauna, looked highly swish, if a tad chichi.
They were even more jealous as they witnessed Maurice
hauling pots of paint up there, swathing the ceiling in
pastel green and the floor in forest green.

But their patience broke when they saw him hoisting
up a luxury car seat. Then an easel on which to paint.
And finally a bookshelf on which to house a small
library and a collection of notepads, into which he
scribbled idle thoughts. Many other workers now
labelled Maurice a 'weirdo' and 'up himself', yet for
Maurice it was the most natural thing in the world.
'It's where we spent most of our time,' he reasoned,
'so why not? I couldn't understand it. Most of them
were sitting on wooden stools.'

The stage was set for conflict with his fellow workers,
but while Maurice's natural inclination was to tackle
dissenters head on, this time he was minded to play
a political long game. With the goal of an easy life
very much in mind, he was determined to get the
other lads onside. During breaks he would draw char-

coal sketches of his colleagues on his easel, then present them with the finished products at the end of the day. The drawings flattered the egos of even the most unreconstructed mouth-breathers in the yard. Maurice was also always on the lookout for abandoned comfy seating, or some old cushions, and whenever he found something he'd offer them to other drivers and beg them to give the seat a try in their crane. Soon enough, Bays 1 to 8 had the happiest crane drivers in the history of shipbuilding.

Maurice joined the local library, and began to fill his spare moments learning some new skill or other. His hunger for knowledge hadn't lessened since his schooldays; if anything, he was getting more ravenous by the day. James remembers that when he and Gene asked for a football goal in the back garden, Maurice went to the trouble of finding out how to weave a net. Using borrowed cord from one of the fishing boats in the docks, he spent three weeks creating a net big enough to hang between the goalposts. Not satisfied with that, Maurice then embarked on a tennis net, even though Gene and James had no interest in the game whatsoever, and there was nowhere to put it up. But that wasn't really the point; if Maurice was going to do something, he was going to do it properly, and do it large. Maurice's net-making years came to a shuddering halt when he strung up a hammock in his cabin, only for it to unravel with him in it and nearly dispatch him out of the door and towards certain doom. 'He was dead creative,' says Gene. 'Possibly too much so.'

Another enterprise which Maurice undertook with

gusto was songwriting. He would listen to his transistor radio in his cabin, and while he enjoyed some pop and easy-listening music – his favourite style was big-band jazz – he felt many of the modern tunes needed a little work. 'I found some of the lyrics of the songs were so repetitive and boring,' he said, before adding predictably: 'I was of the opinion that I could do much better.'

Despite having no discernible musical talent – as his Sinatra pastiches back at school proved, he was effectively tone deaf – Maurice nevertheless began working on an album of song lyrics. In one particularly productive spell, after being inspired by an episode of *The Avengers* on TV, he stayed up and wrote three paeans to the show. Sadly, the first two parts of this triptych – 'Emma Peel' and 'The Mistress Of Mars' – have been lost for ever, but the third lyric survives in its entirety. It was a track he felt had the most chance of becoming a hit, as a result of its topicality.

GIRLS IN MINI-SKIRTS
(LYRICS: MAURICE G. FLITCROFT)

Eleven months of June
Would simply be great
Topless swimsuits and dresses
Would be tempting fate.
But just as appealing
I'm so glad to say
Are girls in mini-skirts
Oh, My! How they please!

Girls in mini-skirts
Revealing their knees.

No matter where you go
In your wanderings
You're certain to see them
Improving the scene
So very appealing
I'm so glad to say
Are girls in mini-skirts
Oh, My! How they please!
Girls in mini-skirts
Revealing their knees.

Now girls in mod dresses
With long flowing tresses
Wearing short skirts
And showing their knees
Are here to stay
I'm so glad to say.

When summer breezes blow,
Or icy winds sting,
In the towns or cities,
How they make them swing,
So very appealing,
In their special way,
Are girls in mini-skirts,
Oh, MY! How they please,
Girls in mini-skirts,
Revealing their knees.

Showing an innate understanding of how a perfect pop single is constructed, Maurice had even penned a middle-eight section. He sent the lyrics, along with an accompanying letter, to Les Reed, the composer of the Tom Jones hits 'It's Not Unusual' and 'Delilah'. Reed wrote back saying that while he quite liked the lyrics, he didn't appear to have been sent any music. This wasn't Maurice's area of expertise, as he informed Reed in a return letter. 'Surely that's the easy bit,' wrote Maurice. 'Can't you do that?' Highly amused, Reed sent back a very encouraging letter informing him of the Songwriters' Guild of Great Britain, and suggesting he might find a collaborator to do the 'easy bit' there.

In his excitement, Maurice promptly wrote to the *New Musical Express*, asking for their opinion of his lyrics, and the chances of them being accepted by someone for publication. They too wrote a very courteous reply, also suggesting that he try the Songwriters' Guild. They did, however, indicate that perhaps if he could think of some kind of tune, his chances would improve vastly.

Encouraged by these responses, Maurice took to penning many more lyrics. He purchased a typewriter and tape recorder – no mean investment in those pre-digital days – and joined the Songwriters' Guild. He disseminated tapes of himself caterwauling his lyrics throughout the music business – very much a lost Bernie Taupin looking for his Elton John – in the hope that one of them would be picked up and become a pop hit. There were, sadly, no takers. Even more tragically, with details of Maurice's mail-out non-existent, none of the copies are known to have survived. A tape-based cultural loss up there with the wiped episodes of *Dad's Army* and *Not Only But Also*, it is a crying shame that The Baritone from Barrow will never be heard belting out the chorus of 'Girls In Mini-Skirts' into a tape recorder as cranes whirr and crank in the background.

Having suffered a major knockback at the ruthless hands of the music industry, Maurice turned his attention to the art world – and, in particular, oil paintings. Unable to afford real oils, he would paint in water-colours or gouache. But just as Maurice would do anything to make his family happy, so they would do their best for him, too, and when Jean won a tidy sum one night at bingo, she treated him to a set of oils and enrolled him in an evening course in oil painting at Barrow College of Further Education.

It was a great time for the Flitcroft family. Gene and James had started school, and so Jean started work as a secretary at the shipyard, doubling their income overnight. They drove a Mazda RX3 coupé, causing heads to turn all over town. They even owned a little scooter for nipping about. When they were old enough, Gene and James were given a scrambler. 'Oh, we were well-off at one point,' admits James with justified pride. And Maurice, by now in his early forties, was both totally content and at the peak of his creative powers.

He was, above all else, a renaissance man. The pastel-green roof of his crane was for him the roof of the Sistine Chapel. 'Girls In Mini-Skirts' was his Monteverdi. The various short stories, poems and ideas for Tarzan novels he scribbled in his notebooks made him the Shakespeare of Stratford-upon-Furness. Yet none of these pursuits would become the one he would be remembered for.

'I often wonder,' mused a septuagenarian Maurice, 'if I'd devoted as much time and effort to the art of drawing and painting, would I have achieved the same level of fame in the world of art that I now enjoy in the world of golf?'

Just as it had done to countless others before him, and just as it would to countless after, golf was about to strike Maurice like a lightning bolt from the sky. Golf, a game with the power to seduce a man and reduce him to an obsessive wreck, a film-noir femme fatale rather than a rom-com sweetheart. It would catch Maurice and reel him in like a helpless fish on a hook, to be either battered to death on a rock or held up as a thing of beauty. For better or worse, the golf bug bit him. There would be no going back.

Hole 7: The Discovery Channel

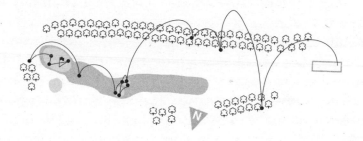

'AT THE age of forty-five years, in the autumn of 1974, I took up the glorious game of golf. Little did I dream that such a simple act as taking up a game would have a profound effect on my life. I would become famous, headline news, hailed as a hero on one hand, held up to ridicule in another.' It is the opening salvo of Maurice Flitcroft's unpublished memoir, the rambling, one-draft, misshapen beast that has until now lain dormant since it was rejected by publishers hands-down in the early 1990s. It is a grand opening, but it belies a very inauspicious beginning.

Until 1974, Maurice had never swung a golf club in his life. It would be safe to say that he had never encountered the game of golf any more than any other working-class man from Barrow-in-Furness.

Maurice was athletic at school and fancied himself a natural talent at every game he ever played, but sport hadn't featured in his life since. That was unless one counted the time he spent swimming and diving – which being pursuits enjoyed on a firmly non-competitive basis, Maurice certainly did not. No one in his family had ever played golf. None of his friends played it. It was as foreign to him as ice hockey, polo or cross-country skiing. So how did he suddenly catch the bug?

Evidence would suggest that two seemingly innocuous and utterly random elements combined to create a seismic explosion, the ripples from which would eventually cause balding heads to shake uncontrollably, and handlebar moustaches of ex-servicemen to twitch with impotent disapproval, in gentleman-only clubhouses throughout the land. Those elements: fell walking and colour television.

In the summer of 1974, Maurice would erase the industrial wasteland of the shipyard from his mind by strolling over the Lake District fells of a weekend. Walking meant he could fill his lungs with fresh air, partake in some much-needed exercise, appreciate the scenery – and, as a bonus, the whole family could enjoy it with him. Jumping in at the deep end – for he knew no other way – Maurice bought walking sticks, compasses, waterproof jackets, boots, socks, gloves and hats for all the Flitcrofts. He enjoyed the experience immensely. Regular walking had given him his first prolonged exposure to relatively unsullied oxygen for years, and the feeling of blood pumping around the old veins encouraged him to return to the world of sport. He was decided: he would take up mountain climbing as a serious pursuit. But at the last minute, something changed, and he took up golf instead of mountaineering. 'In my case and the Open Championship, this could fairly be said to amount to one and the same thing,' he quipped. So what happened?

'We used to have an old rubbish telly in the lounge and we never watched it much,' recalls his son James. 'Then, when we could afford it, we got a colour one and he loved it. I think golf was one of the first things he saw on there, and that was it.'

Maurice's memoir confirms James's supposition: 'When colour TV came in my interest grew. One day in the autumn of 1974, I switched the television on to watch the Piccadilly World Match Play Championship. They introduced the players individually, showed them teeing off, and there was this exciting theme tune: boom ba de boom, ba de boom, ba de boom, and so on. I thought it was great and I remember thinking how marvellous it would be to be part of it.'

And it looked so easy, too! Which very much appealed to Maurice's up-and-at-'em approach to life. Sadly, while golf looks simple on the television, it's arguably the most complicated sport of all. The camera captures the player swinging gently, and their ball landing softly on the green. But there's nothing in vision to betray the delicate physics of finely honed technique, or the nigh-on impossible torque required to send a small, hard ball fizzing through the air, cutting through a strong breeze. But that's the devious seduction of golf, a game which initially gets the heart pumping like a drum-and-bass record – 'boom ba de boom, ba de boom' – before breaking it into a million pieces.

Buoyed up by what was surely the inevitability of becoming the next Jack Nicklaus, Maurice's first move was to order a set of mail-order clubs and some balls. The clubs were Wilson Avengers, because he liked the name, and the balls Ben Sayers, because he'd heard of him. The balls arrived a week ahead of the clubs, and such was Maurice's fervour to get started, he began practising with a walking stick which used to belong to his mother-in-law. It had a long hook on the end, which Maurice had previously put to good use during the blackberry-picking season. He turned it upside down and used the hook end to practise putting on the living-room carpet. Coffee cups laid on their side served as golf holes. 'It could be said that I owe my fine sense of touch on the greens to that walking stick,' he said years later.

When he managed to tear himself away from putting practice, Maurice marched down to the local library and borrowed an instruction manual by the American golfer Al Geiberger. It was a moment of serendipitous symmetry: two years later, Maurice was destined to shoot the highest-ever score recorded by a professional golfer, 121 in the qualifying round of the Open. A year on from that, Al Gieberger would shoot the *lowest-ever* score recorded by a pro, a 59 on 10 June 1977 at the Danny Thomas Memphis Classic. It is still one of only three 59s recorded on the PGA tour. An incredible sixty-two shots separated the two records.

When the set of Wilson Avengers finally arrived, Maurice couldn't wait to try them out. But where to practise? He decided that Sandy Gap on Walney Island was the best place, as there wouldn't be many people about to endanger with any initially wayward mishits. The reason for this is simple: Sandy Gap is one of the most inhospitable environments on earth. Walney Island juts out into the Irish Sea, acting as buffer and wind-break for Furness and the Lake District beyond. Nevertheless, it is still not impossible to see why Maurice thought it would be a good spot to learn the game. When the tide is out, the wet golden sand stretches for ever, like the salt flats of Utah. Admittedly this is only for about two hours a day, and even then the wind lashes so hard it is impossible not to wonder whether one has stumbled into an aerodynamics testing facility by mistake. Maurice's first practice session did not go well: 'I remember my first shot travelling a long way, but that might have had something to do with the gale-force wind that was blowing up a sandstorm around me. Conditions were not conducive for a beginner, or *anyone* for that matter, trying to master the art of hitting a golf ball.'

After his eye-watering introduction to the game of golf, Maurice was determined to find a more pleasant environment on which to master the basics. He ventured to some public fields near his house, where the grass grew over a foot long and the thorny hedgerows seemed purposely designed to swallow up golf balls like greedy children devouring bon-bons. He tried out the shorter grass of his old grammar school, but these were private grounds, a situation that created its own unique problem. And so he settled on Ostley Bank rugby league fields, where he would practise throughout the winter, clipping long irons over the posts and short irons under them whenever time allowed – and there was no match on, of course.

Trevor Kirkwood, a close friend of the Flitcroft family, remembers the first time he saw Maurice traipsing across the fields, golf bag strapped over his shoulder. 'He cut a strange figure, did Maurice. He would wear a waterproof top and wellies, and stand there for hours in rain and snow and God knows what else, whacking golf balls. I think a lot of people thought he was a madman.'

The winter of 1974 proved a baptism of fire for Maurice and his golfing ambitions. It couldn't have been a more miserable introduction. Most golfers decide to take their first swings in the wondrous hazy glow of a summer evening, or stroke a few putts across a green on a spring morning, birds singing in the trees. This is the sporting smack that usually gets a virgin golfer hopelessly addicted. By contrast, there's rarely a more miserable activity in life than playing a series of bad golf shots in the raging depths of winter, four hours of wet feet and plugged lies.

To add to his problems, Maurice had to contend with the enthusiastic attentions of the new family member, an Alsatian called Beau. With Jean and the twins at work and school respectively, it was left to

Maurice to entertain the young scamp. This he did with pleasure, as he loved dogs, but even so, Beau proved quite a handful. 'He would dive in front of me as I was about to hit my shots, making me stop my swing halfway,' said Maurice. 'He completely ruined at least one practice session due to this habit.' The furry prancing quadruped soon got the message when Maurice accidentally landed a 4-iron in its right eye socket, causing what Maurice diagnosed as 'the canine equivalent of a black eye'. But having learned that lesson, Beau quickly picked up a new and different proclivity: catching the ball mid-flight. This made practising chipping a nightmare. 'I'd have a hole in the sand I was aiming at, but I'd never get near it as Beau would snatch the ball before it hit the ground,' moaned golf's answer to Barbara Woodhouse. 'I think that dog had a hugely negative impact on my short game.'

Yet despite the wind, rain and Beau's relentless mischief-making, Maurice kept pushing through, totally hooked, eventually being issued his rightful reward when spring finally sprung. And along came a man and his grass-cutting machine. 'What a difference this made!' he trilled. 'Golf became a different game from the trial of strength it had been during those miserable days of winter, and when the sun shone and the scent of newly cut grass was in the air, my cup of happiness was full.' He began to utilise the lighter evenings summer brought with it. The magic of golf now had him completely under its spell. He'd even made his peace with Beau. 'We eventually settled on a system,' he explained. 'He would stand a yard behind my heels at the ready, then as I started my backswing he would whizz around in a half-circle behind me, ready to dart after the ball as I struck it. That way he would get to chase the ball, but I'd get to see it land first.' Man and dog, best friends, in perfect harmony.

Maurice had stumbled head over heels in love with golf. 'I was practising whenever and wherever the opportunity presented itself,' he said. He was not kidding. He would often take a club into work, on the off chance of being asked to operate the pride of the docks, a large seventy-foot crane overlooking the ocean. During down time, he would crawl out of the cabin and along the arm, whacking old balls into the Irish Sea.

'He had no fear cos of his high-diving days,' explains Trevor Kirkwood. 'He wasn't frightened of anything; he thought nothing of it. Everyone else thought he was crackers – but he didn't care.'

As well as providing the Barrow skyline with a vision more dramatic than the Eiffel Tower, St Paul's Cathedral and the Leaning Tower of Pisa all rolled into one, he kept up his indoor duties too, reading every golf book he could get his hands on. He read instruction books by Jack Nicklaus, Harry Vardon and Peter Allis. He read autobiographies by Arnold Palmer and Tony Jacklin. He read every magazine from *Golf World* and *Golf Monthly* to the American publication *Golf Digest*. But most importantly he read about tournament golf and learned of the major championships

– his interest especially piqued by the British Open.

He discovered that the British Open golf championship – officially called simply the Open – is the oldest and most prestigious golf tournament in the world. It was first played in 1860 at Prestwick Golf Club in Scotland, where Willie Park Snr beat a field of seven other professionals over three rounds of twelve holes. As a reward, he won a 'champion's belt' to hold up his troosers. Soon enough, the Open's first prize of a rather prosaic fashion accoutrement would be replaced by the far more inspiring Auld Claret Jug. A select list of future holders would read like a roll call of the game's greats: Tom Morris Snr, Tom Morris Jnr, Harry Vardon, Sam Snead, Bobby Locke, Ben Hogan, Gary Player, Jack Nicklaus, Lee Trevino, Tom Watson.

Maurice would have read how the Open was played over the finest links courses – links being an area 'linking' the land to the sea – such as St Andrews, Troon, Turnberry, Royal Lytham, Carnoustie and Royal St George's. He would have read how the tournament was organised year on year by a fearsomely conservative group of ex-army majors, rule-makers and ball-breaking sticklers for tradition: the Royal and Ancient Golf Club of St Andrews, who made it their sole aim in life to see that the Open remained the greatest test for the greatest golfers on earth.

Maurice read all this. Yet still decided, having only one winter and summer of golfing behind him, that he was destined to become a part of the Open's illustrious history. 'Was this the road that fate decreed I should follow?' he wondered. 'I reckoned if I showed the same flair for golf as I had shown at other sports . . . if I worked hard, applied myself and practised regularly, who knows? Maybe one day, maybe next year or the year after, I'd be good enough to play in the British Open.' It was rousing stuff. However, there was a caveat to the logic. With an observation of dazzling precision, he added: 'What I didn't realise, however, was that golf is not a game where effort reaps its just rewards.'

Even putting in the long hours would prove problematic. There are three golf clubs in Barrow-in-Furness: Barrow Golf Club, Dunnerholme Golf Club and, the most prestigious and historic, Furness Golf Club, a pristine links perched tantalisingly on the edge of Walney Island, a stone's throw from Sandy Gap where Maurice still practised when the weather allowed. But he couldn't afford Furness, and was turned away from Barrow as a result of several clothing-code infringements. This left only Dunnerholme, a nine-hole course which could be easily turned into eighteen were a player to go round twice. Maurice decided not to bother anyway: he was still employed full time at Vickers, and had a family to look after, so he would rarely get a chance to play more than a few holes at a time even if he wanted to. In any case, Maurice now knew enough of golf, its long history and his own game to convince himself that he had a shot at the 1976 Open Championship the following summer. He would have to practise through the winter, whatever the weather, but that wasn't a problem. 'Ambition is a powerful force. I practised in the freezing cold, gale-force winds, hail, rain and snow. I would carry on with water running down my neck, into my eyes, soaking through my underwear and sloshing in my shoes. And in January 1976, what had started out as a dream and had become an ambition, I set about making a reality.'

But how does one gain entry to the Open? It was called the Open, Maurice assumed, because it was 'open' to anyone. But what did this entail? Just turning up to play? Unlikely. Write a letter? Good idea. But to whom? Why not the man who presented the golf on the television? The man who seemed to know everything and everything about the game? The man whose instruction manual he had devoured every word of? Of course! Peter Alliss!

Mr P Alliss
c/o BBC Television
London

Dear Mr Alliss,

Inspired by the golf I had seen on TV in 1974, and inspired by my two sons, I took up the game in the autumn of that year. Knowing very little about golf apart from what I had seen and heard on TV I remedied this by going to the library and buying a book on the subject. After studying it closely I went to a playing field nearby and put what I had read into practice.

Since then I have read several books on the subject, including two by you, which I found very useful and informative.

Since the summer of 1975, I have dedicated myself to the mastery of the game and consider that I have made a lot of progress, so much, in fact, that I have made it my ambition to play in the British Open.

Now, how does one get to play in the British Open? What do I need to do?

I am not a member of a club, and the chances of me becoming a member in the near future are pretty remote. So how do I go about qualifying? Also, presuming I am good enough, what do I need to do to become a playing professional? I realise the standard is high, but I shouldn't consider becoming a professional if I didn't think the standard of my play was good enough.

If you could find the time to answer these questions, I would appreciate it very much. Should you be able to do so, I am enclosing a stamped addressed envelope for your reply.

Yours faithfully,
M.G. Flitcroft

It must have been a very perplexing letter to receive, coming straight as it did from left field. Alliss clearly gave it little attention, or perhaps simply didn't know where to begin a response, as, sadly, the stamped addressed envelope never found its way back to Maurice's home. As Maurice began to despair that his dream would be shattered under the weight of a golf-bag load of unanswered questions, a helpful librarian alerted him to a new book that had just arrived: *The Glorious Game of Golf* by Peter Dobereiner. Maurice checked it out immediately and rushed home. On opening it in his kitchen, he discovered that the book was a veritable treasure trove of information. The people to write to were the Royal & Ancient Golf Club of St Andrews!

Of course! They would then send an entry form, which the applicant would fill out and send back, along with a small entry fee. It sounded so simple. 'This called for a celebration!' whooped Maurice. 'I made myself a pot of tea.' Then came a second revelation that caused for further celebration, a garibaldi biscuit, perhaps: idly leafing through the rest of the book, Flitcroft stumbled across a feature about a man named Walter Danecki.

Danecki was a 16-stone postal sorter from Milwaukee, Wisconsin, who in the mid-1960s decided to become a professional golfer, only to be thwarted by the US Professional Golfers' Association. They insisted he serve a mandatory five-year apprentice-ship and show proof of playing ability. Undaunted, Danecki turned his attention to the 1965 British Open, assuring the R&A that he was indeed a pro. 'After considerable soul searching,' the forty-three-year-old reasoned, 'I had in all honesty to admit that I was a professional – since it's the money I'm after.' Danecki was given a place in the thirty-six-hole qualifying competition at Hillside Golf Club near Liverpool – and went on to make Open history.

In the first round, Danecki shot what was then a record high score in the Open of 108. It did not stand for long. Danecki shot 113 over the second eighteen holes, for a non-qualifying total of 221, a mere eighty-one over par. Asked why he had bothered coming over to compete, he insisted he usually shot 'around par', and explained that he wanted to return home with 'that pot of gold. I didn't tell my workmates what I was doing in Britain. It would have been a fine surprise for them. I had hoped that I would keep my little secret if I failed.'

There was no chance of that, as Danecki's 221 shots had been heard all around the world, his fifteen minutes of fame ensured by some choice quotes. Trying to remember how he ran up one particular double-figure hole, he said: 'I'll probably wake up at three o'clock in the morning and remember it all clearly, but it's a little foggy now. Maybe it was bunker trouble. No, come to think of it, it might have been out of bounds.' Why did he not go home after the disastrous opening round of 108? 'Nobody likes a quitter.' Did he enjoy playing in Britain? 'I liked playing with the small ball. If I had used the American size, I would have been all over the place.'

Maurice sat in the kitchen, bellowing heartily between mouthfuls of tea and biscuit, as he read about the hapless Danecki. It *was* true: *anybody* could play in the open Open! He immediately took up pen and paper, and composed a letter to the R&A, requesting an entry form. 'The possibility of doing worse than Walter Danecki never occurred to me,' he later said.

When the entry form finally arrived from the R&A, Maurice studied it closely. The answers took some thought. It was just as well the first question – his name – was an easy opener, because things quickly became complicated. Was he amateur or professional? He was an amateur, of course. That being the case, was he able to submit a handicap certificate of one or less? He most certainly wasn't able: he didn't even have a handicap, never mind a certificate. Maurice decided that it was time to turn professional. What was his home club? He wasn't a member anywhere. Should he put Furness? Dunnerholme? Barrow? They might check those. Maurice decided it wouldn't be prudent to explicitly admit to not being a member of a club, so he left it blank.

Maurice sent the form back to the R&A. They would take his word that he was a professional, which Maurice was well within his rights to be anyway. The rules of golf at the time – as approved by an authority no less than the R&A themselves – stated that any golfer who took action for the purpose of becoming a professional golfer, or who played for prize money or its equivalent in a match, tournament or exhibition, would cause forfeiture of their amateur status. And Maurice wanted his shot at that 'pot of gold' as much as Walter Danecki ever did. The R&A also didn't worry about the lack of home club. Plenty of other pros were 'unattached'; this is obviously, they assumed, what Mr Flitcroft meant. He was in!

Confirmation that his entry had been rubber-stamped – he would play in one of five Open qualifying tournaments on Friday 2 July and Saturday 3 July – was received with great excitement in the Flitcroft household. Jean, James and Gene were all supportive of Maurice's brave efforts, believing the amount of time he spent practising guaranteed he'd be the equal of anyone they'd seen on their colour TV. They were almost expecting the Auld Claret Jug to be winging its way to their mantelpiece in Barrow, rather than simply hoping for Maurice to put up a good show. Worryingly, the Open hopeful's celebrations at having gained entry to the most prestigious tournament on earth were overshadowed by the form he was showing in practice.

'My game lacked consistency,' recalled Maurice. 'I would play well one day, not so good the next. I was good with my short irons, fair with my medium irons, disappointing with my long irons, and erratic with my driver and fairway woods.' This was swingeing self-criticism, and words which should go some way to debunk the myth that Maurice Flitcroft was an out-and-out fantasist, the Walter Mitty of golf. But whereas Nick Faldo could later turn to David Leadbetter, or Tiger Woods had Butch Harman to lean on, Maurice didn't have a coach. When things got tough, and the mechanism of his swing broke down, he would turn to the only person he could trust. 'I shared my concerns with my wife Jean and she pointed out there was still plenty of time to iron out any problems. Maybe I could take some time off. Summer was on its way and I could practise for longer in more agreeable conditions. This talk dispelled the faint misgivings I had felt, boosted my confidence and made me feel a whole lot better.'

In fact, there wasn't long until the big day, less than four months, and Maurice's boss at the yard didn't take kindly to a request for time off to practise for the Open. On top of that, every inch the modern man, he was never one to leave household chores to his wife, even in his hour of need. He helped with shopping, cooking, cleaning and washing, as well as the more routine masculine chores of digging the garden and trimming the hedge. (Although his wife helped with those tasks too. 'We make a good team,' he said of their partnership.)

When he could find time to fit in practice, he was on his own. He'd finish work, have his dinner, then head out to Otley Bank and hit shots until it was so dark he could no longer see the ball between his feet. At weekends, he'd get up at 4 a.m. and, after a pot of super-strength tea, head off to Barrow Golf Club where he'd sneak on the course and play a hole or two until the first of the members arrived. Upon being chased away, he would then practise all day on the sands, or at the rugby club, until his fingers bled, before trying to grab more practice incognito as evening fell at Furness Golf Club. 'One of the greens was within range of a street lamp whose friendly glow illuminated the green, enabling me to practise my putting while the rest of the course was shrouded in darkness and mystery.'

This was Maurice Flitcroft's routine, week in, week out, for the four months leading up to his Open debut.

It showed remarkable commitment to the cause in the face of adversity. Say what you like about him, but let no one claim Flitcroft simply disrespectfully turned up to mess about at the Open. He put in the long hours like every other entrant. He just may not have spent them practising any of the right things.

The date with destiny drew ever closer. And with two weeks to go, the exact time of destiny was revealed. Maurice received a letter from the R&A informing him that he had been drawn to play at Formby Golf Club with fellow professionals Jim Howard (Pontypool) and David Roberts (Bedford & County) at 9.30 a.m. on Friday 2 July, 1976. The clock was ticking, and there was no backing down now.

Hole 8: Major Eyebrows and Captain Combover

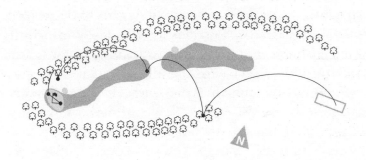

T HE NERVES were jingle-jangling the day Maurice was due to leave for Formby. It was a new sensation for him. He was a man who took to every challenge 'as a duck takes to water or an eagle to flight', but here he was, washing and hoovering the car, gauging the air pressure of the tyres, obsessively checking and rechecking the glove compartment for boiled travel sweeties, cleaning his clubs, and making sure he'd packed enough clothes, especially shirts that had collars and were therefore acceptable on a golf course. He was like a schoolgirl on a first date, only more fidgety and even less self-assured. He felt the same throbbing in his head that he'd felt back in the day, when he'd wholly exaggerated his credentials as a world-class high-diver to secure a place in the Stan

Bonds Troupe. But there was no shame in it: 'I was about to attempt to qualify for the greatest championship in the world, and what serious golfer who had never attempted such a thing before could remain calm and not get excited by the prospect?'

Formby Golf Club is perched on the Lancashire coast just north of Liverpool, and about 30 miles south from Royal Birkdale, where the 1976 Open proper would be held a week after pre-qualification. Only those fortunate enough to make it through the preliminary rounds would star at Birkdale. Maurice was sure he would be one of the lucky players. His elder brother Roy lived about an hour's drive from Formby in a village called Skelmersdale, so Maurice arranged to stay with him and Pat for the weekend. He'd travel down on the Wednesday, then walk the course and practise on the Thursday in preparation for Friday morning's tee-off time.

The plan was executed to perfection until early on Thursday. Maurice had arrived in Skelmersdale on Wednesday evening in plenty of time for tea. Preoccupied with nerves, he was unable to finish the fish-and-chip supper which had been laid on – he didn't even touch his processed peas, usually his favourite component of the meal – but he did notice that Pat didn't use his wasting the good food she had cooked for him as the basis for an argument, as would usually be the case. (Maurice and Pat had long since made a mature pact for the sake of Roy; they were always 'going to spark off each other', but pledged that anything rash said by either party during their

inevitable stramashes would be forgotten once the row
had subsided.) This evening, though, Pat kept schtum,
having been briefed by Roy to consider her sparring
partner's unusually heightened state of nervousness.
Maurice greatly appreciated the gesture, especially as
he wasn't sure he'd have been able to bite his tongue
were the boot on the other foot.

But the meteorological news brought an extreme
weather warning: a Flitcroftian front was about to
move over the Formby region, bringing with it great
heat. Thursday morning, the day before the big event,
was already in phew-what-a-scorcher territory. The
heatwave of 1976 was the hottest since records began.
For fifteen consecutive days, from 23 June to 7 July
inclusive, temperatures reached 90°F (32.2°C) somewhere in England. The first three days in July would
be the hottest of them all, with temperatures reaching
35.9°C (96.6°F). For Brits used to dank cloud and grey
drizzle, it was almost unbearable. Then, on top of it
all, upon arriving at Formby on his reconnaissance
mission, Maurice would turn up the thermostat a
needless notch or two himself.

'I set off to walk the course like a big-game hunter
on safari with my cream shirt, fawn slacks and red
jungle hat, notebook and pencil at the ready, to weigh
the links up and plan my strategy for the first qualifying round the next day.' He was accompanied by his
niece Sandra – Roy and Pat's daughter – who had
kindly offered to show Maurice the route to the course.
She explained her directions calmly and patiently, in
the sort of soothing tones these days generated by

satellite navigation systems in high-end executive saloons. Her efforts were however wasted on Maurice, who was in a world of his own and heard not a single word, taking a couple of wrong turns, learning nothing.

Finally they reached Formby Golf Club and set out to explore the course. But it wasn't long before the relentless sun took a sorry toll. Maurice began by making incredibly detailed notes of every bunker, bush, hump and hollow, making a particular effort to stride out 150 yards to each green from the fairway where he planned to employ his favoured 4-wood, creaming each and every one towards the flag. This felt good. He was acting like a pro now, formulating one hell of a watertight strategy. If he executed this to the letter, ran his train of thought, he had a real chance of making Birkdale the following week. Alas, after two and a half holes, something snapped in Maurice's head: 'It wasn't long before I began to get fed up with this lark and decided to just rely on my judgement.' It didn't help that it was approaching midday, the sun beating down from its most sapping position. He called off the scouting mission and repaired to the clubhouse. This was of some relief to Sandra, who was beginning to feel faint with a toxic mixture of sunstroke and extreme boredom. It's bad enough to walk the course watching someone play if you have no interest in golf; watching them pace out distances between a clump of heather and a pot bunker in a furnace was beyond the pale. Even so, taking her mum's lead during Mushypeagate at the dinner table the night before, Sandra had said nothing.

Back at the clubhouse, Maurice was about to be

given a rude awakening. Incredibly, despite this being the eve of his Open debut, he had never actually stepped inside a golf clubhouse before, used as he was to hopping over fences and playing in the moonlight before scampering off into the darkness, usually with an irate member in hot pursuit. This would be his introduction to the etiquette of the golf club, a labyrinthine tradition of strange rules and illogical diktats. And it would be a baptism of fire. Maurice was about to unwittingly lead his niece not into the family-friendly unisex lounge, but into that anachronism seemingly unique to golf clubs. They were entering the forbidden zone, the hallowed sanctum, the motherlode. They were making their way into – Wagnerian drum roll – the *men-only bar*.

And

he was still wearing

his hat.

The thirsty pair innocently sauntered into the room and waited patiently to order some refreshing squash. En route, Maurice had heard a succession of forced coughs by two ruddy-faced military types in ill-fitting blazers, one sporting waxed eyebrow turn-ups, the other a ludicrous wispy comb-over. Major Eyebrows and Captain Combover had specifically designed their hacks and splutters to galvanise the woman serving behind the bar into action, although she needed no direction. She had already spotted the two hapless rule-infringers.

'Two pints of orange juice and soda please, love,' Maurice ordered, oblivious to the pairs of staring eyes piercing his back.

'Sorry, sir, but you'll have to take your hat off before I can serve you,' replied the bar lady, pointing at the floppy red jungle headgear Maurice had wedged on his head to stave off the intense heat.

'Eh? Why?'

'Because those are the rules,' the lady elucidated calmly and clearly.

Maurice's eyes narrowed. His natural inclination was to assess 'whether the situation was getting heated, and whether it merited a sharp response'. His inner monologue concluded that while it *might* be, at this stage it probably did not. *Yet.* He swiped his hat off his head sharply and stuffed it in his pocket. Maurice was not constitutionally able fully to acquiesce to anything, so he appended the movement with a facial expression that unambiguously asked: 'Satisfied now?' He then repeated his order of two refreshing pints of orange and soda.

Another explosion of coughing erupted from Major Eyebrows and Captain Combover. Maurice wondered whether they'd caught Spanish Flu. The bar lady, finally responding to the coughs, nods and eyebrow-waggles of the retired servicemen towards the interloper from the distaff side, finally gave up wrestling her sisterly urges.

'There is another matter, I'm afraid,' she stammered, replicating the pointed glances towards Sandra. Maurice decided that the heat had caused some kind of collective madness to envelope the immediate environs of the bar.

'I'm not with you,' he responded.

The bar lady was finally forced to state the club's position. 'I'm afraid the young lady will have to go outside,' she whispered, her cheeks deepening to crimson.

'Why?' asked Maurice, immediately snapping into chivalry mode.

'Because this is a men-only bar,' came the only explanation.

'A *what*?'

'This is a men-only bar. Ladies must go outside, or use the lounge.'

Maurice was utterly perplexed. He knew, of course, of the working-men's clubs across the North of England, but they were more often than not populated with women anyway. What was the point of this, he wondered? Yet again, Maurice displayed attitudes years ahead of his time. But he had yet to work out that, if the world was a couple of decades behind him, the golfing firmament was at least another half-century further back. He first confronted the obvious contradiction in the club's policy.

'What are *you* doing here, then?'

'The rule doesn't extend to employees, sir.'

'I've never heard anything so ridiculous in my life. It's a hundred degrees out there and cool in here! We're thirsty. Please, now, we just want our drinks.'

Major Eyebrows had heard enough. He finally folded his *Daily Telegraph*, placed it purposefully on the table, hoisted himself out of his seat, and approached the offending duo. 'Perhaps I can be of assistance,' he pompously puffed. 'She is quite correct, I'm afraid, this is, in fact, a men-only bar. Rules are rules, I'm afraid, old boy.'

Captain Combover, having advanced to the bar in The Major's slipstream, placed his hand on Maurice's shoulder and gestured to the door. The rebel from Barrow was being offered a face-saving out: meekly accept the status quo, smile politely at the misunderstanding, and quietly disappear with Sandra into an area where women were permitted to imbibe orange squash. But he was disinclined to make any sort of grab for the opportunity, preferring to embark on a Hegelian dialectic with his new military chums in search for a higher truth.

'Listen, pal,' Maurice spat, making sure to immediately extract any confusion from the situation, 'this is my niece, and I am playing in the British Open here tomorrow, so if I were you I'd show a bit more respect.' The major was momentarily taken aback by these revelations, as he glanced up and down at Maurice's eccentric safari ensemble. 'If Jack Nicklaus came in here with his niece,' added the Open competitor, 'I don't suppose you'd be so quick to turf them out, would you?'

Aware that several of his cronies were now peering over their *Telegraph*s and listening intently to developments, Captain Combover stepped up a gear to save face. 'It wouldn't matter if old Tom Morris himself were to leap from the grave and stand before me with his wife and daughter, rules are rules and this is a *men-only* bar.' It was a splendid bon mot. The quality of the quip only served to irritate Maurice even further.

'Let's just go, Uncle Maurice, I'd rather go outside anyway,' pleaded Sandra, fully aware of her uncle's appetite for confrontation. What she didn't know was that the last time he defended a lady's honour in front of an authority figure, said authority figure ended up sliding across the top deck of a bus on his chin doing a passable Jürgen Klinsmann impersonation.

'We'll leave if you'd be so kind to tell me exactly *why* women aren't allowed in this bar,' demanded Maurice.

'Because it's the rule of the club, one that's been rubber-stamped by the committee,' spluttered an exasperated Major Eyebrows, highly irked at being questioned.

'Not good enough.'

Captain Combover tried the jauntiness angle – a staple argument of the casual bigot who has genuinely convinced himself that the men-only rule is doing the ladies a favour. 'Well, I am all for women's lib, old boy, but why would a woman want to be in here anyway? It's awful, it's full of men!' The joke fell on deaf ears.

'Not good enough.'

The Major snapped, his manicured eyebrows vibrating like a hummingbird's wings. 'The reason women are not allowed in the *gentlemen's* bar,' he shuddered, 'is because over here is the entrance to the *male* changing room.' Unused to having to explain himself, he marched towards a door adjacent to the bar in order to deliver the killer blow. He flung it open. Through a chink of light at the end of a wood-panelled locker room, several overweight gentlemen could be spotted in various states of disrobe, some talc-ing up, some flossing their clefts with the sharp edge of a towel in the inimitable fashion, most staring blankly back into the bar, like wide-eyed deer staring down the barrel of a shotgun. Sandra let out a shrieking guffaw. Finally a voice from the changing room cawed for the door to be closed with immediate effect, if not sooner.

Maurice conceded defeat. 'OK, *that's* good enough.'

He signalled for Sandra to move outside, bought two orange juices, and scuttled out into the sun after her. It had been an instructive exchange. There was no way he was giving an inch to those two pompous poltroons, who would hide behind some ridiculous rulebook or other while getting some poor barmaid to do their dirty work. His natural instinct was to challenge his supposed betters. Then again, all he had been after was a good reason for the rule. As a good reason existed in that clubhouse, he was quite happy to hang fire the second he was furnished with it. Trouble was, as he had found throughout his life to some cost, authority figures rarely bothered explaining themselves adequately.

Even so, when the situation was boiled down to the bare bones, he was embarrassed at not being able to take his niece for a drink, and utterly amazed that they wouldn't let a woman in the bar.

Having swallowed his pride, Maurice necked his

orange juice with Sandra outside on the patio. The pair gathered themselves up and headed back to base camp at Skelmersdale. After a light lunch provided by Pat, Maurice wandered off to some nearby fields to practise. On the way there he gave himself a pep talk. 'I decided that there wasn't much time left to make radical changes to my swing, so I would have to make do with what I had. I did feel, however, that a satisfactory practice session would do wonders for my confidence.'

He began by hitting some short irons. He was finding the sweet spot, so he graduated to his medium irons, then the long irons. Satisfied that they too were in decent-enough shape, he took out his nemesis: the driver. 'I knew that the ability to hit a good drive was going to be an important factor the next day,' he recalled, 'so it was with some misgivings that I found my driver was not what it should have been.' The trouble was with a certain kind of shot that set off straight and powerful, yet veered horrifically to the left after sailing about fifty yards through the air. This shot is known to most golfers as the snap hook. But Maurice had never played with any other golfers, and had no shared parlance to identify it, so coined a phrase himself: 'The Wrecking Shot'. The harder he tried to fix The Wrecking Shot, the worse it got. When the light faded, he still hadn't found the solution.

Consumed by concern, he trudged back to Roy's. He picked limply at his supper as Pat bit her tongue, and thought about The Wrecking Shot. He had a long hot bath and thought about The Wrecking Shot. He went to bed, tossed and turned, and thought about The Wrecking Shot. Trying anything to take his mind off The Wrecking Shot, he eventually found the perfect solution. He pulled from his suitcase a book he'd been reading, *Golf Rules Illustrated*. He began to read. It was probably right to find out the Rules of Golf. He didn't want to be penalised for any infractions the next day, and maybe this knowledge would counteract any strokes lost with The Wrecking Shot. Within seconds of opening the book, Maurice fell asleep.

He had set his alarm for 5 a.m., but awoke half an hour earlier, bright as a button. After a slurp of tea he was out in the fields again with his driver, in the hope that The Wrecking Shot had miraculously disappeared overnight. To his horror, he discovered it was still there. There was only a matter of hours until tee-off time, and therefore only one solution: forget the driver, and use his 2-wood instead. But any golfer with even a smidgen of experience could have told Maurice that taking an iron off the tee, or at the very most a 3-wood, was the right thing to do if his driver was malfunctioning – especially as a 2-wood is virtually identical to a driver. (It is almost impossible to get your hands on a 2-wood today, even if you tried.) After wasting another hour winging Wrecking Shots around the field with the 2-wood, Maurice eventually put that to one side as well, and decided to use his favourite club, the 4-wood, instead.

He set off for Formby with two hours to spare, which should easily have afforded him half an hour's practice on the range. Unfortunately, having failed to listen to Sandra en route to the club the previous day, he soon got lost, misreading a signpost with devastating consequences. 'I found myself heading in completely the wrong direction,' he said. 'Not sure of the route I should be taking to rectify the error, this necessitated me driving slower than I normally would. All of which began to make me anxious. I couldn't afford any more mistakes. I'd already used up the time I'd set aside for warming up and now I'd be hard pushed to make it to the course on time for teeing off.'

He eventually arrived at Formby with only a few minutes to spare, tearing across the gravel car park in a desperate attempt to find a parking space. First, he needed to buy some golf balls. The club pro, Jimmy Hulme, witnessed Maurice bundling into his shop, wearing a 'shabby cap and a pair of gumboots'. Hulme told him to get out, that nobody needed a caddy. Maurice replied that he was here to play in the British Open, and that he needed some balls. 'How many will I need to get round?' he asked. Barely stifling a rasping bellow of laughter, Hulme spotted an opportunity to make a few quid and sold him a dozen. Maurice then explained that he would require a caddy. With time tight, Hulme busied himself arranging one, telling the shabby pro that someone would arrive at the tee very shortly. An agitated Maurice then raced back to his car to get his clubs and golf shoes.

There was no time to change in the locker room, so Maurice pulled his shoes on while standing by his car, a complete no-no at any self-respecting club and an act which received one or two pained looks from passing members. Were Major Eyebrows and Captain Combover Man to pass now, he would surely be chased down the road, Maurice surmised. He knew he had one too many clubs in his bag, so pulled his errant 2-wood out and hurled it in the boot. Then, red-faced, he scampered off to the first tee, just in time.

There he found his caddy waiting, a teenage lad who made up for his lack of years with callow enthusiasm. Anticipating a hot day, he'd already soaked some towels in iced water and handed one to Maurice. A ball had yet to be struck in anger, but on this blistering day the towel was much needed; Maurice was drenched with sweat after his hair-raising journey. He shook hands with the announcer, who checked his watch and picked up the microphone.

'On the tee,' the announcer trumpeted, 'unattached, Maurice Flitcroft!' A polite smattering of applause.

Maurice turned to his caddy. 'Four-wood please, son.'

The caddy looked confused. 'Erm, there isn't one. You've got a driver and a two-wood.'

Maurice's newly aligned world suddenly span off its axis again. The full horror of the situation snapped into harsh focus. In his haste to make the tee on time, Maurice had whipped his 4-wood out of the bag by mistake and left that in the boot instead of the 2-wood. He allowed his disappointment a verbal outlet: 'Shit.' Jim Howard and Dave Roberts – Maurice's playing partners in match number 10 – shot concerned glances at each other. Then Maurice remembered where he was, and steeled himself. This was it. The British bloody Open. No time for regrets. Time to stand up and be counted.

'Of course, two-wood.' He smiled, winging it already. His caddy handed the club over. 'Thanks, son,' whispered Maurice. And with that, he strode confidently onto the tee.

Hole 9: 121 high-flying disappointments

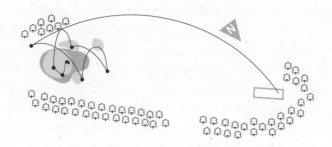

THE OFFICIAL R&A scorer for the 1976 Open qualifying event at Formby Golf Club turned up for
work at 9.30 a.m. Sands Johnson was in plenty of time:
though three-balls had been going out since 8 a.m.,
they wouldn't complete their rounds and need their
cards checked, double-checked and officially verified
by him for at least three, more likely four, hours.

So Sands was able to pooter up the driveway at
Formby at his leisure, taking in the sights, sounds and
smells of a balmy summer morning. In those days,
the first tee used to be visible from the club drive so,
as he passed, Sands glanced over at one of the early
three-balls setting out on their rounds. Sad to see, for
one man it looked as though that adventure had
ended before it had even begun.

'There was this man kneeling on the ground,' recalls Sands. 'He was on all fours, his hands and knees. I just assumed the poor man must have had a bad back injury!'

Sands was mistaken. The man on the tee wasn't suffering any severe spinal trauma, he hadn't tweaked a muscle in his back or even lost a contact lens. The man on the tee was Maurice G. Flitcroft, professional golfer. And Maurice G. Flitcroft was simply going about his business: he was down on all fours to push his tee firmly into the ground, then carefully balance a brand-new Spalding Top Flite XL onto the top of the peg. As Sands went on his way to the recorder's tent, blissfully oblivious, Maurice was preparing to hit his first shot as a top-level sportsman.

Jim Howard and Dave Roberts were watching with added interest. They had no earthly idea what the hell they were looking at. Not only had Maurice already missed his warm-up and nearly missed his tee time, he was also decked out in an ensemble which, even by the standards of mid-1970s golfing apparel, could fairly be described as eccentric: beige slacks, crumpled Fred Perry polo shirt, floppy blue fisherman's hat and tattered Stylo golf shoes.

'Nobody would have worn those shoes,' notes Jim Howard today. 'Bear in mind this was 1976, the hottest summer we'd had in a long time. Well, those shoes were made of plastic. They're a winter shoe.'

Maurice's clubs also rose eyebrows in the highbrow world of professional golf – 'They were catalogue clubs; they'd obviously been mail order,' spotted

Howard astutely – as did Maurice's close resemblance to Marty Feldman, the popular bug-eyed comic star of Monty Python forerunner *At Last the 1948 Show*, BBC vehicle *It's Marty* and the Mel Brooks movie *Young Frankenstein*. 'My first impression was that he looked like a ringer for Feldman,' says Howard. 'His eyes are very similar to him, in fact all his features are very similar to him. If you were to put them together, you'd notice they were very similar.' The fact that Maurice Flitcroft and Marty Feldman shared the same initials would later be commented on, some club members going to the lengths of starting a rumour that Maurice was, in fact, the star comic on an elaborate wind-up.

The possibility of an elaborate hoax – one involving Feldman, that is – wasn't such a fantastical notion. Not only was there an undoubted similarity between Maurice and Marty, one of the comedian's most famous sketches was entitled 'The Loneliness of the Long-Distance Golfer'. A five-minute film, it followed the travails of a hapless hacker slicing his ball hither and yon: onto the back of a moving van, into the bathroom of a nearby house, through a church bell tower, down a train tunnel, into the gullet of a passing crow, each shot taking him further and further away from the hole. Most tellingly for the conspiracy theorists, Feldman hits one shot from the arm of a crane. The punchline being – sorry to spoil it – that when he finally reaches the green (by shooting the crow out of the sky) he finds himself utterly incapable of holing out from six inches, tapping away back and forth long into the night.

Life was about to imitate art, spectacularly so. But despite all the evidence to the contrary, both Howard and Roberts were prepared to give Maurice the benefit of the doubt. 'The way he was dressed,' begins Roberts, 'we thought he was a pro returning from Europe somewhere on his swansong.' The romantic reverie didn't end there. 'Then, when we heard his name being announced in the draw, and that he was unattached, we thought he could have been an American, because obviously a lot of Americans came over to try to pre-qualify and were unattached. So we didn't actually know what to make of him at first at all.'

It would not take long for them to find out. Maurice had the honour, meaning he would tee off first. After crawling around on all fours to find the optimum spot of fresh turf to press his tee peg into, and popping his pristine Top Flite on its top, Maurice rose to become a biped once more, slugged back two deep lungfuls of air and let his breath hiss out slowly. It was like his televised introduction to golf all over again: boom ba de boom, ba de boom, ba de boom. Only this time his heart was doubling as the BBC Big Band. 'I felt everyone's eyes on me as I stepped purposefully forward,' recalled Maurice. 'After lining up my target, I took up my stance, addressed the ball, checked my aim, then swung the club mightily and let fly.' The ball sailed through the hazy summer sky.

Howard had also been studying the mechanics of Flitcroft's drive: 'He just gripped the club, he put both hands down the bottom of the grip, the club came up vertical, and came down vertical. It was as though he was trying to murder someone.'

Maurice's ball had indeed sailed through the hazy summer sky, but almost totally in a vertical direction. Upon landing, it was clear that it had not been imparted with too much forward momentum. It had only just cleared the end of the tee, ending up 40 yards down the track. The decision to use a 2-wood instead of his potentially 'round-wrecking' driver had already backfired. His stoic verdict was that the drive 'was a real high-flying disappointment'.

'To my horror, the tendency to hit a certain kind of shot with my driver also applied to my 2-wood,' he wrote. 'It was not a total disaster. It could have gone straight up, come down, and hit an official on the head. But it didn't, I'm glad to say.' The die was cast. Maurice's next shot was shanked into a filthy patch of rough. Down the fairway, Dave Roberts, whose drive had just crept into the semi-rough on the left, and Jim Howard, whose opening shot was creamed straight down the middle, just over some dangerous cross bunkers, waited patiently. Very patiently. Maurice's third shot, from the rough to the right of the fairway – and several yards before it, too – came off the hosel and squirted off at an odd angle, but did at least get him out of that particular spot of trouble. By transporting him into a fairway bunker.

But the scruffy pro from Barrow was made of stern stuff, and the rest of the hole – if not the round – would be negotiated without further drama. With the burning gaze of Howard and Roberts already causing his skin cells more damage than the blistering sun, Maurice splashed out of the bunker first time, then found the green and took two putts for an opening-hole 7. Three over par, after one hole.

Howard and Roberts, already discombobulated, had not been slow to take action. They could see – after the first hole, after the first couple of shots, even back on the tee – that something wasn't right. Roberts had his wife caddying for him, and she was swiftly dispatched to the clubhouse in order to inform an R&A official.

They arrived at the second tee in the nick of time. Howard and Roberts had cracked their drives away. Then Maurice – the honour now spirited away from him, never to return – had decided that starting the hole between the permitted blocks wasn't to his liking, and begun the process of teeing up elsewhere, closer to the front of the tee in order to make the hole shorter. One of the officials politely told Maurice to return to the designated area and take it from there.

Maurice took 5 at the second, followed by a 6 at the third. It wasn't the most auspicious of beginnings to a round, never mind a professional career, but Flitcroft wasn't the first pro golfer to begin a round 7-5-6 and he wouldn't be the last. 'Even the best players in the world have problems when they land in the rough,' reasoned Maurice, 'and very often they end up shooting high scores. Even higher scores on a single hole than I did, players like Greg Norman, Tom Weiskopf, Seve Ballesteros, to name but a few. Lacking their experience, I just did it more often.' Maurice's logic was watertight. Unlike his game. For while many a professional has indeed begun a round 7-5-6, few follow it up with another three 6s. Fewer still follow that up with a scorecard-wrecking, legend-defining, infamy-sealing, double-figure hole.

'The big one was the par-five seventh,' explains Roberts. 'It's a long hole through sand dunes, nearly five hundred yards. Because of the elements and the weather, the ball was running quite a way, and his bounded into the sand dunes.'

The ball was not quick in coming back out of them. Maurice, his exasperated playing partners up ahead, worked like a dervish to hack his ball out of trouble and back onto the fairway. It became an increasingly futile effort. By now, his idiosyncratic jazz stylings were causing hold-ups, with three-ball after three-ball backed up behind Flitcroft, Howard and Roberts. An Australian voice from a parallel hole was raised in protest, questioning the fisherman-hatted fiend's ability. Maurice stood his ground as proudly as a man can while bumbling around a sand dune and repeatedly swinging a metal stick at a seemingly immovable object.

'An Australian complained that we were holding them up, that he had gone to a lot of expense to get there, as though I hadn't! I don't remember what else he said, but I do remember that I replied that it was an open championship, and that I had paid my entrance fee and was perfectly entitled to be there.'

Whereupon the man stormed off, and Maurice

continued with the task in hand: coaxing his ball out of the sand dune. A task he successfully completed, eventually, after some time. Flitcroft played out the rest of the hole to comparatively little drama, having taken twelve strokes, a full seven shots over par.

Even then, this was a kind reading of events. For a couple of holes later, a member of the three-ball directly following the Flitcroft match, Harry Bannerman, sidled up to his friend Roberts and enquired what the hell was going on.

'What did that guy take on the seventh?' whispered Bannerman.

'He took twelve,' answered Roberts with a thin smile that could easily have been mistaken for the tired grimace of a man weighing up the downside of a lengthy spell inside, with the cathartic joy of wrapping the business end of a 7-iron around a crane driver's neck.

'*Twelve?*' spluttered Bannerman, with a mixture of incredulity and high amusement. 'He took that many shots behind that sand dune!'

'We didn't know how many shots he played, we couldn't see him,' admits Howard now. 'We only found out about three or four holes later that he had probably played eleven or twelve shots in the sand dune. It was very farcical, you know.' Roberts scribbled a question mark next to the seventh hole on Flitcroft's card, and moved on with a heavy sigh.

Thirteen more shots over the next two holes – a 6, followed by a 7 at the par-three ninth – took Maurice to the turn in sixty-one strokes, a massive twenty-five over par after nine holes that seemed like ninety-nine. 'Formby is a course that goes all the way out, and goes all the way back, so you can't come in at the ninth,' sighs Roberts. 'Because we'd have just walked in, you know.'

Just after the turn, Maurice suffered another double whammy. At the par-five tenth, he ran up a card-bothering 11, ensuring the inward leg of his round would be equally as lame as the outward. It was at this point that an R&A official approached him for a quiet word, *mano a mano*. Exactly what was asked has gone unrecorded – all Maurice reported in his memoir was that the official wanted to 'find out what he could about me, judging by the questions he asked' and that the situation soon became 'heated'.

Responding to one of the official's whispered queries, Flitcroft replied with feeling and no little volume. 'I was replying to one of his questions when, to my surprise, he suddenly said "sh-h-h!" which I didn't think very polite, and to which I didn't take kindly. I snapped back that he had asked me a question, and I was answering it.' The fact that Roberts was concur-rently taking his shot just across the fairway, within earshot, did not cross Maurice's mind at that partic-ular moment. 'So far as I was concerned, if our conversation was distracting the player about to swing, that player would have been well advised to wait until we had finished,' he reasoned. 'The fact that he went ahead and played his shot would indicate we were not distracting him. On the other hand, the official could have chosen a more opportune moment to quiz me.'

After the R&A official scuttled off with his tail between his legs, tempers within the three-ball became frayed. On the twelfth Maurice was surprised when a blind wedge shot from deep rough in a hollow generated cries of alarm from Howard and Roberts. 'I could only assume it had just missed them,' said Flitcroft. 'My caddie confirmed this. It was a nice shot out of trouble, for all that.'

The stroke didn't just send an increasingly pensive Jim Howard darting for cover, it also forced him to contemplate deeply existential issues. 'What a way to make a living!' he remarked during a lull in battle, staring straight at Maurice. An innocent aside, but one that raised the crane driver's working-class hackles. His inner monologue ran thus: 'I am surprised to hear a professional golfer make such a remark, not that I have known any before today. Perhaps it is the heat – the temperature is ninety-five degrees Fahrenheit. I will not reply. But if I was going to, I would say that it is preferable to working in a factory, a foundry or down a coal mine.'

Tension also crackled between Maurice and Howard as a result of the former marking the latter's card. Already struggling to keep his own score, Maurice would invariably lose count of his opponent's too. 'So, on a number of occasions,' he explained, 'when I wasn't sure, rather than guess how many strokes the other player had taken, I would ask how many he had taken. It was something I was entitled to do, and he was obliged to tell me. He did so in a grudging manner, which I thought rather churlish of him.'

Maurice was nonplussed at the increasing opprobrium coming at him from all angles. 'The reaction of my fellow competitors to all this,' he would write years later, 'was one of amazement in the beginning judging by their expressions, followed later by a coolness tinged with disapproval.

'I noted this, but I did not let it bother me. Why my apparent lack of ability should have bothered them, I'm at a loss to understand. One thing was for sure: I didn't pose a threat to their chances of qualifying, which should have given them a psychological advantage.'

Nevertheless, Howard was losing all appetite for his Open challenge. A native of nearby Liverpool, he had invited several of his old friends along to their local course to watch him compete for a place in golf's biggest championship. 'Friends of mine had come to see me play, and I ended up with nobody watching me. However, a crowd of two- or three-hundred people had gathered to follow us as a curiosity.'

Word had got round the course of a singular event unfolding. The hubbub whetted Maurice's appetite for nothing so vacuous as fame or notoriety, but old-fashioned glory, an attitude betrayed in his flight of fancy: 'The club probably employed a runner, a fleet-footed young man or woman for such purposes, just as they did in the old days, to carry news of victories on the battlefield, or defeats, back to their waiting masters and the people at home!'

After a steady 5 at the eleventh, a borderline-acceptable 6 at the twelfth, and a not-crushingly-calamitous-given-what-had-gone-beforehand 8 at the thirteenth, Maurice stood on the fourteenth tee gaining succour from the ever-growing gallery following his progress. He was about to play the greatest hole of his professional career to date.

What exactly happened on that par-four – the second-longest on the course at 420 yards – will never be known. But there are two distinct reports. The first was penned by Bill Johnson, the press officer stationed at Formby by the R&A that day, with a remit to keep in contact with the central press office at Birkdale, where the Open proper would be held the following week. Johnson's report details a drive into rough, a hack back onto the fairway, a thinned iron to three feet, and a tap-in for par.

The other report is by Maurice himself, who recollects 'a super 3-iron off the tee'; an 'online' iron shot (albeit one that finished 'well short of the target'); a 9-iron which was 'caught a bit thin', landed just short of the green, bounced and rolled to four feet; and a putt sank 'with the same pleasure I would have sunk a glass of ice-cold beer right then'. Subtle differences maybe, but any golfer will be able to spot the proud flourishes a mile off. Still, a par is a par is a par. A hole had gone by, and Maurice hadn't dropped a shot!

Yet it was too little, too late. Maurice might have made his first professional par at the fourteenth, but the enormity of that effort, and the realisation that, despite the achievement, he was still thirty-eight shots over the norm, took the wind from his sails. That total became an even uglier forty-three over par after he took 9 at the fifteenth. He contemplated walking off the course. 'There was a moment when I wished I was miles away, but that passed. What was I doing thinking such thoughts? I had every intention of completing the round, no matter what, and if I kept trying, who knows? I might still strike some sort of form and salvage something from the wreckage!'

Many lesser men would have taken the easy option of quitting by posting a 'no return' – where a golfer can't take any more and a simple NR is scribbled in the score box to save embarrassment – but Maurice struggled on. He made subtle adjustments to his grip and major ones to his swing, hoping to achieve even a small semblance of form. But he had run out of ideas, and there was nothing left in the tank. It was not to be. After over four hours of struggle against the elements and his own ability, Maurice G. Flitcroft, virgin professional golfer, staggered over the line. He had been a dead man swinging over the last three holes, completing his card with a miserable 5-7-5, coming back, exhausted, in sixty strokes, for a round of 121.

A sizeable crowd had gathered in front of the club-house. Smiling, applauding and cheering, they welcomed the returning non-conquering hero. 'My instinct and reason told me why they were there,' said Flitcroft. 'They were there not so much to greet us, and give a round of applause, but to satisfy their curiosity, see with their own eyes this golfing phenom-enon.'

Howard sent his caddie into the clubhouse to get

some drinks for everyone. Instead of waiting under
the beating sun for the thirst-quenchers to turn up,
he strode off to the recorder's tent. His playing partner
Dave Roberts was already inside it, and in deep conversation with Sands Johnson, who by now had worked
out that the man he thought had a back problem
on the first tee early in the morning had suffered an
altogether different kind of breakdown.

As official recorder, Johnson had to check all cards
as they came in and record the scores. Howard joined
in the discussion. Neither player was particularly
happy: Roberts had shot 82, Howard 86. Both men
were fully expecting to shoot scores in the mid-to-low
70s, and both men were certain of the reason they
hadn't hit their mark. 'They wanted to speak to an
official, they were upset,' says Johnson. 'I asked why,
and they said, "Just look at the scorecard!" I did, and
immediately saw a problem.' It wasn't hard to spot.
Not only did Maurice G. Flitcroft (unattached)'s card
have a three-figure score scrawled across the bottom
of it, next to the seventh hole was the figure '12' and
a massive question mark.

'I had to query it,' says Johnson. 'Both of them
stood there and said, "Well, that's when we lost count."
So they were obviously sick to death about what had
happened. And not too happy with Mr Flitcroft. My
initial problem was with the question mark, but the
fact it was 121 didn't help matters. I was in doubt as
to whether it was the correct score. Looking back,
chances are it wasn't. But they'd obviously got sick of
Flitcroft by the time they'd got to the seventh hole.'

The man himself had yet to make his presence felt
in the recorder's tent. He was still outside, having
waited patiently for Roberts' caddy to return with the
drinks. With shades of *Ice Cold in Alex*, this golfing
John Mills slaked his thirst – no doubt imagining he
was back on the fourteenth green, plucking his par
putt from the hole. The crowd buzzing around him,
Flitcroft – momentarily disorientated – considered his
next move.

He was snapped out of his reverie by an R&A official, who according to Maurice bore 'a resemblance
to John Cleese'. The official certainly shared Cleese's
authoritarian shtick, ordering the supine 'golfer' into
the recorder's tent. Budging not an inch, and
performing mathematical gymnastics in his head,
Maurice worked out that he would probably have to
shoot a round of twenty-three the following day to
qualify for the Open proper – in other words, he
would have to record a minimum of thirteen holes in
one – and decided to take his leave of the competition. Addressing the Royal & Ancient John Cleese,
the Marty Feldman lookalike announced his formal
withdrawal from the 1976 Open Championship on the
spot.

It was a spot from which Flitcroft was immediately
relieved, the official hauling him up off the grass and
then shoving him in the back to propel him towards
the recorder's tent, where Jim Howard, Dave Roberts
and Sands Johnson were waiting. 'In other circumstances, this might have called for a punch on the
nose or at the very least a push from me in return,'

Maurice contemplated later, 'but because of the occasion, I limited my response to a few well-chosen words.'

A crowd began to fill the scorer's small tent. Johnson sat behind a table, alongside his fellow officials. Maurice remarked at the time that they all seemed very sombre: 'Stony-faced would be the best way to describe them.' But years later he would revise his description of the scene, taking a bizarre sideswipe at both golfing protocol and the output of Britain's public-service broadcasters: 'They were rather like magistrates sitting on a bench waiting to pass judgement on some poor misguided soul who, fed up with the endless soaps, sit-coms, foreign films, quiz shows and repeats, not to mention the boring and pretentious golf commentaries by Alex Hay and Bruce Critchley on television, stubbornly refused to pay for a TV licence.'

Scores were checked, cards signed, hands shaken. Although Johnson harboured understandable doubts about the total this Flitcroft character had run up on the seventh, he was in the pleasant position of being presented with an official no-brainer. 'As far as the card was concerned, the 121 was OK. It was signed by Flitcroft and the marker, and as far as we were concerned, both of them had agreed the score and it was put in. With a question mark!'

A piece of golfing history had been officially rubber-stamped. Maurice's 121 – 49-over par – was the worst-ever round recorded since the Open Championship began in 1860, comfortably beating Walter Danecki's previous high of 113, set in the 1965 qualifier at Hillside

Golf Club, less than six miles down the Merseyside coastline.

Maurice took his leave of the scene, and with it the 1976 Open Championship, passing 'John Cleese' on his way out. He had one last shot to take. 'Here was an opportunity to even the score. I knocked him with my shoulder as I was passing. He must have thought he was to blame, because he apologised. I didn't enlighten him and, honour satisfied, I left the tent.' Petty perhaps, but if anyone had deserved to leave Formby Golf Club having recorded at least one small victory, it was Maurice. Newly buoyed and feeling at least a foot taller, he picked up his bag, threw it over his shoulder, and sauntered to his car, the day's work done.

Back inside the tent, Sands Johnson spotted an old friend, journalist Bill Johnson, the sometime northern golf correspondent for the *Daily Telegraph* and present at Formby as an R&A press officer. Sands knew that Bill shared a love of the lighter side of the game, so approached him with a smile on his face. 'I think you have got an interesting story here, Bill,' he whispered. Bill knew that if Sands gave him a heads up, he should follow the trail. He raced out of the tent and found the object of curiosity unlocking the boot of his car, just about to put his bag in the back.

'Excuse me. Mr Flitcroft, is it?'

Maurice turned. 'Aye.'

'Hello, Maurice. My name's Bill Johnson. Do you fancy a quick drink? I'm buying.'

Maurice had turned his thoughts to getting back

to his brother's flat, and putting his feet up after a long day. But then his sixth sense kicked in. He had a sudden feeling that what he had just done was going to hit big. His clubs still strapped across his shoulder, Maurice slammed the boot of his car shut. 'After you,' he gestured, and followed Johnson towards the clubhouse. His life was about to take a dramatic turn leftfield, like a typical Flitcroftian Wrecking Shot.

In

WHITE COURSE   **FORMBY GOLF CLUB**   **PAR 72**

(Standard Scratch Score 72)

Player _Maurice G. Flitcroft_   Competition _1976 Open Qualifier_

Handicap _n/a_   Date _2nd July 1976_

Marker's Score	Hole	Length in Metres	Length in Yards	Score	Strokes Rec'd	Par	Won + Lost - Halved 0 Points	Marker's Score	Hole	Length in Metres	Length in Yards	Score	Strokes Rec'd	Par	Won + Lost - Halved 0 Points
	1	370	405	7	12	4			10	469	513	11	4	5	
	2	348	381	5	7	4			11	355	388	5	11	4	
	3	466	510	6	3	5			12	372	407	6	5	4	
	4	286	313	6	14	4			13	349	382	8	15	4	
	5	148	162	6	17	3			14	384	420	4	9	4	
	6	370	405	6	6	4			15	369	403	9	2	4	
	7	453	495	12?	1	5			16	113	124	5	18	3	
	8	316	346	6	10	4			17	432	472	7	8	4	
	9	166	182	7	16	3			18	358	392	5	13	4	
Out		2923	3199	61		36		**In**		3201	3501	60		36	
								Out		2925	3199	61		36	
								Total		6127	6700	121		72	

Holes won _____

Holes lost _____   Handicap

Result _____   Nett | 121 |

Players's Signature _M G Flitcroft_   Marker's Signature _____

PLEASE REPLACE DIVOTS

Hole 10: Impregnable Quadrilateral, pregnable Open

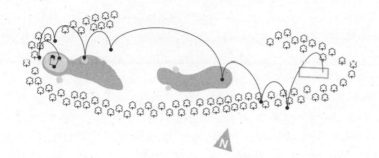

WHEN THE news of Flitcroft's 121 reached golf's highest office, Keith Mackenzie – the secretary of the Royal & Ancient Golf Club of St Andrews, the man who ran the Open, the head honcho, the chief, the bigwig himself, *el presidente* – was involved in a question-and-answer session with a group of school-children, extolling the virtues of the game in the hope of inspiring a future Open Champion. In scenes eerily foretelling George Bush receiving news of the 11 September atrocities while reading *The Pet Goat* to a class in elementary school, an R&A blazer sidled up to Mackenzie, whispered the breaking news in his ear, and left His Excellency sitting in front of a room full of kids, wearing an expression of bewildered and queasy disbelief. Just like Bush, it would be a while

before Mackenzie would regroup and wage a dispro-
portionate and unjust war. But for now all he could
do was stare into space, as he wondered how such a
cataclysmic event could have befallen him on his watch.
Because up until this moment, his reign as secretary
– and grand mufti of the Open Championship – had
been a regal procession.

During the 1960s, the Royal & Ancient made a
collective conscious decision finally to embrace the
twentieth century. Institutionally conservative with a
small C, the R&A wasn't going to do anything so radical
as allowing women into the clubhouse. But they did
at least accept the need to embrace one aspect of
modernity, the modern commercial world, if only to
ensure their flagship championship was to maintain
its status as one of the biggest golf tournaments in
the world.

Founded in 1860, the Open Championship is by far
the oldest of today's four major golf tournaments. The
next to come along, the US Open, only did so in 1895,
with the US PGA following in 1916 and the Masters
bringing up the rear in 1934. But the concept of these
four 'majors' – the four most prestigious titles in tournament golf, the Grand Slam – wasn't formulated until
1960. And looking back at how it all panned out, the
Open so very nearly missed the cut.

It wouldn't have been for a lack of history. From
the mid-nineteenth-century all the way up to the
Second World War, the Open was a big noise. By the
1930s, it had joined the US Open and the British and
US amateur titles to form what we now refer to as

the Old Grand Slam, but back then was snappily entitled the Impregnable Quadrilateral of Golf. (It's a
wonder commentators wished to change that delicious
tongue-twister!) But come the 1950s – by which point
widespread professionalism had rendered the amateur
titles worthless to the world's best players – the Open's
status as one of the biggies suddenly began to look
unsure.

The US tour was totally dominant in terms of playing
quality and strength in depth, and the intrinsically
inward-looking nature of American sport ensured the
US Open became by default the world's most prestigious title. Meanwhile, the Masters Tournament, two
decades old and held at the picture-pretty Augusta
National Club in Georgia, had fast become golf's most
glamorous shindig. And the scheduling of the US PGA
Championship – a mere week after the poor old Open
– regularly decimated the field of Britain's pride and
joy: most American professionals were dissuaded from
crossing the water by the lengthy difficulties involved
in transatlantic travel at that time, and anyway the
purse on offer by the R&A was considered laughable
by the cigar-chomping Yanks.

The jig looked up for the Open and its symbolic
Auld Claret Jug. But two men would save the tournament's status, and rekindle its glory.

The first was the new blue-eyed boy of professional
golf, Arnold Palmer. Between 1921 and 1933, his
countrymen had dominated the Open, winning all
bar one of the titles. Walter Hagen won four, Bobby
Jones three, the latter completing the Impregnable

Quadrilateral of Golf in 1930. In 1946, the legendary Sam Snead won the first post-war event. And in 1953, the great Ben Hogan added the Open to his Masters and US Open titles won earlier in the year: the Hogan Slam as it eventually became known. Hogan's Open win was all the more remarkable for the fact that he had never previously been bothered to enter the tournament, and would never find the motivation to do so again.

In 1960, Palmer won both the Masters and the US Open, and decided to enter the Open for the first time, in order to emulate Hogan's feat of seven years earlier. He wasn't worried about the paltry size of the cash on offer: he'd worked out, along with his agent and friend Mark McCormack, that his brand value was bound to soar with the legendary status a Hogan-style haul would bring. Problem was, with the amateur titles long consigned to history, there was no Impregnable Quadrilateral to aim for. And not being Ben Hogan, he could hardly win a Hogan Slam. So, while getting tight on booze one night with a few pals prior to his 1960 Open bid, Palmer came up with the idea of something to try to win himself. Something even better than Hogan's feat: the modern Grand Slam of Masters, US Open, Open and US PGA. Palmer's sportswriter friend Bob Drum ran with the idea, the British press picking up the concept with glee. Palmer failed to win the Open that year – so bang went his Slam! – but he'd be back in Britain to become Open champ in 1961 and 1962, after which Jack Nicklaus would become obsessed by the tournament, too. The British Open's shine was slowly being restored, and it was all thanks to the Americans.

But despite the best efforts of Palmer, the R&A still needed to actually do something proactive themselves. Which is where the Open's other saviour comes in. His name was Keith Mackenzie. It would be a name that would send shivers down Maurice Flitcroft's spine until the day he died – a day that couldn't come soon enough as far as Mr Mackenzie was concerned. From day one, the two were destined to become mortal enemies.

In any other arena, Mackenzie would have been nobody's idea of a forward-thinking go-getter. A bluff, rotund, balding man whose constitution was 50 per cent flesh, 30 per cent blazer and 20 per cent gin, he was exactly the sort of bumptious gent one would expect to see wedged in a leather armchair by the fire in his club, rolling a large ball of expensive cognac around a glass, sucking on an ivory pipe, and loudly bemoaning loss of empire. In the world of golf, however – and more specifically the club of the Royal & Ancient, St Andrews, Fife – Mackenzie was the very model of a modern major-general.

During the Second World War, he had seen service in the Indian Army. His time with the Gurkhas was spent largely sauntering around the golf courses of Calcutta, where he had time to hone his game: not long after being stationed on the subcontinent, he had whittled his handicap down to 1. If there were any doubts as to whether his time in India was charmed, they were dispelled in June 1947, when, returning home from service, the 2 a.m. flight carrying him caught fire at 14,000 feet. The pilot nose-dived in an attempt to put out the flames, but the ploy was doomed to failure, and he was forced to crash-land in the desert. The plane broke in half, exploding into a ball of fire. Thirteen people were killed, while others were badly injured. Mackenzie was not one of them. He extricated himself from the wreckage, dusted himself down, and waited for help. He did not wait in vain, a spotter plane soon locating him, a needle in a haystack. 'I was one of the lucky ones,' he recalled years later. Understandably, he developed a morbid fear of flying, though it was one he forced himself to overcome, not least, it was rumoured, because he'd been given free travel for life by the company whose plane bit the dust.

The business world came calling, and Mackenzie set up camp in Burma, where he became a marketing executive for Shell Oil. He kept his hand in on the golf course, getting involved with local clubs at committee level, and in 1967 spotted an advertisement in *The Times*, which he had regularly flown out from London, for the post of secretary of the Royal & Ancient Golf Club of St Andrews.

The club had been founded in 1754, parked itself next to the already famous Old Course in the small Fife seaside town, and set about becoming the biggest cheeses in the game. They accepted responsibility for writing the Rules in 1897, took over the sole running of the Open in 1920, and entered a pact with the US Golf Association to carve up the governance of the game worldwide: the USGA would run things in the States, Canada and Mexico, while the R&A could oversee the rest. So to say the role of secretary was a prestigious one is something of an understatement.

The blustering Mackenzie naturally felt he could handle the role with ease, and sent in his application, despite not being entirely sure of his ability to find St Andrews on a map. Once he got there for his interview, the super-confident marketing guru admitted to the committee that he'd never been to the place in his life before. Startled by his candour – the other candidates had spent large amounts of time delivering mealy-mouthed platitudes on the magnificence of Fife – the committee were won over by Mackenzie's plans for golf. He wanted to develop the game commercially, with a view to ploughing the millions he'd raise back into the sport. That meant exploiting the R&A's number-one brand: the Open Championship.

The R&A had dipped its toe into the murky waters of the modern world in 1966, allowing on-course advertising to be displayed around Muirfield. Mackenzie was not impressed. 'I recall that there was an advertisement near the first tee for a certain firm's bananas,' he recalled. 'That put me off eating those particular bananas.' The response was Mackenzie in microcosm: on the one hand, he was needlessly pugnacious and stubborn; on the other, he was battling to retain the understated and elegant aesthetic of the grandest tournament in the world.

Mackenzie promised to turn the Open into a cash cow, without tarting it around shamelessly. The R&A

bit and offered him the job. Slowly, a more modern Open began to take shape. At his first Open, the 1967 championship at Hoylake, Mackenzie ensured the fruit-hawking ads of the previous year were spirited away. He was taking notes. From now, the devil would be in the detail: for example, there were no scoreboards at Hoylake, a blackboard and chalk in the press centre the only concession to signage. Mackenzie unveiled new leader boards the following year, the simple principle being that paying spectators who had some idea what the hell was going on were more likely to come back. And pay again. Simple logic, but previously beyond the ken of the claret-soaked clan at the R&A, who sat gleefully open-mouthed as the money slowly dripped in. Mackenzie went on to introduce hospitality areas and product exhibition zones, ideas which would eventually grow into the modern tented village.

Yet Mackenzie knew the Open was nothing if the best players in the world didn't bother to compete in it. 'He determined that his ambition was to refurbish the Open,' explains Bill Elliott, the much-respected golf correspondent for the *Observer*. 'And the key to that for him was getting the Americans to come back.' Of course, it helped that Arnold Palmer had flown over and won the title in both 1961 and 1962, and that there had been further American success in 1964 and 1966 with victories for the ill-fated Tony Lema (a superstar in the making who would die in a plane crash in 1966) and Jack Nicklaus. But US involvement was still thin on the ground. Mackenzie got to work.

'You might say that, in those days, I went over to try to recruit players for the event,' said Mackenzie on his retirement in 1983, 'though it wasn't really recruitment; rather a case of talking to players and letting them know that, if they came over to play, accommodation would be arranged for them and that they would generally be looked after.'

Mackenzie's work did not go unnoticed by the game's top figures. 'He did a tremendous amount for the R&A, badgering – bullying, almost – people to come over and play in our Open,' says the BBC's voice of golf, Peter Alliss, today. 'He did a tremendous amount of furthering. He'd travel to the Masters every year, and badger the players to come over and play in the Open. Organised it so he could find them hotel rooms and everything.'

Sir Michael Bonallack, Britain's most successful amateur golfer and the man who would eventually succeed Mackenzie as secretary of the R&A in 1983, considers his predecessor to be 'largely responsible for making the Open what it is today', a point Bill Elliott readily agrees with. 'The Open's position in world golf had slipped quite dramatically away during the 1950s and 1960s, and Keith was the key figure in re-establishing it as a significant championship,' says Elliott. 'He blew smoke up the Open's backside. The main players suddenly realised: Hey, I think we should pay some attention to this Open Championship. And so the Open was up and running again.'

By the mid-1970s, the Open was being regularly contested by top stars from the US Tour such as

Nicklaus, Lee Trevino, Gary Player, Tom Weiskopf and Johnny Miller. Top stars meant the Open could attract larger and larger crowds, and offer significant prize money. This, in turn, ensured even more of the world's top golfers turned up to play. The all-new modern Open was a success story, which was good news for the health of both the R&A coffers and Mackenzie's ego. The secretary now regarded the championship as very much his own baby. He was every inch the master of his own domain.

What Keith Mackenzie said went. In 1976, he instigated the practice of ensuring the winner's name is engraved on both the Auld Claret Jug and the winner's medal before the victor receives them at the closing ceremony. To this end, he gave the engraver a whopping twelve minutes to complete both tasks.

'Please, Mr Mackenzie,' begged the poor man entrusted with the job, 'please never let Severiano Ballesteros win, because to do that in twelve minutes on the cup and the medal is going to be extremely difficult.' The quip was half joke, half plea for a more realistic timeframe in which to perform a highly delicate task. It fell on deaf ears.

'Chum,' replied Mackenzie, 'you had better start practising.' (Three years later, when Ballesteros did win the Open, the engraver managed to complete the job, albeit minus the last 'S' on the medal. In fairness to Mackenzie, he gave the engraver 'full marks' for his efforts, as he 'had spelt Severiano full out, not shortening it to Seve'.)

Mackenzie particularly enjoyed baiting journalists. At the 1978 Open at St Andrews, there had been a telecommunications strike ahead of the event, and no new phone lines could be set up. The R&A secretary pulled out all the stops – but only to order the construction of a pigeon loft beside the press centre with a sign beside it reading, 'Park your pigeons here'. A distinctly unamused press pack was forced to walk en masse into the nearby town centre to make copy-filing arrangements with owners of pubs, restaurants and shops.

At another Open, Mackenzie nearly caused a strike by golf writers on the eve of the championship, by suddenly announcing that journalists would no longer be allowed in the locker room to interview players. Mark Wilson, covering the event for the *Daily Express*, recalls that 'peace was only restored when he surrendered with one final swipe at the press. "You lot are the most important people of all with your pre-championship publicity value for ticket sales," he told us. Then he added: "But once the first ball is hit you are just a bloody nuisance."'

'Everybody had a run-in with Keith Mackenzie at one time or another,' recalls Peter Haslam, then editor of *Golf World* magazine. 'He was very strict, a rules man through and through. And he often made his own rules, and you didn't cross them. We all had instructions on where we could go on the golf course: you can go inside the ropes, but only in certain places.'

This fastidious approach led to an incident at Carnoustie, where a Japanese photographer was spotted by Mackenzie 'prancing about all over the fairways, getting in the way of the players, trying to photograph them from about five or six feet, and doing things like that'. It transpired that the snapper had not been briefed properly, as he didn't have particularly good English. This didn't cut much ice with Mackenzie, who decided to hold a 'de-armbanding ceremony' outside the press centre.

Bearing in mind that Japanese culture is built very much on honour and the retention of dignity and face, ostentatiously stripping this gentleman of his accreditation was not the most tactful of acts. Mackenzie was reminded of this in trenchant terms when he ran into the unfortunate photographer again in Tokyo years later, by which point he had put down his camera and become a journalist instead. 'He revealed that he was the photographer who had been de-armbanded at Carnoustie,' reminisced Mackenzie. 'By then, his English was much better,' he added drily, recalling a foul-mouthed tirade which this time crossed cultures effortlessly.

In the 1978 Open, having already put up the backs of the entire Fourth Estate with his pigeon-loft jape, Mackenzie appears to have totally lost the run of himself after a threat was made to Tom Watson's life. Watson's brother-in-law had received a call in the United States from someone with an English accent who repeated the phrase 'Don't let Tom play today' three times. Having phoned Scotland Yard, the brother-in-law then rang the R&A head honcho. Subconsciously making the snap decision that a smoothly run tournament is worth more than the ongoing life of an Open champion, Mackenzie simply didn't bother to pass on the message to Watson. Instead, after discussions with local police, a plain-clothes officer was tossed a BBC TV armband by the secretary. This allowed him inside the hallowed ropes without raising alarm, whereupon he could follow Watson around the course as an undercover body-guard. If anyone approached to enquire about the position of BBC cameras, Mackenzie suggested the hapless copper should simply 'tell them to push off and mind their own bloody business'. Exactly how this plan would have put off, say, a sniper from going about his task went unrecorded. Happily, Watson made it round without meeting his maker.

Though Mackenzie's self-importance could be tire-some, he was nevertheless a popular figure in the world of golf. Getting the new Open winner's name on the trophy toot sweet may have caused the engraver a severe pain in the eyepiece, but the players were always appreciative of the gesture, as were the top six in every Open for the top-quality champagne Mackenzie insisted they shared with him.

'He wasn't everyone's cup of tea,' admits Peter Alliss. 'He was an untidy sort of chap really. But he was a character. Gruff voice, good sense of humour, he was a good secretary.' Mark Wilson agrees, talking of a 'truly great and powerful character' who was 'honest and strong enough to always stand in front of the press and argue his case, no hiding behind his office door'; while Peter Haslam remembers a 'wonderful man' and 'most affable fellow' who once extended him an impromptu invitation to dinner in an exclusive Monte Carlo eaterie and thought nothing of picking up what would have been a very hefty bill.

But Mackenzie's pomposity would always win out, and it was to be his Achilles heel. 'In many ways he was warm-hearted and generous, and rather kind,' says Bill Elliott, 'but he was completely R&A, he was completely golf, above all other things. He is painted by many people as the cliché of the golf club secretary, the master of his own little universe, and in some ways he fitted into that. He stood fools not gladly at all.'

And so it was that, on 2 July 1976, Mackenzie would encounter what, for him, was the perfect embodiment of a fool: Maurice G. Flitcroft (unattached). 'It got to the point where Keith nearly had a heart attack at the mere mention of his name,' recalls Sir Michael Bonallack. Mackenzie was about to become the Eliot Ness to Maurice's Al Capone, the Herbert Lom to Flitcroft's Inspector Clouseau, the Wile E. Coyote to an uncatchable Road Runner.

In a delicious irony, Mackenzie had also been the unwitting Dr Frankenstein to Flitcroft's monster. As R&A secretary, it had been Mackenzie's duty to arrange the qualifying tournament for the Open. Personally responsible for vetting all player entries, he would assign each Open wannabe to a tee time at one of four qualifying courses. The best scores at each venue would secure a place at the Open proper. Mackenzie had arranged four qualifying competitions at courses in the Southport area. However, shortly before they were due to take place, he was informed that there had been a rather serious administrative error: the R&A had accepted too many entries! There would not be enough tee times at four courses to go round.

The solution was obvious: withdraw the extra players. A polite letter of apology and a refund of their entry fee would do the trick. But despite his success in turning the Open into something of a cash cow, Mackenzie didn't see the benefit in the R&A turning down easy money. A commercial man to his bones, he decided instead that, by holding qualifying at a fifth course, the R&A would trouser thousands of pounds' worth of extra revenue for very little effort.

Mackenzie appeared unannounced at Formby Golf Club early one afternoon to announce his cavalier decision. 'He appeared shortly after lunch,' said Richard Doyle-Davidson, then secretary at Formby. 'To be honest, he looked more than a little dishevelled. Half pissed, in fact. But there was no doubting the urgency of his request. I decided we could do it.'

By ordering that fifth qualifying course at supershort notice, Mackenzie had inadvertently secured a place for Maurice, who would otherwise have been out. Mackenzie had been the author of his own tragic downfall. His personal fiefdom had been stormed, and he had rolled out the red carpet himself . . . and left the front door ajar. Not that it mattered, because Maurice had come crashing in, boots first, through the R&A's front window.

The man who had saved the Open, and almost single-handedly changed the direction of professional golf, sat rigid in front of the schoolchildren as the full consequences of his drunken folly played out in his mind, the flesh on the bones of a nightmare.

'What shall we do, sir?' asked the bearer of bad news. There was a long pause.

'Make some phone calls. We should be all right,' announced Mackenzie, with as much confidence as he could dredge up, 'as long as we keep this out of the press.'

Hole 11: Maurice talks to the press

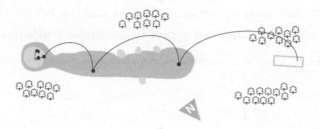

BILL JOHNSON ambled from the car park to the clubhouse, with Maurice trailing in his wake. The brand-new holder of the record for the worst-ever round in the Open Championship wasn't entirely sure if he was doing the right thing. He wanted desperately to get back to Roy's house and attempt to make some sense of what the hell had just happened. His 1976 Open bid was in tatters. Having genuinely believed he was in with a shout of winning the tournament, these were 121 hard facts to take.

Then again, there was no way his round was going to go unnoticed. The press were bound to mention it somewhere, surely, so it would only be prudent for Maurice to put his side of the story. A quick drink with this guy wouldn't do any harm. He picked up his stride, dumped his clubs against a nearby wall, and followed the journalist into the clubhouse.

They entered the bar and it quickly became clear that the news of the record-breaking round had spread. Mouths were agog everywhere. It didn't help that Maurice was still wearing his fisherman's hat and spiked golf shoes. And who should be sat in their usual seats but Major Eyebrows and Captain Combover. Had they even moved during the last twenty-four hours? Maurice wondered. However, his entrance into the bar affected an entirely different response from them this time around. Instead of looking over their newspapers disparagingly, they snapped them shut and stood up. Was that even a nod and a smile they cast in his direction? 'Lots had changed since I'd last been in there,' Maurice reflected. Indeed it had: he'd clearly amused the two old duffers so much they were willing to waive the rules this time. Discombobulated, they were now at a loss as to whether to hurl him out or buy him a drink. It was a moral dichotomy that would divide club golfers the world over.

Bill Johnson tried to stave off any negative vibes from members by holding up his palms in mock surrender. 'I know, I know,' he mouthed apologetically. The unspoken message was clear: please leave me to deal with this, everything's in hand, and I'm working here. The pair were allowed to pass through the bar in peace. Maurice was unable to resist blowing his two friends a cheeky kiss.

Johnson found a cubbyhole to set up camp, out of

the still-sizzling sun and away from the gaze of the
still-jabbering public. A sizeable crowd – much more
animated than a gathering would normally be at a
mere *qualifier* – was hanging around outside the clubhouse, and sniffing around the recorder's tent.
Rumours were bounding around like wild deer, and
the sharper punters were acutely aware that whatever
was going down in Flitcroft's wake was probably much
more important than anything happening out on the
course.

Bill asked Maurice if he wanted a drink. Maurice
replied that a glass of water would do, so long as the
stuff wasn't too chalky. (The water that came out of
the taps back in his Barrow home was, in his opinion,
the softest and tastiest in the country.) He had run
out of cigarettes, though. 'Could I cadge one?' he
asked. 'I think I might have smoked 121 out on the
course.' Johnson said he could do better than that,
heading for the bar, whispering to the steward behind
the counter, then coming back with a couple of cigars
which appeared thicker than the shaft of Maurice's
driver. Plus two very generous brandies. The men
chinked glasses as Maurice – allowing himself to relax
for the first time in the day – started sucking on the
end of his Cuban cheroot.

Having settled the puffing Barrovian back in an
ample armchair, Johnson excused himself for a
minute. Every journalistic alarm he possessed was
whistling, clanking and screaming in his head. A huge
story had fallen into his lap, and he absolutely had
to interview this imposter: who the hell was he, and

why was he playing in the greatest golf tournament in the world despite a clear and almost total lack of ability? This was potentially huge. It would make a great scoop for the *Telegraph*. But he wasn't here as a freelancer today, he was here as an R&A press officer. There was one at each of the five qualifying courses, all with a hotline to the main Open press centre, already set up at Royal Birkdale for the tournament proper the following week. Most of the national golf scribes were holed up there – and they had to be informed. He couldn't keep this gold to himself.

Johnson rang the number and announced the arrival of golf's Walter Mitty to the press pack. He was left with explicit instructions to keep Maurice at the course at all costs, even if it meant kneeling on his chest or tying him to a snooker table. Even from six miles away, Johnson could just about hear a chorus of half-written stories being ripped up, desk chairs tipping over and cars hysterically wheelspinning out of Birkdale, en route to Formby, where all the action suddenly was. Forget writing about how Big Jack was feeling a twinge in his elbow, or the balletic beauty of new boy Severiano Ballesteros's swing: here was a genuine Open record-breaker, the story of the year coming nearly a week before the tournament had even begun!

It was going to take the press pack a while to get to Formby, though, affording Johnson the opportunity to quiz the man himself. He returned to the table, only to find Maurice's head almost completely obscured by a thick cloud of cigar smoke. He also noted that both brandy glasses had been divested of their contents. Squinting through the Cuban mist, Johnson could just about make out a satisfied smile spread across Maurice's face.

Johnson popped back to the bar and ordered two more brandies. And another cigar. He placed them down on the table, along with his notepad. The pair engaged in some easy-going chat, both men knowing the small talk would inevitably segue into an interview sooner rather than later.

After ascertaining the raw facts about Maurice – his name, where he was from, and what he did for a living – Johnson moved the conversation quickly onto golf, trying his hardest not to allow an eyebrow to shoot up upon hearing the round was Maurice's first-ever eighteen-hole sortie. 'I wasn't really ready for this championship,' admitted Maurice, showcasing for the first time – but not the last – his mastery of tinder-dry understatement. 'I was trying too hard. I didn't think I was ready but my wife Jean and my thirteen-year-old sons encouraged me to play. I felt the pressure of the big event. I was just a bit flustered. To be frank, I was a bit erratic.'

Johnson put it to Maurice that his slow play had ruined the chances of Jim Howard and Dave Roberts, who had shot 86 and 82 respectively. Howard, for example, had shot a 73 on the practice day before the official qualifying round, and would go on to take 74 shots during his futile second qualifying round, post-Flitcroft. Those two scores would have seen him qualify for Birkdale; as it was, Howard never did make it to the Open proper.

'I did feel sorry for my partners, as I am sure they can play better,' replied Maurice, 'but I was only slow when I got into trouble in some of those bushes.' Bill proffered the suggestion that he probably visited quite a lot of bushes running up a round of 121. But that particular point was left hanging, as Maurice, affecting not to have heard, nonchalantly tossed back the last of Johnson's brandy and rose to leave, safe in the knowledge that his extraordinary bid to reach Birkdale would be accurately reported. He had instinctively liked and trusted Johnson, who he felt 'got' what he was trying to do.

By now, a phalanx of press photographers had arrived from the Birkdale press centre. They had been waiting patiently in the corner of the lounge for Johnson to finish his interrogation, and now it was their turn. One of the photographers approached Maurice and asked him if he would be willing to be photographed. Maurice baulked. He knew instinctively that if he agreed, his cover would be totally blown; should any press reports be accompanied with even the smallest picture of himself, there would be no way he could wheedle his way into next year's tournament and try again. There was also the small matter of his top set of false teeth. They had begun to play up, the adhesive melting in the intense heat, and would drop down almost every time he opened his mouth. They just about stayed in place when he clamped his cigar in between his teeth, but he was fighting a losing battle.

With the state of his dentures and next year's qualification tournament in mind, Maurice politely turned the offer down, and slipped out of the bar quietly. Despite his protests, the persistent snappers followed him, begging for a photograph. But Maurice was adamant that he didn't want his picture spread all over the newspapers. He picked up his bag, which had been lying outside the clubhouse, and wandered towards his car again, anonymity and dignity intact. But waiting for him by his car was his caddy. In all the hubbub, Maurice had forgotten to pay him his £3 fee. It was this small oversight that led to Maurice abandoning his decision to go to ground, and instead offering himself wholesale to the baying press.

All he had left in his pocket was a single five-pound note, soaked through with sweat after spending four hours in his pocket on the baking links and rendered almost worthless. 'Any of you got change for a fiver?' Maurice asked the photographers, waving a soggy blue picture of the Queen in the air. 'I've got to pay my caddy.' There were waves of giggles.

'How much was it?' piped up one of the photographers.

'Three pounds,' confirmed Maurice. 'But he deserves double,' he added, no doubt factoring in the extra miles the poor lad found himself covering while zig-zagging along Maurice's convoluted route around the course.

'I'll take care of it,' replied the photographer, who immediately – and ostentatiously – handed seven pounds to the bag carrier.

'My caddy's delight knew no bounds,' reported

Maurice later, ever the thoughtful employer. 'A broad smile spread over his face and he jumped for joy.'

But as a result, Maurice suddenly found himself morally beholden to the photographer. It would be extremely bad form to insist on leaving without posing for photos now, after one of the photographers had settled his debt. He sighed at the prospect of a long day getting even longer, but in truth he wasn't *that* annoyed. Despite still fretting about his chances of slipping through the net again in twelve months' time – and with cramp setting in his jaw as a result of clenching his dentures together to avoid oral embarrassment – something inside of him knew he'd regret not allowing the press to take a photograph or two. The decision had, serendipitously, been spirited out of his hands. For the rest of the day, Maurice decided to go with the flow.

He whipped off his floppy hat and gurned awkwardly. The photographers insisted he put his titfer straight back on. After a quick kneejerk grumble – he didn't care either way, but he didn't like being ordered around – Maurice popped the hat back on. He also, having nearly spat his teeth onto the floor while moaning, whipped the free-floating dentures out of his mouth and into his pocket. He snapped his lips firmly shut, and allowed a huge grin to spread across his face. He looked, as every paper would comment the next day, just like a poor man's Marty Feldman. It was as though the lonely long-distance golfer was here in the flesh. The pictures would become iconic, appearing across the national media the next day, the definitive Flitcroft mug-shot.

The photographers demanded some action shots. Maurice suggested that the obvious place was the course and, oblivious to the fact that professional golfers were strewn across it desperately attempting to earn themselves a place in the 1976 Open, marched towards it, 8-iron in hand. 'The photographers wanted pictures that would reflect my epic struggle with the game and the course,' said Maurice, 'pictures that would complement the written accounts.' They selected a none-too-secluded spot running along the edge of the course, where trees and bushes were at their thickest, the grass tallest, the undergrowth most resembling a jungle. Maurice was detailed to wade in.

It was time for catharsis. 'Finding new strength after my rest, I entered into the spirit of things and thrashed about heroically,' recalled Maurice. 'I uttered such expressions as, "Take that, you bastard! And that! And that! Let that be a lesson to you! You've been asking for it all day, now it's my turn you swine! Take that! Oh, take yourself off!"'

Maurice, bringing his club almost vertically up and down through the thicket, the stub of a panatela sticking out of his mouth, was lost on the journey into his heart of darkness. It was difficult to know what was moving at the greatest speed: the head of Maurice's 8-iron, the shutters of the cameras or the heads of the photographers performing double-takes and looking at each other in amazement at the unique *mise-en-scène* set out in front of them.

The snappers continued to fill up their films, stopping only to wipe the tears of laughter streaming down their faces. 'I was enjoying myself no end,' Maurice would remember. 'No longer under pressure, I gave full rein to my feelings, swinging away with ever-increasing enthusiasm and vigour, scattering divots and grass and leaves everywhere.' All the while, traipsing past in the background, Maurice's fellow Open hopefuls were still out on the course, looking on in stunned disbelief.

Maurice finally put down his club, throwing it gently over the thicket and back out onto the path, near his bag. Dripping with sweat, he clambered out of the rough to a tumultuous round of applause from the ranks of photographers. He shook every man by the hand. Finally, the photographer who had paid Maurice's caddy for him slipped a little something into the player's pocket as well. 'Buy yourself a drink,' he said with a smile, before walking off. Once the last cameraman had disappeared around the corner, Maurice dipped into his pocket and took a peek. It was two crisp pound notes. Dry ones. 'I reckoned I had earned them,' decided Maurice.

By now, so many journalists had arrived from Birkdale that Bill Johnson was forced to set up a de facto press conference in order to achieve some decorum. With his stint in the undergrowth having been met with such approval by the photographers, Maurice began to taste the sweet old nectar of performing for a crowd once again. It was a feeling reminiscent of his diving days, but this time he wouldn't have to risk life and limb, he'd just have to talk. Which was something that came naturally to him (especially now he'd taken his dentures out).

Maurice sat down behind a table, rows of journalists gathered around him. Bill noticed the difference in Maurice straight away: meek and mild when he was chatting one-on-one earlier, this instantly infamous professional was coming out fighting his corner with Flitcroftian fervour.

The first burning question was fired at golf's hottest property: what could he put his bad score down to? 'I rushed to get here and I had no time to warm up,' answered Maurice. 'I was hot and bothered on the first tee. But I started to put it together towards the end of the round. I hit some really super shots.' It was the opening salvo in a litany of non-sequiturs and dry asides that would have the hacks stifling giggles like schoolchildren in assembly.

'I suffer from lumbago and fibrositis, but I don't want to make excuses,' he continued, doing exactly that. 'I was never happy with my driver. I had only just mended it after breaking it when I hit a brick instead of the ball. And I left my 4-wood behind in the boot of the car, and I shouldn't have. I'm deadly accurate with that.'

What part of his game did he need to tighten up? 'Well, I struggled around the greens with my chipping. Problem is, when I practise at home my dog Beau usually catches the ball before it hits the ground, so I never see how it reacts. I misjudged a lot of chips today because of that dog, but I can't be too hard on him, he's only a pup.'

And what about his putting? The journalists had heard of some epic struggles on the greens. 'I thought I putted pretty well,' he argued. 'Apart from the five putts on the eleventh. Actually, I'd like to take the opportunity to praise Formby Golf Club for the quality of their putting surfaces, as in texture and pace they resemble my living-room carpet which I practise on every night.'

The most crucial issue had yet to be addressed: why the hell had he done it? Why had he opened himself up to almost certain humiliation, when it must have been clear a car crash of a card was unavoidable? The press pack were expecting a response in parts humble, self-deprecating and apologetic. What they got was a categorical statement of intent, an unashamed call to arms.

'I've always been a bit of an athlete, and thought it would be nice to play in the Open with Jack Nicklaus and all that lot,' began Maurice. 'It would give me some encouragement. If I don't make the grade I will give the game up and take up painting, at which I am good.

'But I have made a lot of progress in the last few months. After all, in eighteen months, I haven't reached my peak. Some of those top stars have been at it for years. They are well past their best. All those other guys have already realised their potential. I'll go away, tighten up my game, and come back next year.'

Jim Howard quietly watched the performance from a detached distance, and with amused admiration.

'He was very good,' he says. 'All of a sudden he came alive. He was pretty good in there!'

He was far from the only member of Maurice's audience to be impressed. The collected journalists had been convulsing with laughter at the relentless barrage of deadpan wisecracks. Who was this guy? A comedian? A clown? (Rumours that this was an elaborate hoax orchestrated by that man Marty Feldman had indeed by this point started to circulate, put about by some of Formby's scattier old boys.) But Maurice was no clown. In fact, as much as he was enjoying the limelight, it hadn't been his intention to be humorous. He appeared to be just telling the truth. 'I'll see you next year, fellas,' he said finally. If he was messing around at this golf malarkey, and simply playing everything for laughs, his poker face belied nothing.

For the third time, Maurice headed towards his car. Finally, his day's work really was over. He stowed his clubs in the boot and pootered serenely away. The drive back to Skelmersdale afforded him time to reflect on the events that would change his life for ever. 'I wasn't disappointed that I hadn't qualified,' he said. 'I had known from the start, before I set foot on the first tee, that things hadn't worked out as I anticipated, that there were too many shortcomings in my game for me to realistically expect to qualify. Nevertheless, I had expected to do much better. That was the annoying part – knowing I had the potential to do better. But would people believe me? And did it matter what people believed? Well, yes! I had my pride and like most people, wished to be well thought of, admired and respected.'

His mother, of course, was one who thought well of him. Contacted by one enterprising journalist, she would outdo Maurice with the quote of the day. Having been informed of her son's record 121 score, she asked: 'Does that mean he's won?' When it was explained that, no, the polar opposite was in fact true, and that a high score isn't a signifier of great golf, she sighed and responded: 'Ah well, they all have to start somewhere.'

Maurice arrived back at Roy's flat and broke the news of his 121, to some consternation. Over tea, he explained what had happened, and suggested he might be in the papers tomorrow. Roy, Pat and Sandra were unsure whether it was a good thing or not, but Maurice told them not to worry. He was sure everything would be OK in the long run. He took his leave and drove back up the M6 bound for Barrow, whereupon he planned to sit in his favourite armchair with a mug of tea and relay the events of the day to Jean and the twins, every inch the returning hero. En route, he mulled over his next move. 'In other circumstances, my poor performance would have gone unnoticed, but I had done it in public in a qualifying round for the Open Championship. I couldn't undo what had been done, but I could redress the balance. As things stood, it would be twelve months before I got the opportunity to try again, but that didn't matter. Twelve months would give me plenty of time to sort my swing out and put my game together. There was nothing I could do about it except resolve to do better the next time. That there would be a next time was a certainty.'

But back at Formby, a 'next time' was already looking increasingly unlikely. A mere couple of minutes after Maurice had wrapped up his press conference and taken his leave of the stage, an incandescent Keith Mackenzie had telephoned the club. He was desperately trying to implement a full press embargo on this embarrassing event. Jim Howard and Dave Roberts were issued with their instructions. 'We'd been told not to say too much by the R&A because obviously this wasn't going to bode well for them,' recalls Howard. Mackenzie's orders were explicit: Howard and Roberts could have their entry fees back, but they had to embark on the most futile round of their entire careers the following day. 'We were compelled to play the second round, even though we had no chance of qualifying,' says Howard. 'We were given our thirty-pound entry fees back. We were the only two people to ever have our entry returned by the R&A, but we didn't want it back. We both would have just rather gone home.'

But it was far too late for the R&A, and deep down Mackenzie knew it. The Open – his Open – had been completely desecrated by this shameless publicity-seeking interloper. On being told the harrowing news from Formby that a *press conference* had been held for the man, he bit the bullet and rang an R&A colleague stationed at the press tent at Birkdale, demanding to be told the terrible detail. As the Flitcroft quotes crackled down the line, Mackenzie allowed his head to fall into his hands. It stayed there until he heard the pay-off: 'I'll see you next year, fellas.' At which point he slowly lifted his head with a new, steely determination. As long as Keith Mackenzie was in charge of the Open Championship, there was only one certainty: for Maurice Flitcroft there would be no next time.

Hole 12: Headlines and hard times

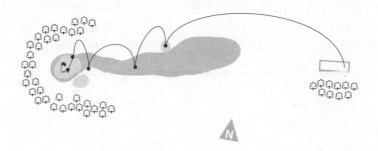

MAURICE FLITCROFT woke on the sunny morning of Saturday 3 July 1976 and tried his best to pretend it was just like any other day. He got out of bed, made a pot of tea, drained a cup, and casually lit a roll-up. The pretence didn't last. The caffeine and cigarette kicking in, Maurice leapt to his feet and hotfooted it down the newsagent, unable to contain his curiosity for another second.

He would not be disappointed. The press, in super soaraway summer silly-season mood, had had a field day. A JOKER WHO DROVE 'EM WILD AT THE OPEN, blazed the *Daily Mirror*'s front page. THE AMAZING ADVENTURE OF MAURICE, THE ROYAL AND ANCIENT RABBIT was the *Daily Mail*'s take on events, as the paper asked, 'However did one of Britain's worst golfers get into the Open? Maurice proved beyond a doubt that he is quite the worst golfer ever to compete in the British Open.' Meanwhile the *Daily Express* ran with GATECRASHER OF THE CENTURY, subtitling the piece, 'Or how a crane driver made a fool of the Open in 121 ways.' It began: 'You could tell there was something different about Maurice G. Flitcroft from the start . . .' before relaying the whole 'hilarious episode' starring the 'gallant rabbit'.

The *Sun* went for a surprisingly restrained headline – A BRITISH OPEN CHUMP: TRICKSTER TAKES 121 – but really went for it with their opening salvo: 'Stuntman Maurice Flitcroft saved his greatest performance for the Royal and Ancient Golf Club. For he fooled them into accepting his entry for next week's Open Championship – and promptly shot a record-breaking score of 121 in yesterday's qualifying round!' Unlike Maurice, the *Daily Record* played it straight down the middle with 121 – AND MAURICE DRIVES INTO HISTORY. Even the United Kingdom's newspaper of record, *The Times*, joined in, reporting THE OPEN RECORD SCORE SOARS HIGH AS A CRANE.

Only the *Daily Telegraph* refused to play along, reporting Maurice's feat grudgingly by hiding it away in the middle of a downpage report and pointedly refusing to mention the player by name. 'Scoring was wretchedly poor,' it sniffed, 'many being in the 80s and one imposter getting 121.'

Back at the house, Maurice pored over the articles with Jean and the twins. They were met with mild approval. 'The accounts were basically fair, humorous and almost-but-not-quite accurate,' ruled Maurice, characteristically damning with faint praise. Nearly every article had made some mention of his ballpark resemblance to Marty Feldman. 'I may be prejudiced, but on the whole I don't think the pictures did me justice. Partly because I had left my dentures out, and I have only myself to blame for this, and partly because they were taken not before or during the round but after, when a certain amount of tiredness and strain was beginning to show.'

Why the national media would queue up to photograph him *before* he took 121 shots to smash the Open record for rank amateurism was not dwelt upon. He did, however, mull over his decision to pose for the photos *sans* prosthetic dental accoutrements. 'I had left my dentures out because I hadn't had them long and I wasn't used to them. Having said this, I must admit I rather liked the picture in the *Mirror*, which showed a lot of character and humour and that indefinable quality they call charisma – even though I say it myself.'

Maurice briefly contemplated suing the *Sun* for calling him a 'chump' and a 'trickster', insisting melodramatically that the broadly sympathetic story 'amounted to no more than a scathing account by someone who obviously lacked any sporting instinct, not to mention a sense of humour, the type of person who might support fox hunting and hare coursing and complain if the fox and the hare should outwit the hounds and the unspeakable people chasing them'.

Jean talked him out of this ludicrous response, not a difficult job seeing Maurice's mood was generally buoyant. Still, it was typical that, even in his moment of triumph and rare acclaim, this master of belligerence was able to find something to raise his heckles.

Indeed, although Maurice on the whole enjoyed these initial fifteen minutes of fame, he had some doubts about the price of celebrity – or infamy – from the outset. Once he had read the papers, Maurice walked to a pub near his Laurence Avenue home to meet up with Bob Herbert, a journalist from the Barrow-based *North West Evening Mail*. Herbert had requested an interview with the new local boy made good, and would encounter a reticent Maurice already struggling with some internal contradictions.

With the sun blazing outside, the two sat in a dark corner, both cradling half-pints. 'He didn't want to talk at first,' says Herbert, 'though eventually he did. He may have looked for attention years later, but the first time, I don't think he appreciated the fact he'd been rumbled. He enjoyed the limelight, having been involved in the Open, but the fact that everyone suddenly knew that he was a fraud was a bit of a disappointment to him.'

The Barrow journalist, who coincidentally remembers enjoying Maurice and Eddy Bruce's one-off performance as Fumble & Tumble at the local lido as a youngster – 'They were good fun, he were funny. At least I think so. This was back in the late 1940s, early 1950s, remember!' – was in no doubt of Maurice's determination to make it in professional golf. 'As far as he was concerned, he was a serious golfer even then. I don't think he was joking. He was going to join a club, he was saying: "Then I'll make my mark!" He didn't spell it out there and then, but it was fairly clear that this wasn't it as far as golf was concerned. He was obviously hoping to get back into the Open. It was bad that he was discovered so quickly. He thought it was a game he could conquer, and he wanted to show people just how good he could be. He was absolutely serious about that.'

But while Maurice's self-image was that of a top-class professional golfer in the making, he couldn't help projecting a comic persona. Once again, his recalcitrant dentures were affecting the levels of gravitas. 'His top set weren't secure,' laughs Herbert. 'So every time he spoke, they'd drop down and he'd clinch his teeth and he'd reset them. And he'd start talking again, and they'd drop again. It was really distracting.'

The two men parted company with a friendly handshake at 1.15 p.m. Maurice told Herbert he'd have to go back to the house, pick up Gene, then take him to an inter-school sports day on Walney Island. 'He said, "I've got to go because I have to take my son who is running in the so-and-so race at 1.30 p.m." Now, it's a ten-minute drive at least, and he's not even left the pub yet. I have no idea whether he made it.'

It quickly became clear that the general consensus regarding Maurice was positive. Sands Johnson, the official scorer at Formby who had the honour of rubber-stamping the worst score in the history of the Open Championship, recalls today that the membership at the golf club – even Major Eyebrows and Captain Combover, on whom Maurice had made an indelible impression days earlier – 'all enjoyed it. To be honest, they decided it was not desperately serious. Well, it was serious from an R&A point of view, and a golfing point of view, but it was more of a joke than anything else.'

The positive opinion held by the open-minded members of Formby appeared to be shared across the country. A contemporary letter from a Mr Derek S. White in the *Daily Express* was headlined BEST GOLF STORY YET and read: 'What a tonic it was to read the endeavours of Maurice G. Flitcroft. I laughed until the tears ran down my cheeks. As a five-day member, subject to all sorts of rules and regulations, I have nothing but admiration for his nerve – dare I say cheek – for showing up the game as he did. He proved a point – but at least his partners had a drink with him. I enjoy a game of golf for the fun of it. But too many golfers take the game far too seriously.'

This prevailing mood was caught by the *Daily Record*, who followed up their story with another jaunty article headlined, MAURICE G. FLITCROFT ... SUPER-STAR! 'I got a kick out of that,' admitted Maurice, almost as happy with the fact the accompanying photo was 'in colour, no less!' than the gushing headline. 'I really didn't play up to my form,' he told the Scottish paper. 'I was aiming for the low eighties and could easily have got there if I had been a bit luckier. I also missed out by not knowing the rules all that well.'

The light-hearted tone was dispensed with, however,

as a stony-faced Maurice stated his intentions for the following golfing year. 'Next year the Open is at Turnberry, but before that I have to get my handicap down to one,' he predicted. Then he cleared his throat and announced: 'That shouldn't be a problem. I am already training seriously.'

Keith Mackenzie, meanwhile, had put the R&A into a state of DEFCON 1, the maximum measurement of military readiness, for the potential press fallout. While the rest of the country enjoyed a gentle smile at this silliest of summer stories, the R&A chose to press the red button and go nuclear.

An official R&A response was issued forthwith. 'There was no way of vetting this man's entry,' they announced. 'It is, after all, only the second time since 1965 that somebody has tried to make a fool of themselves and this great championship,' they continued, referencing Walter Danecki's jaunt around Hillside. 'When you consider that this represents two people out of a total of about 4,500 entries, it is not too bad.'

Mackenzie justified letting Maurice's entry through the net, arguing that 'it is difficult to check the credentials of unknown players, particularly with an entry the size of the one this year, which was over seven hundred'. No mention was made of his last-minute gin-soaked decision to pocket nearly £4,000 for the R&A in fees by allowing a whole tranche of players – Flitcroft included – in at the last minute to compete at Formby.

The R&A statement continued: 'We don't like

anybody making a monkey out of the Open Championship. People will be asked why he was allowed to play. The answer is that professionals do not necessarily have to be members of the professional associations to enter. Not every country has one, and if players were excluded for this reason alone, the championship would no longer be "open". This is a vulnerable point and will be looked at. We can write and ask players to give details of their golfing ability, but what guarantee is there that it would be correct information?'

It was a defensive tactic. But just in case anyone thought the R&A were simply resigning themselves to an attack by an army of Flitcroftian freedom fighters, they responded to Maurice's 121-gun salute with a salvo of their own. It was meant to draw a definitive line under the matter: 'He will not enter again. If he tries to play next year, we will be waiting for him.'

That promise was, if one is being charitable, an understandable response from a professional organ-isation embarrassed by an imposter gatecrashing their party, while the whole sporting world looked on and laughed. But Mackenzie wasn't finished with Maurice – and what he did next provided the spark that ignited a fire within Maurice that would burn for the next twenty years. It would also be an effective rallying cry for those who would congregate behind Maurice in his battle with the R&A.

The Monday after the 1976 Open concluded, Mackenzie ordered a letter to be written to the English

Golf Union, pointing out that, as Maurice had declared himself to be a professional on his Open entry, he was technically unable to join any golfing establishment as an amateur. If he was ever to make an attempt to do so, he should be immediately debarred. It first appeared to be the petulant act of a man still glowing with red-faced pique. In fact, on closer inspection, it was a calculated masterstroke worthy of a James Bond villain.

In effect, Mackenzie had created a catch-22 for the interloping scamp. As Maurice had declared himself a professional, he therefore had officially renounced his amateur status. This meant he couldn't join a club as an amateur. He could technically play on any course as a professional, but needed certification provided by the Professional Golfers' Association to do that. Problem was, he couldn't get a PGA certificate until he got his handicap down to 1. And he wasn't going to manage that without joining a club and playing in amateur competitions, which, of course, as a professional, he was now unable to do. Complicated and convoluted, yes, but the letter to the English Golf Union was a stroke of genius by Mackenzie. It is tempting to picture him, sat on a red leather swivel chair behind a large oak desk in his wood-panelled St Andrews office, dictating it to a minion while cackling and stroking a white cat sat in his lap.

Maurice was shafted. Mackenzie had cleverly used the little man from Barrow's artifice against him. Checkmate. Even if he'd had Severiano Ballesteros's talent, Nick Faldo's coach and Jack Nicklaus's bank balance, the cleverly worded missive meant he would never legitimately return to the Open. It was a cunning move. But it was one to which Maurice would react with the belligerence of his youth.

'Oh, Maurice was furious!' says his old friend Trevor Kirkwood. 'The R&A effectively banned him from joining a golf club ever again. How could he get better and prove himself? He couldn't. But he wasn't going to give up after that. He thought it was unfair of Mackenzie. Unsporting.'

It is true that the R&A were unable to ban Maurice from paying a green fee at a club and getting onto courses that way. 'In those days, golf courses were looking for as many people as they could to get in,' explains Peter Haslam, who was editor of *Golf World* magazine at the time. 'It's not so bad these days because now there's as many people playing golf as they want. But in those days if Maurice suddenly turned up with a twelve-pound green fee, they'd grab his hand off. They wouldn't even ask for his name! And in any case, he could turn up and say, "I'm Fred Jenkins, I play at Barrow links and have a handicap of twenty-six." It would not have been feasible to totally ban him, even if the R&A wanted to.' Even so, as any club golfer knows, playing at municipal courses once or even twice a week does not a low handicapper make. And in any case, that wasn't something Maurice could afford. He felt he'd been the victim of a terrible injustice born of class prejudice. He was adamant he had done nothing wrong. The Open was *open*, after all. He had tried his best. And he reasoned that his

Maurice in his diving days.
The chirpy rider is his aquatic
collaborator Eddy Bruce.

Maurice G. Flitcroft
Acrobatic Stunt & Comedy High Diver

37 Hartington Street,
Barrow in Furness,
Lancs.

Maurice poses legs akimbo while a
fellow diver points the way to greatness.

Maurice heading
for the drink
after being
struck on the
head with a
mallet; all part
of the fun of
Grin & Splash.

A study in golfing antithesis. A 19-year-old Seve Ballesteros with the errant 46-year-old crane driver.

From first to last: Maurice plays it cool with eventual 1976 Open winner Johnny Miller.

The greatest meets the worst? The Barrow Rabbit maintains a respectful distance from The Golden Bear.

Maurice claims he was 'never a trophy hunter', but his eyes, fixed on the prize, betray him

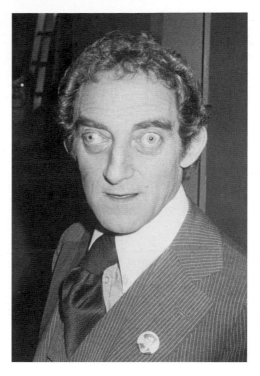

Conspiracy theorists suggested Maurice
was comic legend Marty Feldman in
disguise – and the initials M.F. proved it.
(*Right*) Feldman as Flitcroft
lining up a putt.

'Yes!!!' Maurice celebrates
missing a putt by only
two inches with this nod
to Bruce Forsyth.

Keith Mackenzie, Maurice's
nemesis at the R&A, 20% flesh,
80% rulebook.

A round with Alliss. The commentating legend fails to dissuade Maurice from aiming a 3-iron through a clump of trees.

Maurice in his Gene Pacecki disguise.

Comic Tom O'Connor and TV-AM presenter Anne Diamond look on as Maurice showcases his skills on the morning of the 1983 Open

'This is the first time we've been out of the house since the gas oven exploded.' Maurice entertains Michigan hosts Terry Moore (right) and pro-host Buddy Whitten (far right) with his after-dinner speech.

'I'm more frightened driving on the wrong side of the road on 12th Street than I am by the R&A.' Media star Maurice being interviewed by sportscaster Tom Cleary for WZZM-TV-13 at Grand Rapids.

Maurice enjoys a post-round repast with Tim Moore, Mike Meyers of British Airways USA and Terry Moore. 'You have to hit the right people with the right idea at the right time,' said Terry. 'We were lucky that Mike responded to the Flitcroft story.'

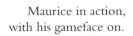

Maurice in action, with his gameface on.

Maurice looks adoringly at wife Jean. 'Whenever I needed sugar in my tea, she would provide it. She was a magician.'

Maurice's portrait of his beloved wife.

A Picasso-influenced abstract of Jean, possibly from Maurice's Red Period.

Maurice's claim to be 'the new Van Gogh' doesn't seem so far fetched in this self portrait.

Future world disco-dancing hero James Harlequin Flitcroft (left) and Gene Van Flitcroft (right) cut some rug in a competition circa 1980.

Maurice on the famous Swilcan Bridge at St Andrews, home of golf, ahead of the 1990 Open.

Maurice in his dotage, outside Laurence Avenue, the HQ for many an assault on the R&A. He never got rid of the clubs – or gave up on his dream.

Maurice's swing, as analysed by *Urban Golf* pro James Day: (1) Sound fundamentals at address, though the ball is a little far back in the stance; (2) Oh dear! His left shoulder is too high, it's going to be hard to get this back on track; (3) He's done quite well, though it's going to be difficult to square the club head; (4) See how hard he's had to work to stop the ball going right. Look how high his right shoulder is and how rolled his left foot is. This shot went high and right, or maybe even a duck hook!

failure ensured the rest of the field effectively had one fewer player to compete against for qualification. So why was everyone getting so angry?

Maurice kept his powder dry for a while. It helped that his attention had been deflected elsewhere. The week after his 121, he achieved his ambition of attending the 1976 Open – in a manner of speaking, anyway. The *Sunday People* had offered him £50 plus expenses to go to the final day's play at Royal Birkdale, where it was hoped Maurice would be surreptitiously photographed with whoever the eventual winner was. Maurice declined the offer, holding out for £100. He got his money, but only upon agreeing to keep a low profile at all costs and not advertise his presence at the event.

The day proved a total farce. It began when Maurice was given directions to meet the *People*'s journalist at a service station just off the M6 motorway. 'Shortly after leaving the M6, turn onto the road to Southport. You will see a service station on your right. A little bit further on is a lay-by on the left. Meet there on Saturday morning at 11 a.m.' The only cliché missing in the instructions was an order to look out for a woman standing under a clock wearing a red rose carrying a tatty copy of a novel. Maurice embraced the spy-thriller aesthetic wholeheartedly, buying a 'sporty trilby' and a pair of dark sunglasses so he could 'conceal my identity from the enemy when I arrived at Birkdale'. Naturally, Maurice put his hat and shades on the *People*'s expense account; the paper were presumably grateful he had not got totally carried away with the spy theme and purchased a fur Homburg and two one-way first-class train tickets to Minsk.

Maurice – who had taken the family along with him for the day – met the woman from the *Sunday People* without further unnecessary drama, and the party made their way to Birkdale. On arrival, the first job was to go and look at the Open trophy, the revered Auld Claret Jug, which was on display in a tent. Maurice was unimpressed. 'I have never been a trophy hunter,' he proudly explained. 'Just taking part in a competition and succeeding was reward enough. That doesn't mean I never welcomed the opportunity to win a cash prize or its equivalent.' At which point Maurice had fully drifted off into the realms of fantasy. Not only was he imagining winning the trophy; he was now pondering various alternative prizes, given that the one previously lifted by the likes of Jack Nicklaus, Tom Watson, Gary Player, Arnold Palmer, Peter Thomson, Bobby Locke, Sam Snead and Tom Morris Snr wasn't up to his exacting standards. 'I think most trophies are ugly things, in some cases monstrosities. More to my liking would be one of those miniature bronzes by Henry Moore, which I am sure would look infinitely better on my mantelpiece or sideboard.'

The rest of the day was spent tracking potential champions – the already legendary Nicklaus and a nineteen-year-old Severiano Ballesteros – and the eventual winner Johnny Miller. Maurice packed off Jean, James and Gene to look around the tented village, or watch the golf, or whatever else they wanted, and got down to work. This entailed racing around just ahead of the leading players, stepping out onto the fairway as they passed, and walking alongside them while the photographer took a cheeky shot or two. 'It involved not a little artifice and quite a lot of dodging about from one spot to the other,' complained Maurice. 'I didn't like the plan. It wasn't my style. But short of causing a fuss or upsetting someone, this did seem the only way in the circumstances.' Never usually shy of causing a fuss or upsetting someone, Maurice was also conscious of the £100 fee weighing down his wallet.

The job eventually done, Maurice did get to snatch a few minutes watching the golf. One of the more vivid Opens, the 1976 staging is memorable for the blistering weather, Miller's stunning six-shot victory and the emergence of the young Ballesteros, who would go on to become one of the game's greats. Maurice's total recall of the rest of his day at Birkdale, however, amounts to enjoying a can of ice-cold Pepsi-Cola – 'so refreshing!' – and some fish and chips, bread and butter and a pot of tea once reunited with his family.

Maurice had certainly enjoyed his Warholian fifteen, and even made a little hay while the sun shone, although he was certain he had missed out on many other media opportunities. In the mid-1970s, those were thinner on the ground anyway – the mainstream media in the UK consisted of three terrestrial television channels, newspapers with tiny sports sections, a small smattering of specialist sport magazines, and no internet (although Ceefax had just been launched) – but Maurice was also stymied by having no telephone in his house.

'I missed out on a lot through not being on the phone,' he sighed. 'I received lots of messages and telegrams from newspapers wanting to do stories, but not having a phone made things difficult to negotiate terms. I would get a message asking me to ring them from a public phone, reversing the charges, of course. There were times when I would have liked to think things over before making a decision, when I would have liked to say "call me back", or "I'll give you a ring and let you know", but not being on the phone made that difficult, not to say, but to do.'

The R&A, in effect, got off lightly. Today, a Maurice Flitcroft would surely be granted a regular lucrative column in one of the many bulbous stand-alone newspaper sport sections, and a spot or even a programme on one of the many digital TV sport channels. His face would adorn scores of magazines, from irreverent golfing titles like *Golf Punk* to the lads' mags. His efforts would be deconstructed by the broadsheet press. He would become an instant viral sensation on the internet, clips of his swing appearing on YouTube. His shots would be the loudest heard around the world since the days of Gene Sarazen. No doubt some entrepreneur would sign him up to release a tongue-in-cheek instruction DVD. A sell-out stunt-diving tour would be arranged. His lyrics would be set to the music of a novelty single. An original Flitcroft painting would be hung somewhere in Tate Modern. And should the offers of work finally dry up, there would always be a fortnight in the jungle: *I'm Maurice Flitcroft, Get Me Out of Here*!

Instead, Maurice pocketed his £100 from the *Sunday People*, a spy-hat-and-glasses comedy combo, and an unexpected £8 cheque received from the BBC after conducting an interview with a local radio station from the confines of a red public pay box.

The Monday following his trip to Birkdale, Maurice went back to work. He received a mixed reaction: some were hostile, thinking the celebrity 'up himself'. But his closer friends on the cranes greeted him with a cacophony of banter, cries of 'fore!' ringing around the shipyard hanger. An impromptu ceremony was held, and Maurice was presented with a crude approximation of a golf club that someone had made out of a scrap of steel which had been lying around. Maurice took the ribbing in good grace, even showcasing his swing with the club to whistles and wild applause.

He used some of the *People* money to put down a payment on a new gleaming-red 50cc Suzuki scooter, to replace the five-year-old one that transported him to and from work. 'It was more in keeping with my new Superstar image,' he noted wryly, adding that he had purchased the vehicle 'from the showroom of former Isle of Man TT Motorcycle Champion Eddie Crooks'.

As he went wheelspinning around Barrow on his shiny new charge, passers-by would wave at Maurice. True, some of them would be screaming abuse – 'Give

it up, you sad bastard! You are *useless*' – but most were
happy to see the joker who drove 'em wild at thé
Open. He was clearly going to remain a star on the
insular peninsula for some time to come.

Even so, Maurice quickly settled back in his old
routine. A month passed of the same old, same old.
Ever the golfer in his mind, life began to drag without
something in the middle distance to aim for. The beautiful summer of 1976 was some compensation, and
Maurice took his family walking in the nearby Lake
District at the weekends. Beau would accompany
them, too, now enjoying extra pats and ear scratches
from strangers after his mention in the papers.
Occasionally he would take his clubs, and spray a few
balls around the Lakeland fells. His competitive juices
flowing after his Open experience, Maurice also
played a lot of tennis at his works sports club.

But it was not enough. One day at work, as he
daydreamed while sitting in his crane, the foreman
blew his whistle. Thinking someone wanted a lift,
Maurice sat bolt upright and prepared to get the
machine moving. But the foreman called up: there
was a letter from America for him at the personnel
office! In a stroke, the existential weight of the day-
to-day grind was lifted from Maurice's shoulders. Too
excited to go through the laborious process of moving
his crane back to the wall and climbing down the
ladder, he leapt from his cabin and shimmied down
two guy ropes.

The letter was from a golfing collective in the States
who called themselves Eagle Ho! They had been

impressed with Maurice's story, which had been retold in the *Chicago Tribune*, and were requesting an auto-graphed picture of their new hero. 'It was my first-ever letter from America, and it left me with a warm feeling,' said Maurice. 'I was thrilled to learn my fame had spread to the United States. I replied soon after-wards, sending them a short account of my attempt to qualify for the Open, and an autographed picture as requested.'

The renewed attention – received from afar, and from a glamorous location like the USA, to boot – made up Maurice's mind for him. Mackenzie's atti-tude in the immediate wake of Formby had seriously rankled, and had been eating away at him ever since. Even if he had brought shame and heartache on the world of golf, as the R&A claimed by saying he had 'made a monkey' of the Open, there was no bloody way he was taking their bullying lying down. Plus, Mackenzie's ruddy-cheeked Services bluster really rubbed him up the wrong way, reminding him of the idiots he had run rings around in the Army. Maurice even wondered whether the clowns at the R&A could be classed above the mandrill he had goaded as a child. They certainly couldn't be very smart, Maurice surmised. After all, didn't they realise whose cage they had just rattled?

'If the R&A had just laughed along with the joke, even through gritted teeth,' says Maurice's friend Trevor Kirkwood today, 'he would probably have left it. He would have been sad, because he loved golf. But I think he'd have just gone away. But the way the R&A came down on him like a shithouse after Formby. That meant Maurice was always going to get back in that Open by hook or by crook. He was a determined bugger.'

Like Mackenzie before him, ahead of the 1976 qualifiers, Maurice made a snap decision that would change the history of the Open Championship. He decided to enter for the 1977 Open, and to hell with what the R&A said. 'There was the winter to get through,' announced Maurice, channelling Percy Bysshe Shelley, 'but "O wind! If winter comes, can spring be far behind?" And after spring, the summer, and the Open championship!'

He faced an even tougher hurdle than before. While Maurice had been scooter riding, fell walking, crane driving and daydreaming, the R&A had busied themselves by shoring up the Open's defences. Mackenzie oversaw a root-and-branch overhaul of the qualifying process. The previous system saw the best scorers from four qualifying courses automatically gain entry to the Open. Now there would be a two-stage qualifying event: regional tournaments would be held around the country, the cream advancing to a final qualifying round at a single venue. In addition, the R&A reserved the right to demand evidence of playing ability from any potential contestant. As well as digging a moat around the outside of their walls, the R&A had also invested in a new portcullis. And just to be sure, Mackenzie was positioned on a top turret with a pot of boiling oil.

Flitcroft decided to stride right up to the castle walls

and shake his fist in rage anyway. 'Dear Sir,' began his letter to Mackenzie on 18 November, 1976:

I wish to enter for the 1977 Open Championship. As my intentions are serious, I do not wish this application to be treated as a joke. Having read reports in the papers of the new arrangements for qualifying, I consider that I have as much right to enter as anyone else, providing I fulfil the necessary requirements.

It is with this view in mind that I would like you to send me full details, so that I may plan my training schedule and next course of action.

Incidentally, barring accidents, I consider I am the man most likely to succeed in 1977.

I shall look forward to hearing from you.

Yours faithfully,
M.G. Flitcroft

Mackenzie took less than a fortnight to respond. His letter offered a 'personal opinion', which suggested it was most unlikely the R&A committee would accept Maurice's entry as a result of the 121 shots he took at Formby earlier in the year. The brief missive concluded by advising him that he 'would recommend most strongly that you do not enter for next year's Championship'.

Mackenzie's personal opinions and recommendations meant less than nothing to Maurice, who simply sent his entry form to Mackenzie in January anyway, along with a letter. 'Dear Sir,' it began, Maurice unable

to scrawl his name even though he knew full well who
he was writing to:

> *I would like to say in support of my application, that*
> *what I did last year in a qualifying round of the Open*
> *should not be allowed, in all fairness, to prejudice your*
> *decision in respect of my entry for this year's Open. I*
> *will have had 12 months to prepare for this year's Open*
> *and I can assure you I have not wasted my time.*
>
> *In view of the fact that the regional qualifying*
> *rounds being held this year to sort out the high shooters*
> *from the low shooters are a consequence of my perform-*
> *ance last year, I think it only right I should be allowed*
> *to compete in one.*
>
> *I am not in a position at the present moment to*
> *provide any written proof of my ability, for what such*
> *proof is worth, but I am prepared to prove my ability in*
> *person on a course, such as St Andrews, but preferably*
> *Turnberry. Notwithstanding that such a course of action*
> *would be tantamount to imposing stricter qualifying*
> *requirements from me than from the rest of the field.*
>
> *Yours faithfully,*
> *M.G. Flitcroft*

Much of the logic was sound: Maurice was certainly
not in a position to provide any proof of his ability,
having effectively been banned from every course in
the country. However, only Flitcroftian philosophical
processes could conclude that, as it was his actions
and indeed his very existence that necessitated the

addition of an extra qualifying round designed to keep him out, he had therefore earned the right to compete.

Mackenzie wasn't having a bar of Maurice's circular philosophies. He informed the player that he had 'ample opportunity' to give evidence of an improvement, simply by entering, and recording favourable results in other tournaments open to professional golfers. The snub was leaked to the press, who mentioned Maurice's failure in passing. DRIVE ON, MAURICE, chirruped the *News of the World*, BUT ONLY CRANES. A lame headline, but one which gave Mackenzie immense pleasure.

But Maurice was determined to land his quarry, and had anticipated such a response from Mackenzie. Considering it highly unlikely that an entry in his name would be accepted, Maurice had hedged his bets. For the first time – but certainly not the last – he filled out a form using a pseudonym, a combination of his twin sons' first names: James Vangene. 'They wouldn't accept my entry under my own name,' he told Dick Nelson for WGVU-TV in 1988, 'so I thought what I'd do is enter under an assumed name and . . . erm . . . that is what I did.' It was the first use of a tactic that would form a large part of his legend.

The bumbling R&A, not expecting Maurice to launch a pincer movement, accepted Mr Vangene's entry – sent from Maurice's stepson Michael's flat in Kensington, West London – without question. He would be entered in the preliminary qualifying round at the South Herts Golf Club in North London. But as July closed in, Maurice decided his game was not hitting the heights it had done the previous summer. He was in terrible form. During the winter months, wearing wellies and overalls, he had shanked a few balls around the local playing fields, which had resembled nothing more than a peat bog. It was his only practice. Playing like he was, even a score of 121 would be a pipe dream. With a heavy heart – and fibrositis caused by 'an intensive programme of preparation' – James Vangene wrote to the R&A and pulled out of the 1977 Open.

His most recent golfing moments having been spent knee-deep in a quagmire, Maurice decided he might stand a better chance playing in a tournament held later in the year. The German Open, he noted, was played in early August, a full month after the Open. He fired off an application under his own name. Again he hedged his bets, this time also entering the Dutch Open, which was to be held a week after the German version, under the unusual monicker of B. Maury.

It was at this point, at the start of June, that Ian Wooldridge of the *Daily Mail* contacted Maurice. If any paper could be described as the essence of old-school golf in the 1970s distilled, the Daily Mail, with its small-c conservative Middle England values, was it. And Wooldridge, the chief sportswriter on the paper and one of the most respected journalists in the country, was of a piece with it politically. Yet something drew him to the Establishment-baiting Flitcroft. (The year before, he had famously delivered the line of the decade by describing Maurice's 121 as 'a blizzard of bogeys ruined by a solitary par'.)

'Ian would have been slightly torn,' says Patrick Collins, chief sportswriter of the *Mail on Sunday*, of his long-time friend and colleague who died in 2007. 'He quite liked the reactionary stance of golf. He thought the R&A were preserving something sacred. And yet there was a side of Ian that would have been absolutely taken with somebody who was just determined to take the piss. And I could see his idea of a decent story overcoming his reactionary side!'

Wooldridge managed to get hold of Maurice via a Flitcroft family friend's phone, and asked him if he was planning to play in the 1977 qualifiers. Maurice said he had been banned by Mackenzie, but was hoping to compete in the German and Dutch Opens to compensate. However, such was the cost of making it to mainland Europe, he'd probably have to camp out in a tent the night before his round.

Wooldridge immediately promised that, if Maurice went to either Germany or the Netherlands, he'd see to it that the *Mail* covered his expenses in return for exclusive coverage of his exploits. 'The idea of playing a jape on the Germans – right up Wooldridge's street, that was,' laughs Collins today. 'He would have been absolutely thrilled at the idea of turning over the Germans. He would have seen it as some sort of retribution!'

In what would be Maurice's biggest piece of media exposure since his exploits at Formby, Wooldridge gave over his following week's column to the Europe-bound player. THE OPEN GOLFER WHO HIT A CENTURY IS TO RAID EUROPE, screamed the headline. The column relayed the news of Flitcroft's entry in the German and Dutch Opens, noting that though no place had yet been offered in either tournament, the word 'if' 'would not appear to come into the final analysis of this curious business'. Maurice, displaying his trademark ice-cool logic, explained that 'should they turn me down, I shall immediately re-apply under another name'.

An eyebrow arching higher than one of Flitcroft's skied drives, Wooldridge suggested that Maurice's ambitions were akin to 'my own determination to become resident conductor of the Berlin Philharmonic after one lesson in tonic sol-fa'. But Maurice was talking up his game, arguing that 'the way I'm playing at the moment, I should say that I'm nearly down to scratch. I'm very disappointed at being barred from the British Open in front of my own spectators.'

Whether Maurice's chops were up as much as he claimed is open to question: one of Wooldridge's colleagues took Flitcroft to play at a course in the Lake District, witnessing a round of 114. 'Flitcroft pointed out that he'd modelled his game on Gary Player,' relayed Wooldridge's man, 'but this was not entirely substantiated by his first drive, which had more height than length and landed in the rough a hundred yards distant.' Later on, Maurice had insisted on using his 4-wood while only 70 yards from the green. 'We were soon preoccupied searching for the ball in the bushes behind the greens,' ran the report.

But Maurice's attack on mainland Europe was destined to failure. His entry to the German Open was, amazingly, accepted. But when he rang the *Daily Mail* sports desk to speak to Wooldridge about covering his travel expenses and accommodation, he found the journalist was on an assignment in the USA. Maurice asked the woman who answered Wooldridge's phone whether anyone was taking his place. 'She became quite peeved and said *no one* could take his place,' harrumphed Maurice. 'She was obviously a fan.' He attempted to rephrase the question, but the communication between the two had broken down irreparably. In the absence of any instructions left by Wooldridge for the desk to follow, the *Mail* were unwilling to commit to covering Maurice's expenses. 'He probably didn't believe that I would succeed,' presumed Maurice, once again looking for conflict where there was none.

Under these reduced economic circumstances, Maurice decided to give the German Open a miss. He wrote a regretful letter to the tournament organisers, explaining that the *Mail* had 'changed their mind' about covering his expenses, and that anyway 'it was too late to book a ferry as they were fully booked owing to the holiday season'. He had been left with no alternative but to withdraw.

But the episode with Wooldridge didn't leave Maurice totally bereft. In the paper, the columnist had written about the player's plans to camp in a tent, eating out of tins, as a consequence of his tottering financial status: 'Merely, it goes without saying, until he can cash his prize-winning cheques.' Maurice's brain whirred into gear. 'This sarcastic reference gave me the idea for a name,' he explained. 'After substituting pay for prize-winning, adding it to cheque, then changing the spelling, I came up with Pacecki (pronounced Pa-check-ey).' It was such a snappy joke, it easily survived Maurice's painful deconstruction, although he failed to mention that the surname was also a phonetic nod to Walter Danecki.

The need for a decent pseudonym or two was quickly becoming apparent: Maurice G. Flitcroft was a marked man. He attempted to join the European Tour qualifying school, in order to become a playing member of the Professional Golfers' Association, enter tournaments, and prove to Mackenzie he was worthy of a place in the Open. 'My entry for the 1977 Open was not accepted as Mackenzie said I had ample time and opportunity since the 1976 Open to prove my ability by recording results in events open to professional golfers,' wrote Maurice in a letter to Professional Golfers' Association secretary Ken Schofield. 'But that's nonsense because I am not a member of the PGA.'

In Maurice's opinion, simply claiming he was a professional was enough. Schofield patiently and politely pointed out that players needed an accredited handicap of 1 or better, and in any case the PGA had no record of his registration as a pro. 'Our job at the Tour in those days was to try to avoid such Walter Mittys getting through our entry safety net,' says Schofield. 'I guess when Maurice outed himself in such public circumstances, he had, in fact, blown his cover.'

It was also clear that Keith Mackenzie's letter of 1976 to the English Golf Union was having the desired effect: Maurice was persona non grata in the world of golf. His reputation also preceded him when he persuaded a junior member at Barrow Golf Club to take him round for a very rare eighteen holes. Maurice and his playing partner enjoyed the round, until the very last hole, when Maurice reached the green with a 'super U-shaped fifty-yard pitching wedge' while under intense critical scrutiny from a large number of members who had congregated by the windows of the clubhouse.

As Maurice lined up his putt, an official, hot under the collar, stormed out of the clubhouse and demanded a word. Maurice shot him a glance. The official, aware that he was committing a breach of golfing etiquette, retreated momentarily and let Maurice putt out. 'I sank my putt, to cheers from the gallery,' recalled the player. 'Then, as much for the benefit of those watching as anything else, made a victory gesture and gave a yahoo!' The gesture was, for the record, not a million miles from celebrity golfer Bruce Forsyth's trademark riff on Auguste Rodin's *The Thinker*, the pose he always struck upon taking the stage at the beginning of *The Generation Game*. Nice the official found it not, the official found it not nice. 'You have brought the game of golf into disrepute!' began his pompous rant. 'You have made a mockery of the game!'

Maurice's riposte befitted his earlier pose of a man caught in sober meditation.

'Bullshit!' he parried, considering it 'the most appropriate word to use to describe what he was saying, much stronger than nonsense and poppycock and rubbish'. With that response, all bets were off. 'The words flew thick and fast after that,' recalled Maurice, 'like sparks from a log fire that's just been stirred up. I ignored my companion's low-voiced caution to take it easy, and continued in full flow, not stopping until I'd made it quite clear that his views, and those of the R&A, were not my own.' That disclaimer issued, it came as no surprise to Maurice when he was informed he was no longer welcome at Barrow Golf Club.

Maurice's name might have been mud, but the organisers of the 1977 Irish Open were only too happy to let Gene Pacecki play in their event at Portmarnock, County Dublin. Sadly, like Open hopeful James Vangene earlier in the year, Pacecki suffered a pre-tournament dip in form prior to his first outing as a professional. 'I was confident of my ability to hit good shots with my short irons,' said Flitcroft/Pacecki, 'but I was erratic with my medium and long irons, and while I enjoyed using my driver, I couldn't guarantee that I would split the fairway every time I used it.' Maurice's fibrositis was also playing up again; Pacecki used the ailment as an excuse to withdraw. Administrators at the European Tour, who were affiliated with the event, asked Mr Pacecki for a medical certificate for their records. It was at that point Maurice considered the correspondence to be over.

Maurice nonetheless concluded that the likes of Mr Pacecki had a glittering future in the game. 'I forfeited my amateur status, and any faint chance I might have had of becoming a member of a club and getting a certificate, when I entered the 1976 Open,' reasoned Maurice. 'But what I could do was enter under another name from another address and hope that they would continue to accept these entries on their face value.'

In the winter of 1978, Maurice fired off applications for the Irish, Spanish, Italian and French Opens as James Vangene, and for the Open as both himself and Gene Pacecki. Only one application was successful – and incredibly it wasn't a small-fry tournament, but the mother lode. To Maurice's astonishment and delight, the R&A wrote back to Pacecki's Kensington address, informing him that he had been drawn to play in one of the pre-qualifying rounds at South Herts Golf Club. He had five months to hone his game and prove everybody wrong. He was back in the Open, but this time he vowed he would be remembered for his brilliance and not his hopelessness. In short, it was time to get practising.

Hole 13: Practice makes imperfect

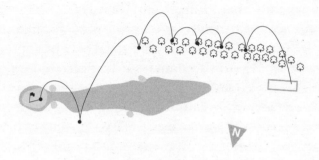

'I REALISED THAT to achieve success in the '78 Open, I would have to put in a lot more practice. This meant taking the occasional half-day off work for this purpose.' Maurice was serious about honing his game all right, but 1977 would prove a tough year. Relations between worker and bosses at Vickers had, after an uncharacteristic half-decade of détente, become slightly heated again. The catalyst had been his escapade at Formby the year before, when Maurice's superiors were startled and unhappy to find their employee on the front page of the national newspapers. It wasn't that he had brought shame on the company – they didn't care a jot about that – but that he had been supposedly off sick with a 'heavy cold' that week. When hauled over the coals regarding the matter, Maurice was tempted to tell the management that his high score had been the fault of the imaginary high temperature he had been suffering, but for once thought better of making the quip.

Despite this good grace, industrial relations deteriorated. In the middle of 1977, he was demoted from the cranes to the boiler room. His lovingly decorated cabin was torn to shreds by its new applicant, the rudimentary Spartan aesthetic of bench and levers restored. Maurice became more and more disillusioned with his new job, and he showed it, being warned several times to change his attitude. This conflict and dissatisfaction finally came to a head in early 1978 when Maurice was 'forced to challenge the authorities' about conditions in the boiler room, 'as a result of which I was sacked'. Maurice took the blow of being technically laid off as a blessing in disguise, especially since, as a long-serving worker, he received a generous redundancy package. He was now unemployed, but it afforded him the time he needed finally to master the game of golf.

There were no repercussions at home. The Flitcroft clan were a modern outfit, and a loving one who all pulled in the same direction; Jean was not overly concerned at becoming the family's only breadwinner. Gene insisted that it didn't bother her one bit: 'She had a good job at Vickers and just told Dad to get on with his golf. We weren't really a money-oriented family, us. As long as we could get by, we were all right. And Dad had supported us for years, so we didn't mind supporting him.' His conscience clear,

Maurice would now dedicate his life to golf. And if he'd learned anything about the pursuit, it was that if you wanted to succeed, you simply had to practise.

But where? Having been banned from Barrow Golf Club after Bruce Forsythgate, finding Furness too expensive and staffed by officials unimpressed with his sartorial stylings, and considering Dunnerholme simply too far from home, Maurice set about looking for a suitable public space in which to hone his craft. What he really needed was an area large enough to practise his driving, with grass clipped enough to polish his short game. The boggy strip near his home where he used to practise was now too overgrown. He needed to look slightly further afield.

He seemed to have found the answer when he stumbled across the lush and inviting playing fields of Park View School, less than half a mile from his Laurence Avenue abode. He knew that, strictly speaking, he wasn't permitted to play there. But upon finding a gap in the vandalised chain-link fence, he ventured in to find a tailor-made practice facility fit for any budding Jack or Seve. There were acres of football fields to cream drives across – and, best of all, a neatly shorn cricket pitch off which to clip wedges. Unfortunately for Maurice, the wicket had been painstakingly cultivated by the school janitor, a frustrated cricket nut who had long harboured dreams of a career as a groundsman at Headingley. The strip was his pride and joy, and he became understandably incandescent with rage when Maurice began regularly to tear up divots with mistimed swishes of his wedge. High-speed chases involving the irate waving of fists became the order of the day.

Often, as Maurice scampered back towards the perimeter of the grounds and through the hole in the fence to safety, he would try to reason with the janitor, arguing that eleven- to sixteen-year-old schoolchildren did not necessarily require a quality of wicket that would grace a Test ground; in fact, balls bouncing off jagged divot-holes at unpredictable degrees would probably improve the children's batting technique. Never once did the janitor, in hot pursuit, agree with Maurice's reasoned thesis. 'I was incredibly unpopular with him,' remembered Maurice with typical understatement.

Tiring of the caretaker's constant interruptions, Maurice moved to the football pitch. There were advantages: the size of the pitch meant Maurice could let loose with his driver without fear of losing a ball. The disadvantages, however, soon became painfully clear. The football area was much nearer to the main school building – and wherever there are school buildings, there are invariably schoolchildren.

These little vindictive buggers took great pleasure in hurling abuse at Maurice from a safe distance. When that didn't get the reaction they were after from this oddball, they began hurling boiled sweets, sticks and stones, and whatever other projectiles they could lay their hands on – including, much to Maurice's bemusement and chagrin, unspent bullets. Maurice experienced only a small amount of satisfaction when he concluded that at least they weren't being fired from a gun.

He tried ignoring the kids but noted that playing it cool only seemed to make the situation even more amusing for them. He tried walking away but the youthful rabble would follow him 'like a pack of hyenas'. And he tried shouting at them – but this seemed to give them the most pleasure of all. He even tried setting Beau upon them, but the placid canine had far too sweet a nature to scare the children and would often end up joining their side, being coaxed away by some child waving a sausage roll in his direction. After they started feeding him sweets, Maurice was forced to leave his beloved dog at home, fearing for its dental health. Not having Beau with him to anchor his mood swings and temper his patience further destabilised Maurice. The kids were getting under his skin. It was time to take offensive rather than defensive measures.

One day, suffering under the sort of wanton attack that would make Bomber Harris blush, Maurice took a moment's thought, then raised a 4-iron into the air and made a frenzied charge towards his miniature aggressors, while loudly stating his intentions: 'I'm gonna kick your arses!' The phrase, Maurice conceded years later, 'rather contradicted the threat of the raised club'. It had the desired effect, though, scattering the children like feline-feared pigeons. Still, back they would come, time and again, as if drawn by an unseen force, to goad him once more.

Maurice became aware that these ever-repeating fracas were occurring less than 100 yards from the school staffroom, where they had become cult viewing.

A group of teachers would gather to watch the spectacles unfold, sipping their cups of tea and dipping their digestives while watching a man in his late forties take swings at their charges with what was essentially an iron bar. To his surprise, not one teacher came to the aid of either himself or the children. Maurice theorised that this could only be a deliberate policy: that the staff believed that he would eventually be savaged by the little wolves and discouraged from returning. If that was true, they didn't know Maurice Flitcroft at all.

There followed weeks of routine pitched battles. Maurice would regularly turn up just after first bell at 9 a.m. and embark on a solid two hours of driving practice. On the stroke of 11 a.m., he would be attacked by marauding gangs of ten or fifteen highly amused children entertaining themselves during their mid-morning break. Sticks, boiled sweets and sods of turf would be hurled at Maurice's head with some velocity and, often, some success.

After twenty minutes of sparring, the children would repair to their classrooms, at which point Maurice would pull his wedge and putter out of his bag and practise his short game on the cricket pitch while the janitor took an early lunch. Another hour later, upon the janitor's return, Maurice would be chased away, occasionally taking refuge, cowering like a hunted animal, under nearby trees. There he would partake in his own luncheon, a repast of cheese-and-chutney sandwiches, pickled egg and sponge cake, washed down with lemon squash.

By half past one, with the kids fed and watered and classes back up and running, Maurice would emerge from the woods to practise his long game. Here he would hone his driving until the final bell, whereupon the school buildings would be divested of its pupils. He noted that the children became particularly excitable at the end of the day. Thrilled to be released from their lessons, they would be at their most daring; if Maurice did not collect up all his balls in time, the bigger children were almost certain to sprint onto the grass and claim any loose Dunlops and Top Flites – though Maurice would usually get them all back, thrown as they were with no little intent at his forehead. This would invariably lead to heated exchanges: occasionally Maurice would be chased by the foul-mouthed predators, all the way back to his front door.

At least this gave the trudge back home added cardiovascular benefits, but Maurice was forty-seven years old and it was a taxing routine. However, it was one he was forced to embark on whether he liked it or not: he needed to sharpen his game if he were to make the Open in 1978, there were no other local areas suitable for serious practice, and he needed to play during the day as it was dark more often than not by four thirty. The Easter holidays were too close to the Open to wait for; he would simply *have* to go in day after day to face the abuse.

Sadly, the twin-pronged attack from kids and caretaker was not the only obstacle placed in his path. Maurice describes in detail his correspondence with the local education authority and the local police. The headmaster of Park View eventually decided that something had to be done about Maurice's routine, however much it entertained his staff during boring lunch hours and kept many of the bolder kids out of mischief elsewhere. The local Assistant Director of Education was informed of the daily fracas, and he wrote to Maurice explaining that playing golf on school property 'constitutes a potential hazard to the children who use the fields'. It was also pointed out that 'the consent of the relevant authorities' had not been given. He was asked to 'desist from playing golf on the site at all times, otherwise I will be forced to refer the matter to the county solicitor'.

While Maurice saw no reason to bow to the assistant director's wishes, and continued to make use of the playing fields – which as a sometime taxpayer he considered a community resource – he did attempt to keep a lower profile, in the hope of keeping everyone happy. Unfortunately, his efforts came to naught, and he continued to become embroiled in confrontations with staff and children – 'my tormentors' – both of whom genuinely began to wear down his resistance levels and haunt his subconscious. He would wake up with a start in the middle of the night, pyjamas wet through, Jean asking him whatever was the matter. Even a simple task like making a pot of tea became a psychological battlefield, the slightest tap in the pipes while drawing water for the kettle causing him to spin round on his heels, half expecting a catapulted pebble or grass sod to be winging its way towards his face. It was a condition he'd witnessed only once before – and that was in shell-shocked soldiers during his tour of duty in Italy shortly after the Second World War. That it had come to this for golf's next superstar!

Sadly, Maurice's new low-profile approach – as well as being utterly unsuccessful – was not considered an acceptable response by the authorities. The county solicitor was called into action. He sent Maurice a concerned letter, repeating the demands of the Assistant Director of Education to desist from playing golf at Park View. The missive also noted that 'while playing golf, you swore at, and threatened to hit some of the pupils. I am further led to believe, when a member of staff approached you, you verbally abused him and threatened him with a golf club.' Maurice was told in no uncertain terms that, if he did not stop playing on the fields with immediate effect, legal proceedings would commence on behalf of the County Council. He was also ordered to lay off the abuse, else the police be hauled into the equation, too. Maurice felt that the accusations of verbal abuse and physical threats were a bold and saucy melodrama, and responded accordingly.

Dear Sir,

I was so incensed by your letter that I was compelled to put pen to paper immediately. I believe I'm being singled out because I am a golfer. There are other members of the public who avail themselves of the

playing fields (football, cricket, heavy petting, etc.) but
they are allowed to continue unhindered.

I have never struck a child with either club or ball
and I hope I never will. I believe they are more in
danger from flying hockey sticks, the odd bullet and the
large quantities of broken glass which litter the fields
than they are from my practice.

May I also add that it is a barefaced lie to say I
chased and threatened a member of staff with a golf
club. I do admit to engaging in a heated discussion
with one member of staff causing me to become
animated whilst holding a club, but this could only be
construed as threatening by the most sensitive of souls.

While I have your attention, I would appreciate it if
you took time to look into the behaviour of the pupils at
Park View School. They are the most ill-mannered anti-
social children I have ever encountered. I have two
young sons of my own and would be horrified if they
were allowed to behave in such a way at their school.

I put it to you that it is I who consider myself to be
the one threatened.

Yours,
Maurice G. Flitcroft

Despite stating his case, the threat of police involvement forced Maurice to stay away from Park View.
Taking on the school, its pupils, the mandarins at the
council, their legal representatives, and potentially the
Old Bill, with all the concomitant worry and stresses,
would take up too much time and energy. If it hadn't

done so already. He couldn't afford to engage with these enemies: the 1978 Open was suddenly only a matter of weeks away. Anyway, Maurice had a much more dangerous foe of his own making to deal with, one that had been almost forgotten in the mêlée: that vicious and unrelenting snap hook with his driver, known to himself as The Wrecking Shot.

A hook occurs when a player turns his wrists too much at impact, causing the clubface to strike the ball (assuming the player is right handed, as most are and Maurice was) in a right-to-left path. The ball initially flies straight, but due to the spin imparted at impact, it suddenly veers to the left, as if being sucked towards trouble by some meteorological Hoover. It is regarded as the most destructive shot in golf, because the whipping action needed to create it generates much more power than the technical glitches associated with other bad shots (such as the slice, fluff or sky) where the clubhead is delivered at a comparatively low speed, therefore limiting any subsequent damage. In fact, the hook is regarded as the 'good golfer's bad shot', and has been instrumental in the downfall of some of the greats of the past, including the legendary Severiano Ballesteros.

But this gave little comfort to the legendary Maurice Flitcroft. The Wrecking Shot simply had to be stopped. There was nothing for it: he needed to ramp up the practice. With Park View at least temporarily out of bounds, he would have to travel further afield to find a suitable practice area, even if it meant a two-hour daily round trip. At least Beau could re-join him, which was timely as the pet had acquired the equivalent of a doggy spare tyre round his midriff during his sabbatical from golf-ball chasing.

Maurice scoured the suburbs, then the countryside, and eventually found an answer in Grange-over-Sands, a mere one-and-a-quarter hours' drive away. There he found a stretch of grass between a housing estate and a sandbank which protected the estate from the roaring sea. It appeared at first glance to be a horse field, but finding no horses present, Maurice emptied his shopping bag full of balls and began to warm up. However, trouble would follow Maurice around all his life, much like his faithful old cur, and even on this windswept tundra, it was soon yapping at his heels again.

One afternoon, as he was beginning to discover the root cause of The Wrecking Shot – even to the point of hitting 'one or two straight ones' – a guttural cry came from behind him: 'Oi! The eff you think you're doing?' A rough-looking young man, as wide as he was tall, his shaved head balanced on an even thicker neck like a pea on a plinth, was bearing down on Maurice. A young girl, no more than four years old, was holding his hand.

'Just ironing out a few problems with my swing,' laughed Maurice, deciding levity might cause the man to temper his aggressive tone.

'Not while I'm here, you won't!' he replied. 'If you hit my daughter with one of those things I'll effing kill you.'

Of all the problems Maurice anticipated en route

to lifting the Auld Claret Jug, being 'effing killed' on a piece of wasteland by a homicidal skinhead wasn't one of them. But a glance at The Thug's daughter, with her sweet smile and sparkling, innocent eyes, allayed his fears. Surely The Thug wouldn't 'effing kill' him in front of her? Granted, he'd already seen fit to swear like a debauched seaman in front of her, but murder is still a massive leap from mild profanity.

'You'll wait till we're past yon fence, you hear me?' ordered The Thug. Heartily relieved, Maurice gave him the assurance he demanded. Off father and daughter went, following the hedgerow which separated the estate from the field. Maurice waited patiently but noticed The Thug appeared to be taking his time to reach 'yon fence' some 300 yards away. Considering the relative speed in which he was approached, Maurice couldn't help thinking The Thug was deliberately dawdling in order to impinge on his practice time, which, with the light already fading, was dwindling by the minute.

With The Thug now fully one hundred yards away, Maurice felt safe to hit a couple of chip shots. His range with the club, even allowing for a catastrophic miss-hit, was only some 60 yards. Nevertheless, The Thug took umbrage at the literal breaking of the pact and issued forth a warning: 'Oi! What did I effing tell you?'

'I'm just practising a few chip shots!' Maurice hollered. 'They won't go near you!'

'You'll be practising for a new brain operation if you hit one more of those!' retorted The Thug, with a blatant disregard for the physics of both golf and medical science.

Waving his towel in the air like a white flag, and apologising profusely, Maurice was content to sit out the stand-off. The Thug continued his meander up the side of the hedge, now procrastinating further by showing his daughter every berry and bird's nest present within it. Surely this fellow had never bothered much with this stretch of topiary before, Maurice wondered, yet here he was now showing the sort of regard for nature that would shame David Bellamy.

The Thug and his offspring almost at the fence, some 280 yards away, Maurice began to warm up again, taking slow-motion practice swings with his driver, well away from a ball so as not to upset the truce. However, from the other end of the field, it looked to the presumably short-sighted Thug that Maurice was once again disobeying his precise instructions, and that his daughter's life was in grave danger. The Thug lifted her onto the fence – seemingly to give her a good vantage point to witness the carnage that was about to unfold – then strode with extreme purpose towards Maurice.

'What did I effing tell you?' he screamed as he raced across the field.

'No ball! No ball!' implored Maurice, pointing at the collection of balls some six feet away. 'I was just doing some practice swi—' But it was too late.

'He covered the ground incredibly quickly,' observed Maurice years later, 'and seemed to succeed in lifting himself fully off the ground as he neared

me, launching himself at my chest with both feet.
Being pretty nimble, I managed to get out of the way,
but could do nothing about the left hook he delivered to my chin soon after. How ironic that I should
have been there to cure my left hook and ended up
receiving the boxing version, square in the mouth.'

What followed was something out of a Laurel and
Hardy film. The two took up cudgels, Maurice a
4-iron and The Thug a shorter 7, which considering
their difference in height almost made the match even.
Both combatants rounded each other for some time
until the first blow was struck in earnest, The Thug
managing to smack Maurice's right forearm. The pain
was such that Maurice feared it might be broken, but
instead of retreating like a wounded animal, the blow
only seemed to enrage him and spur him on. The
red mist descended. Letting out a primal scream, he
rushed at The Thug with hitherto untapped levels of
determination and ferocity, whirling the 4-iron above
his head and flying towards his opponent, a helicopter
hijacked by a deranged maniac. He crumped it into
The Thug's ribs (a move Maurice would be so proud
of, he would repeatedly recall it to pressmen well into
the 1990s). This powerful and direct approach forced
The Thug to re-evaluate his tactics. He retreated and
scarpered up the field to gather up his waiting
daughter and flee for his life. Maurice's application
and determination had once again allowed him to
overcome a seemingly insurmountable obstacle.

One problem, however, remained stubbornly
unsolvable. With The Thug now fully out of sight,

Maurice began to repair his Wrecking Shot again – but succeeded only in hitting seven balls straight over the sandbank and into the Irish Sea, before the light became too dim and it started to rain.

Worse was to follow. Driving home that night, Maurice's scooter spluttered to a halt, forcing him to walk home. The next day a mechanic diagnosed its ailments as being terminal – and besides, had Maurice not noticed his tax had run out two months ago? With no vehicle to travel further afield, he was left with no alternative. He would have to go back to Park View School.

In May 1978, Maurice returned – quietly, and with some hesitance, as he was running the risk of legal and police action – to the killing fields of Park View. However, to his astonishment, he found that the pupils who had so haunted him previously now welcomed him back with open arms, shaking his hand and hugging him. 'Could it possibly be that these children had missed me?' wondered Maurice. 'That I actually brightened up their lives? That they looked forward to going to school, just for the prospect of goading me? And that in my absence life had become dull?'

Maurice soon found that his theory was indeed correct. After the initial love-in, the children soon backed off to their normal position some 15 yards away, and began the sod-pelting and abuse-throwing, as per the norm. Realising he, too, had moves to make in this dance, Maurice raised his club above his head and charged at them screaming. The children obliged in their usual fashion by yelping with excitement and scampering behind a tree or bin.

To his surprise, neither the staff nor the law caused him any heartache. Maurice assumed it was because, this being the business end of the summer term, nobody could be bothered to raise Cain with the holidays coming. In truth, it was probably because Maurice failed to show up on the school fields with the intense regularity of earlier months. Subconsciously, Maurice was afraid of making The Wrecking Shot any worse than it already was, and decided it would therefore be beneficial to pare back his practice sessions with the Open coming up. He rationalised this by remembering how, back in the 1940s and 1950s, professional footballers would be starved of the ball in training during the week, in order to 'make them want it more' by the time of the match. A staunch Manchester United fan of yore, he concluded that if this approach had been good enough for the Busby Babes, it was surely good enough for him.

Hole 14: The difficult second album

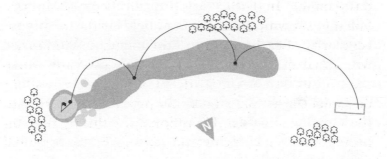

Dᴇʙᴜᴛ ʜɪᴛs are notoriously difficult to follow up. Hollywood auteur Orson Welles failed dismally to construct another movie as assured as *Citizen Kane*. Mancunian barre-chord specialists Oasis were only heading in one direction after *Definitely Maybe*. And the Irish-American novelist J.P. Donleavy, despite fifty years of trying, could never dream up an anti-hero to top *The Ginger Man*'s Sebastian Dangerfield, who shook a fist of rage against the world and never stopped battling his foes, whether real or imaginary.

Maurice Flitcroft – a scattergun creative like Welles, a working-class hero to rival the Gallagher brothers, and an irrepressible force of nature in the mould of Dangerfield – was about to experience his own second-album syndrome. Because while the 121 at Formby in

1976 took the world by storm, Gene Pacecki's perform-ance at the 1978 qualfiers at South Herts Golf Club would fall under the media radar, even if it was equally spectacular in its design.

Bizarrely, considering the effort he'd put into practice for most of the year, Maurice was taking his foot off the gas at the point most other professionals were really stepping up their preparations. He had already, in order to avoid both the law and The Wrecking Shot, cut back his visits to Park View over the last month. And now he took the unusual step of taking off the entire week prior to the Open. South Herts was, after all, near to his stepson Michael's flat in Kensington – so what better excuse for a family holiday in the capital?

Maurice, Jean and the twins spent the week gadding around London. They visited the British Museum, the Tate Gallery – where Maurice was particularly taken by some Henry Moore miniatures on exhibi-tion – and the Mad Dog Skate Bowl, where James and Gene showcased their skateboarding skills. No golf practice found its way onto the itinerary.

Unfortunately, that would show out on the course come qualifying day. On 3 July 1978, Maurice G. Flitcroft – in the guise of Gene Pacecki – turned up on the tee at the very last minute. Unlike at Formby, where he had taken the wrong turning on the way to the course, this was very much more by design than accident. 'I didn't want to get there too soon, because I wished to keep a low profile and be seen by as few people as possible,' he said. 'My main fear was that someone would recognise me, and see through my new image.'

To create this 'new image', Maurice had grown a massive handlebar moustache, and was sporting an all-dark-blue outfit of shirt and slacks, a complete contrast to the light-coloured all-out assault on the senses he wore while sashaying around Formby. Despite looking like a low-grade pimp, he raised little suspicion when he reached the first tee. 'My fears proved to be groundless. No one challenged me. No one said: "I say! Aren't you Maurice G. Flitcroft?"' Nevertheless, Maurice was still consumed by nerves. 'The fear of my true identity being discovered didn't disappear until I came face to face with the starting official, was addressed by the name of Gene Pacecki, and handed my scorecard.' Like James Garner handing over his fake passport to a Nazi for the first time in *The Great Escape*, Maurice was comprehensively eyed with excruciating suspicion by the official, before being waved on to much relief.

That relief did not last long. The opening hole at South Herts is a short par four, easily drivable at around 300 yards. A good player will fancy their chances of a birdie, and maybe even a flying start with an eagle. Maurice, however, sliced his opening drive into deep rough on the right-hand side of the fairway, where it nestled by a staked tree. The proximity of the sapling allowed him a free drop, although this did not relieve him of the thick, tangled rough he was in. Inexplicably deciding to take a 4-wood – a clean connection, even from the rough, was likely to send the ball skittering hysterically through the green and miles beyond – Maurice topped the ball, which moved less than twenty yards up the rough on the right.

Maurice pulled his pitching wedge from his bag, and took his medicine, chipping out onto the fairway. Another two shots later, and he was on the edge of the green in five, twenty feet from the hole. Whereupon, to the widespread amazement of all in the immediate vicinity, he drained his long putt and 'escaped' with an opening-hole 6, two strokes over par.

Maurice could not sustain his good momentum, such as it was. An R&A official had clocked his hacking around in the rough with a 4-wood, and had decided to keep an eye on developments. Three more holes of erratic play would be enough for the black-blazered official to take decisive action. He approached Maurice and suggested it might be 'better for everyone concerned' if he withdrew from the competition, as his 'poor form was in danger of effecting the chances of his fellow contestants'.

A trenchant exchange of views then took place, Maurice pointing out that he had spent a lot of time and money preparing for the event, and in any case the awful state of his form was 'a debatable point'. To prove this, he insisted on teeing up at another hole. It was not the time for The Wrecking Shot to rear its ugly head. Maurice sent his next drive left; upon hearing his ball pinball around the big trees which lined the side of the hole, he decided to withdraw – but only if he could get his £35 entry fee refunded in full. It wasn't long before the official, sensing a simple

resolution to a tricky problem, was sending Gene
Pacecki away from the course with a chequey in his
grip. Maurice's day out as Pacecki had lasted just five
holes and had been dismally unsuccessful, but at least
he had got his money back.

Having got on with the R&A official, whom he
considered an amiable fellow despite his professional
links to the hated Mackenzie, Maurice had briefly
toyed with the idea of telling him who Gene Pacecki's
real identity was. But he wanted to play in the Open
again, so decided not to. It did mean, however, that
there would be no publicity for Maurice this time
round; the story of Pacecki's failure would not make
the newspapers. This was mainly, of course, because
no record had been smashed as it had been at Formby:
'Bad Golfer Plays Badly' isn't much of a story in itself.
And especially as that Bad Golfer didn't, on the face
of it, appear to be the infamous Maurice Flitcroft. But
it did also vindicate the R&A's new policy of holding
regional pre-qualifying tournaments ahead of a final
qualifying round, in order to weed out any clowns.
That is what had happened here, the bid of Pacecki–
Flitcroft being snuffed out almost before it had begun.
And not one sorry stroke of it had infiltrated the
public consciousness.

The lack of coverage gnawed away at Maurice's
soul. But he took some succour in that it meant Gene
Pacecki still had a future on the professional circuit.
There was other good news, too. Across the Atlantic,
a strange cult had been gathering momentum for over
a year. Word had reached Maurice that his grinning

face adorned the must-have garment of the sporting season. The renowned *New York Times* golf writer John S. Radosta had penned a light-hearted paean to Maurice in the February 1977 issue of *Golf Digest*, anointing him 'Gatecrasher of the Year' for his exploits at Formby. The piece had gone down well with the readership, whose number included Jim Johnson of Richmond, California.

'I can't tell you how much I enjoyed your piece on Maurice Flitcroft,' his letter to the magazine began. 'I'm not sure why but his refreshing story will be remembered long after we've forgotten how Big Jack designs par fives. Just looking at Flitcroft's face makes my day. I may put it on the head of my driver. I printed it on a T-shirt which I am sending to John Radosta. As long as he wears it, he will never be a loser!'

Alongside the letter, the magazine printed a photograph of Radosta squeezed into the garment, which pictured a denture-free Maurice as Marty Feldman, under which the legend HE TRYED was almost perfectly mis-spelt. Despite looking like a character from a Woody Allen film who is experiencing a Manhattan mid-life crisis, the paunchy fifty-something Radosta nevertheless gave off an air of effortless super-cool, as only a New York writer from the late 1970s could ever do. Flitcroft had inadvertently conquered one of the most fashionable metropolises in the world, at the point the city had reached its trend-setting apogee.

Back at the coalface, Maurice's plan for Open glory

at the 1979 event took a shattering blow. Still unemployed, in January he enrolled in a building construction course at Barrow College of Further Education. A dubious Government initiative, the idea was to furnish trainees with skills such as painting and decorating, bricklaying, plastering and carpentry. In reality, it meant sending out the unpaid men onto wastelands which required reclaiming. Using pickaxes and spades, Maurice and his fellow trainees were forced to clear land, then dig foundations for public-sector buildings.

It was a time-consuming occupation, not unlike an actual job, and as a consequence it ruined Maurice's new stringent practice regime. But he consoled himself with the fact that it afforded him some much needed physical exercise. Maybe brute strength was the area he needed to improve, he thought. He took the least desired job of all, digging trenches, because he thought the action of swinging an axe into the ground 3,000 times a day might build up some sort of core strength, and help him garner some much needed torque in his golf swing. He swung that axe all through winter, but when spring came along, he was stunned to find that his plan had backfired as only a Flitcroftian scheme could. 'I had to reprogramme my tired muscles and get them used to swinging a club as opposed to a pickaxe,' he recalled, 'with the result that I made some poor swings. There was one in particular, with a 4-iron, that I buried in the ground behind the ball just like I would have done with the pickaxe, hurting my wrist in the process.' It took

Maurice months before he was able to hold a club again. Any chance of playing in the 1979 qualifiers as Gene Pacecki was gone, though Maurice sent the R&A an entry form in his own name anyway, just in case it annoyed Keith Mackenzie, which it surely did.

In 1980, Maurice applied again, twice. The entry under his own name was, of course, dispatched straight into Mackenzie's waste-paper bin. His other entry, as Gene Pacecki, was accepted. What's more, it earned him entry straight into the final qualifying round at Gullane Golf Club, just up the coast from Edinburgh and home to Muirfield, host of that year's Open. To throw Mackenzie off the scent, Maurice had asked his stepson Philip, now resident in Switzerland, to post it from his address. To the player's surprise, entrants from outside the United Kingdom and Ireland were exempt from the regional qualifying rounds.

Maurice drove up to Scotland, taking James as caddy. He had never been across the border before, and after five hours of pootling along B-roads from Barrow, soon got lost around Edinburgh. After viewing the castle from several angles, repeatedly heading in and out of the city centre, he eventually bit the bullet and, fighting the natural reaction of every anti-authoritarian fibre in his body, asked a local bobby for directions to Gullane. Pronouncing the word to rhyme with Elaine, Maurice was questioned by the officer.

'Gull-ayne?' asked the policeman.

'Yes,' snapped Maurice.

'Gull-ayne?'

'YES.'

A pause. 'Do you mean "Gullun"?'

'CHRIST! If that's what they call it in Scotland, then yes.'

The constable, momentarily rocked back in his boots, issued directions. Maurice, having not considered that the locals might actually have the inside track on the pronunciation, but pleased at having put another authority figure firmly in his place, continued on his way. He finally made it to the East Lothian coastal town as dusk was falling, Pacecki's early-morning tee-off time looming. Maurice drove around to find a suitable place to park the car and pitch the tent he had taken with him as a money-saving device. This was easier said than done. The Gullane sky quickly turned pitch black as Maurice repeatedly turned his car at right angles to the road, shining the front beams into field after field. More often than not, passing cars would be forced to stop and wait as Maurice executed laborious three-, five-, or sometimes seven-point turns on the narrow roads, first to peer across the land, then to get out of everyone's way and stop holding them up. Similarities between his attitudes on the golf course and on the nation's highways were not impossible to spot.

Eventually, after a couple of hours of fruitless search, Maurice found an open stretch of land that seemed fit for purpose. He parked the car at the side of the road, helped James lug the tent from the boot, wandered across some treacherous terrain – all shadowy humps, hollows and long, thick grass – and pitched the tent in a clearing. The two clambered into their sleeping bags, and were soon off to sleep, a long day ahead for Gene Pacecki.

Maurice awoke a few hours later in plenty of time for tee off, the sun not long risen. This would be just as well, because when he poked his head out of the front flaps of the tent, he quickly noticed that it was pitched between two fairways of a golf course. A few hundred yards away, albeit on a different hole, a greenkeeper was preparing a green. Nothing unusual in that, but a quick 360-degree scan revealed green-keepers busying themselves everywhere, plus officials with walkie-talkies strutting, pointing and generally looking officious. Well, thought Maurice, I've found Gullane all right.

Maurice took one look at the location of his neon-orange tent and calculated that he and James had about five minutes tops to get off the course before being spotted. Getting recognised on the first tee would be irritating enough; being rumbled for accidentally camping on the course would surely sully his name for ever in the circles frequented by the golfing cognoscenti. Some thirty years later, James remembers the occasion very well: 'It just looked like some field when we pitched the tent. We hadn't a clue where we were. Then we woke up in the morning and there were people everywhere. This one guy was on the other side of the fairway. Imagine his face when Dad popped out the tent in his Y-fronts for a few morning stretches.'

Once the tent was packed away, Maurice began to

see the plus side of waking up *on* the course, a luxury usually afforded in tournament conditions only to the top professionals and by means of the nearest hotel. He could check the weather, the pin positions and generally get a feel for the run of the thing. 'Accuracy off the back tees would be of paramount importance,' he decided. 'Any drives that were sliced, hooked, pulled or pushed would be almost certain to go into the long, thick grass, some of it nearly waist high, that comprised much of the rough.'

After searching in some of the rough for lost balls – and finding about a dozen – Maurice took his leave of the course's environs and found a nearby field in which to hit a few shots. The state of his game caused him great anguish. 'I began to have some doubts about playing. This was partly due to feeling that I wouldn't have been drawn to play in the final qualifying competition if I hadn't been entered from Switzerland. However, I had considered I would be justified in playing if I could be certain of putting up a good performance. But when, for some inexplicable reason, I started to hit poor shots with my 9-iron, a club with which I was usually confident, I began to have serious misgivings.'

This uneasy feeling once again manifested itself in a piercing pain tearing through Maurice's head, the same throb he'd felt before his diving debut and his first Open tilt. It doesn't need Pamela Connelly-Stephenson to work out that these episodes weren't strictly a coincidence, but migraines born of internalised stress. Maurice's mind may well have been in denial that his Open attempts caused him obscene levels of stress, but his body wasn't, and on this occasion it all became too much. Maurice lay stricken in a cow field somewhere near Gullane, staring up at the skies.

'He had to withdraw,' says James. 'His head was splitting. He could barely walk, never mind play golf. And he was worried he would be wasting a place someone else could have, so he withdrew.' Gene Pacecki's place would go to one of the standby competitors. It was a gallant gesture, and one that proved Maurice's respect for the Open, and for his fellow golfers, whatever Mackenzie and the R&A assumed. Maurice instead spent the day curled up in his sleeping bag at a roadside lay-by. One thing was for sure, this Open attempt wasn't going to make the *Nine O'clock News*. The day after, a fully recuperated Maurice went for a stroll around the Open tented village at Muirfield, buying a new set of budget clubs – although not replacing his precious putter and 4-wood – and a punnet of strawberries to take home for Jean. It would have pushed it to have called the trip a success, but Maurice felt it at least 'rekindled memories of camping out when I was in the Boy Scouts'. And at least Pacecki's cover was *still* not blown.

Pacecki's positioning well under the R&A radar meant he was accepted again in 1981, though this time Maurice had applied from a UK address and therefore had to play in the regional qualifying. As in 1978, Pacecki – whose increasingly labyrinthine biographical details now stretched to an American nationality as well as the Swiss citizenship and a British property – would play at South Herts Golf Club. As James had escorted Maurice on his trip to Gullane, this year would be Gene's turn to accompany his dad. Deciding against camping, they hired a van, in which they planned to sleep the night before the tournament. But on the motorway journey to London, Maurice's repressed stress again rose to the surface. This time it manifested itself in a bout of monomania, Maurice becoming unreasonably agitated by one particular group of motorists: truckers.

He grew irritated by just about every other articulated lorry he would pass. Perceiving any manoeuvre made by a trucker as a flagrant act of bullying – especially their irksome habit of demanding he move out of the outside lane, even though he was 'usually doing the legal limit of 70 mph' – Maurice spent a large proportion of his journey through several English counties leaning out of the window, giving passing HGV licence holders the benefit of his in-depth knowledge of the Highway Code. 'They were bowling along without a care, drunk with the feeling of power and invulnerability that driving such vehicles imbues in them,' he later clambered onto his soapbox to say. 'If I had my way, I'd take the licences off these idiots. All juggernauts should be banned from motorways. Not only would this benefit the environment and wear and tear on road surfaces, it would also reduce the stress suffered by the private motorist on such journeys.' For the umpteenth time, Maurice was demonstrating how far ahead of his time he was when it came to society's big issues.

This forensic yet passionate dissection of the UK's transport policy inevitably brought on a migraine. Maurice was forced to pull into the lay-by and lie down in the back of the van. As Gene couldn't drive, he walked to a service station and called Michael.

'My wife had to drive me to this lay-by on the A1 where I found Maurice half dead in the back of a van,' remembers Maurice's stepson. 'His migraine was so bad I had to drive them the rest of the way to London. He was having terrible headaches. I'm sure it was because of his golfing exploits.'

But there was no way Maurice was going to bale out at the last minute two years running. Once ensconced in Mike's Kensington flat, scoffing cold chicken and swilling tea, he soon forgot the madness of the motorway and his migraine simmered down to a gentle throb.

Gene Pacecki's tee time in the morning was at 10.35 a.m., and for once Maurice allowed himself plenty of opportunity to prepare. He got to South Herts just before 10 a.m., and after finding the car park full and dumping the van down a nearby lane, made it to the club a whole half-hour before teeing off. It gave him time to crack a few drives down the practice range – though much good all this would do him.

One of Pacecki's playing partners that day was Mark Sharman, who now works as a professional at the Quantam Golf School in Essex. Back in 1981, he was a twenty-two-year-old with hopes of reaching the

Open. Sharman's first recollection of Maurice was that 'he dressed well', a statement which breaks all records for understated sarcasm.

'There were some pretty bright colours on display,' recalls Sharman. 'It wasn't subtle. He wasn't shy. Bright clothing, baggy-sleeved sweater. But that was fine until he picked up a golf club. And then you really did start to wonder. And as the round went on and on, there was less and less to wonder about. He was all over the place.'

Maurice, remembering how he had sliced his drive on the opening hole in 1978 into deep filth on the right, decided to hit this one down the left, which would then fade into the centre. Over-compensation was always on the cards. He pulled one into the rough on the left, still leaving a shot of over 100 yards to the green at the short par four. Nevertheless, he found his ball in a reasonable lie. 'All that remained for me to do was hit a simple pitch shot onto the green and two-putt to par the hole,' he reasoned. 'There was a bunker guarding the green on my intended line, but in the belief that bunkers should be ignored rather than feared, I took my 9-iron and boldly went for the green.' With grim predictability, Maurice's shot plugged straight into the bunker. He splashed out, but took three putts to get down. It was yet another double-bogey 6 on South Herts' opening hole for the US pro Gene Pacecki.

Maurice's drive on the fourth – another par four – sailed into a clump of trees on the right of the fairway, making 'a helluva clatter'. After a long search, the ball was found on the other side of the trees, in the rough running down the side of another hole. Maurice lifted a sweet 8-iron back over the trees and onto the correct fairway, thinned a 3-wood up the track in the vague direction of the green, and bumbled a pitch onto the green. Two putts later, Maurice had secured another 6. He considered this quite a professional outcome considering the manner of his drive, but others were beginning to question his talents.

'There's one thing looking for the odd shot, but it was literally every hole,' says Sharman. 'You were hitting down the fairway yourself, then had to go looking for his ball. What was a bit difficult was that I suffer from hay fever. I was a bit concerned that, though I was taking tablets, they might run out!'

As in 1976 at Formby, play was backing up around the course.

'We let at least one group through,' recalls Sharman, although he thinks it might have even been two or three. 'It was painful. You did get some funny looks: you'd give them a shrug of the shoulders back.'

Word got round the course that a madman was playing in the Open.

'There are people who aren't orthodox, but there's a sound, and a way the ball flies,' explains Sharman. 'But he didn't look orthodox, he didn't make that sound, and he didn't make the ball fly!'

Pacecki had taken fifty-six strokes by the time he reached the tenth tee, a personal best for Maurice. He would take a fifty-seventh and a fifty-eighth and even a fifty-ninth, but those would be Pacecki's last shots in the 1981 Open Championship. Two R&A officials had been waiting for him to take his drive at the tenth. It is fair to say they were not gripped with the anticipatory excitement of superfans. Maurice's drive on the hole would be his worst of the day, no little achievement considering the dross that had preceded it.

'He hit quite a bit behind the ball and just topped it,' reports Sharman. 'On the tenth, you go down a hill and then up, and after three he'd not got to the uphill bit. Which is about fifty or sixty yards, if memory serves!'

One of the blazers politely suggested it was time for Mr Pacecki to cash himself in: 'Do you think you've had enough now?' Maurice had, in fact, been considering walking off the course ever since the seventh hole, so minor were his chances of making the final qualifiers. But he was damned if he was going to be marched off the course by an official without a fight. Maurice argued that he didn't believe his play was affecting his fellow competitors, or anyone else for that matter. Having said that, if he was guaranteed a full refund of his entry fee . . .

Within a quarter of an hour, Maurice had been taken back to the clubhouse, issued with a freshly written cheque, and was heading off the premises, once again without being unmasked. What's more, Maurice was quite right: his play had not affected his playing partners, as Sharman got through the regional qualifier to the final qualifiers, and only just missed out on the Open proper at St George's, ending up as an unused reserve.

'I think I could have been annoyed big time, because it's the Open qualifying, you're nervous and everything else, but I was hitting it well,' says Sharman. 'It was a relief that he had gone at the tenth, but then I had something else to deal with because we were waiting for people to play as a two-ball! But it's all part of golf. I've had lots of experiences through the game, and that was just another one really. It's just good that I was playing reasonably well, so it didn't affect me.'

Maurice wasn't too displeased with his performance, nor the fact that Pacecki's play was again considered unnoteworthy by the mainstream media. He wanted his next foray into the newspapers to be a spectacular success. And while his nine-hole score wasn't anywhere near qualifying standard, he was at least improving. 'I wasn't unhappy,' he wrote. 'Plus I had the satisfaction of knowing that I had beaten the system once again.'

Later in the year, Maurice attempted to gain a place as himself in the Bob Hope British Classic, a pro-am charity event which ran from 1980 to 1991 under various guises but never really caught the public imagination like the comedian's similar ventures in the States. Maurice went straight for the kingpin, addressing a letter to Hope. He told the story of his 'magnificent failure' at Formby. 'My inclusion in the tournament would attract a lot of attention and consequently a good deal of publicity,' he argued. The letter finished with a flourish. 'One last thing. They do say that one good turn deserves another – and I did go and see your Road Films.' Maurice had amused himself greatly with this pay-off – 'It was a humorous note I hoped he would appreciate' – but three weeks later Hope wrote back to him, saying that while he wished he could give him some encouraging news, all the amateur spots in the tournament had already been filled. He also added a corrective PS, thanking Maurice for watching his Road 'Pictures'.

Pro-am tournaments are, as the name suggests, laid-back affairs where professionals pair up with amateurs of varying quality, who usually pay for the privilege, a charity benefitting. Maurice was offended at the slight. 'It wasn't an amateur spot I wanted, but an invitation to play in the tournament as a professional, which I believed the organisers could extend to me if they so wished.' Maurice changed tack, writing to another comic involved with the tournament, Bob Monkhouse's former sidekick Dickie Henderson. This time, the correspondence was intercepted before it reached the talent, a terse reply stating that only players with tour cards would be considered. Maurice's pique was raised, and years later he reflected, with no little *schadenfreude*: 'At the time I was disappointed at being given the cold shoulder but later was glad not to have been associated with the tournament because of the bad press it got, which played no small part in its early demise and disappearance from the British golfing calendar.'

Demise and disappearance were the order of the day, because in 1982, Gene Pacecki suddenly reached the end of his Open journey. While Pacecki's efforts at the 1978 Open failed to set alarm bells ringing in the hallowed corridors of the Royal & Ancient, golf's governing body weren't about to ignore the signs a second time. One three-hole meltdown could be written off as unfortunate, and certainly was quickly forgotten. A second slapstick jaunt by the same player was unlikely to be missed by the penpushers, though. Mackenzie had been informed of Pacecki's perform-ance in 1981 and, having done some impromptu homework, was in no mood to let another Flitcroft rampage all over his tournament. Little did he know! But while Mackenzie remained blissfully unaware of Pacecki's author, he was at least on hand to snuff out the creation. Pacecki dutifully filed an entry form for the 1982 Open, but this time he would be knocked back. Spectacularly. Not only did Mackenzie go to the extraordinary lengths of immediately sending a terse telegram to Pacecki stating 'your entry received but not accepted', he also followed up the snub with a letter. It was the equivalent of running over a rabbit with a ten-ton truck – then getting out and whacking the roadkill over the head with a shovel, just to make sure.

This forced Maurice to change tack the following year. He was determined to make a splash, vowing that 1983 would go down in history as 1976 had done. This time he wouldn't go unnoticed. So the world braced itself for the sporting comeback of comebacks, one which would rival Muhammad Ali, Jack Nicklaus and Lance Armstrong, it was time for . . . FLITCROFT II: THE RETURN OF THE DIVOT.

The quest to play at the 1983 Open began in the usual fashion. He first sent the R&A a request for entry under his own name. A tactic he had used while also applying as Pacecki, this was designed to throw the R&A off his scent. This year, though, rather than a request for a form, the letter was a brazen demand to play in the first Open to be held at Birkdale since 1976.

Dear Sir,

I would appreciate it if you would send me an entry form for this year's Open.

Alternatively, to commemorate my first abortive attempt to qualify in the Open, when it was last held at Royal Birkdale in 1976, might I suggest you just send me an invitation.

Someone has got to stop these foreigners coming over here to play in our major events and walking off with the trophies and large sums of money that go with them. I would welcome the opportunity to put a stop to this rot.

Yours faithfully,
Maurice G. Flitcroft

Exactly how Mackenzie responded to this missive, effectively a repeated prod on the lapel of his blazer, has gone unrecorded. We can only guess whether the letter hit the bottom of the waste-paper bin before or after half a bottle of gin was decanted into a tumbler and knocked back in order to ease the pain. But one event certainly took place at R&A HQ that week: an application to play in the Open was accepted from an up-and-coming Swiss professional called Gerald Hoppy.

Determined to bring his A-game to the Open, Gerald Hoppy – the golfing artist formerly known as Maurice Gerald Flitcroft, as well as Hoppy Johnny to his mum – set about practising as much as he possibly could. This meant once again running the gauntlet at Park View School, where the kids posed Maurice more difficulties than the likes of Keith Mackenzie ever could.

His return, however, was met with hysterical scenes from the schoolchildren. None of them had attended the school during Maurice's earlier period as a Park View regular, but he was a legendary figure with the kids nonetheless, tales of near riots having passed into school lore. The new breed took to hurling boiled sweets at the harmless old man – now fifty-four years of age – and they threw them with gusto. Maurice once again played his role of agitator by running at them with murderous intent. For a brief moment, Barrow's two factions co-existed in relative harmony. But not everyone was so enamoured to see the quixotic character back at the school. A week after his triumphant return, Maurice received a letter from the headmaster, which made reference to the letters of years previous and, cutting to the chase, warned that 'any further trespassing' would see the matter escalated, at great speed, in the direction of the courts.

Maurice responded by appealing to the headmaster's better nature.

Dear Sir,

You may be unaware that I am practising for the British Open golf championship which is now a matter of mere weeks away. Unfortunately for both of us, your school fields represent my only chance of making a good fist of it in the competition proper.

I suggest you confine your directives and threats to the people within your charge, with a view to stamping out hooliganic and criminal behaviour.

Yours,
Maurice G. Flitcroft

The gambit did not work. The head of the local police force contacted Maurice by letter, informing him that he had been asked by 'several interested parties' to appeal to him to stop playing golf at the school. He told Maurice that the teachers had been instructed to phone the local nick should he be spotted doing so again, and that a prosecution for trespassing would be forthcoming. Maurice decided it was time for the gloves to come off.

Dear Chief Inspector,

With due respect, I was so enraged by your letter I have looked into the legality of your position. Having studied the matter in the local library it would appear to me that trespassing is not yet a criminal offence or for that matter is the art of hitting a golf ball.

Has the headmaster also mentioned the countless other members of the public who avail themselves of the fields, without permission? Will they be arrested too I wonder?

Yours,
Maurice G. Flitcroft

Considering morality and righteousness to be firmly on his side, Maurice continued to utilise the public facilities of Park View in order to pursue his Open dream. But with teachers, local authorities, the police and, quite possibly, the Army ready to pounce, the inevitable denouement to the episode was not long in coming. Practising his short game one lovely May afternoon in the forbidden zone by the cricket pitch, Maurice spotted two policemen making their way towards him across the field. Maurice had run this moment through his mind again and again – but now it was for real. And it was time for action.

Scooping his practice balls into a carrier bag, Maurice headed for a hole in the wire fence – cut by his own hand five years earlier and thankfully still there, otherwise Maurice would have been shredded into a hundred chorizo-shaped chunks, such was the speed in which he approached it – and once through he stopped for breath on the main road. However, the policemen were one step ahead of him and soon pulled up alongside in their car. They issued a final warning in no uncertain terms: if he was caught practising on the fields again, he would be arrested for causing a breach of the peace.

Maurice acquiesced, reasoning that a stint in prison would be unhelpful to his Open prospects. But before walking home, Maurice stopped at the roadside to tally up the number of balls in his bag. Scarpering from the police at short notice had forced him to neglect his customary ball inventory. Golf balls were expensive and had a tendency to lose themselves, so it would be extremely wasteful to wantonly leave any on the playing field. On completing the count, Maurice found himself short of two balls, which he must have overlooked in his hurry to escape. They were top-class balls, too, in mint condition. So he headed back through the gap in the fence and onto the field in search of them. Sadly, no sooner had Maurice stepped back onto the field to commence his fine-tooth-combing of the grass, than sirens were blazing and he found himself sporting handcuffs.

'The officers were not interested in explanations,' remembered Maurice. 'The senior of the two policemen, in fact, was quite peeved, shouting at me in an aggressive manner. His colleague, not wishing to be outdone perhaps, or accused of not pulling his weight, took hold of my right arm and, ignoring my protests that I didn't need his assistance, proceeded to hustle me from the playing field. I was then bundled into a police van, driven to the station and read my rights.

'During the journey I made it clear to both officers that I wasn't happy about the way I'd been manhandled and that I'd made note of their numbers with a view to lodging a complaint. As my upper right arm was throbbing blue murder, I added that if my Open campaign was ruined by an injury, they'd be hearing from my solicitors and should expect to pay compensation.'

At the magistrates' court two weeks later, Maurice was charged with 'causing a nuisance and disturbance on the educational premises of Park View School'. He pleaded not guilty and, according to his solicitor, 'put up a good fight' during a discussion of the finer points of the law with the presiding magistrate, but he was found guilty and ordered to pay £50 in fines and £59 in costs, a total of £109. Maurice was particularly galled at having to pay compensation to a part-time teacher, called as a witness for the prosecution, who put in a claim for losses suffered as a result of having to close a shop he kept to attend the court hearing. Maurice now added teachers and magistrates, the petit-bourgeois middle classes, to his imaginary hit list. This was another episode to fuel his working-class consciousness.

Yet despite these troubles, Maurice managed to keep his eye on the bigger picture. Paying off the fine in weekly instalments wouldn't be too much of a problem. What did present a problem was finding an alternative place to practise in order to sort out his swing for the Open, which was now less than two weeks away. He returned to the rugby club where, over the fortnight, he knocked his game into the best shape possible.

On the morning of his fourth Open attempt, Maurice's ever-supportive wife Jean helped to create Gerald Hoppy, gluing to his face a spectacular drooping moustache favoured by Mexican revolutionary Emiliano Zapata, and placing a ludicrous checked deerstalker hat upon his head. But despite his dashing look, Hoppy/Flitcroft's performance in the 1983 regional qualifier at Pleasington, near Blackburn, got off to a familiar start.

Reports vary as to the quality of his opening shot. Maurice's account describes 'a beautiful drive' hit 'straight down the middle', which was 'much appreciated by the watching gallery'. His playing partner Michael More, a young assistant professional from Turnberry, recalls him 'topping his drive on the first hole. He immediately asked his caddy for the seven-iron, which I thought was very strange as he hadn't looked at his lie, or seen how far he was from the green. His caddy was a strange chap as well.' For the record, Hoppy's caddy that day was a pony-tailed gent trading under the spectacular monicker of Troy Atlantis. It was his son Gene.

What is not disputed is what happened next, as Flitcroft slipped into something of a funk. He was, if you'll excuse the excruciating but frankly unavoidable pun, Hoppy mad.

'Maurice took his seven-iron off his caddy and stormed off,' says More.

The momentary loss of cool severely affected

Maurice's already fragile confidence. 'My swing slipped out of its groove,' he admitted. 'I thinned my approach to the green and took three to get on. Then I took three putts to get down.'

More decided to ignore Hoppy almost immediately. 'Me and the guy I was playing with just wandered off, and left him to it,' said the super-sanguine More. 'You just do your own thing. To an extent, you just switch off what other people are doing, and just concentrate on your own game. So no, he didn't really disturb me. I very quickly realised he shouldn't be there, so I just ignored him.'

Sadly for More, that professional approach meant he missed a comedy treat. On the second, Hoppy took four shots to get from tee to green, whereupon it all began to go outrageously awry. With the ball only five feet from the hole, the Swiss pro suffered less a rush and more a tsunami of blood.

'I wasn't surprised that I missed holing out with my first putt, and disappointed that I missed with my second, but I was surprised that I missed at my third and fourth attempts.'

Head down, Maurice was battering the ball around the green with increased panic, a man in the sweaty grip of yip mania. 'I was certain they would go in, but they didn't; each one turning away at the last moment to stay out.' For the Marty Feldman look-alike, it was a scene almost identical to the punchline of the comedian's 'Loneliness of the Long Distance Golfer' sketch, when dusk fell as the hapless player took hours to poke a ball into a hole.

Maurice's playing partners watched with growing amazement as Gerald Hoppy took shot after shot, with no thought whatsoever for golfing etiquette. The hapless putter takes up the story himself: 'Gene told me later that one of my fellow competitors had become quite agitated at my non-stop attempts to sink the ball, and thinking perhaps that coming from Switzerland, I wouldn't understand English, had sought to convey to me by means of some frantic hand signals that I was putting out of turn. It must have been quite funny, but I had been so engrossed in what I was doing that I had never noticed.'

Having begun with a 6-9 two-gun salvo, Hoppy's game went from bad to worse. He took 8 on the third hole, before a 'series of misfortunes' led to a 10 on the sixth. Following the pattern of Flitcroft at Formby and Pacecki at South Herts, word spread once again that a golfing maniac was roaming the course.

The R&A official who eventually threw him off the course first caught up with Hoppy on the par-three eighth – but there was some initial confusion as to who was the imposter.

'All three players had missed the green,' says the official today, who prefers to remain anonymous. 'Flitcroft was short, but not so noticeably that you'd think he was out of his depth. And his resulting chip to the green was decent. In fact, just taking their approaches to that green, you wouldn't say he was the worst of the three. I knew of Flitcroft, obviously, but I had never seen him so I couldn't recognise him. I was trying to work out which one was which, and all I saw was a chip, I didn't see a full swing or anything. However, it didn't take long for the truth to out when I looked at his card.

'Flitcroft's partners were delighted to see an official. They knew pretty well why I was there. They said, "Can you do anything about this?" so I said, "Well, let's have a look at his card." His card was horrendous, sevens and eights and all sorts of things, he was well over par. He hadn't got a leg to stand on; he shouldn't have been there anyway. I was as polite as I could be. I suggested that he should retire. To which he was not very amenable. I said, "Well, come on, you're obviously not being very fair to these guys, you're destroying their chances." And he had his son with him, walking around with him in a pair of ordinary walking shoes and carrying around with him a bag over his shoulder like a ladies' handbag. Anyway, he said, "Well, I would like to play nine holes." So I said, "Right, I'll let you play the next one if you go off at the ninth green." So we did that, and his son said, "Come on, Dad, come on, Dad, you've had enough of this." So off he went.'

Gene was asked years later what was in his ladies' handbag. 'Probably my dancing shoes,' he replied. 'I wore hiking boots to caddy but they didn't fit my look when I got off the course. I was a world-class dancer and top DJ, you see. I wasn't going to walk around in any old shoes.'

As for Hoppy, he'd gone out with a bang, taking eight at the ninth to reach the turn in sixty-three. His card read: 6, 9, 8, 6, 5, 10, 6, 5, 8. Had he played the

second nine as well, there was every chance he would
have beaten Maurice Flitcroft's Open-worst record of
121.

As it was, Hoppy was out, much to More's chagrin.
'We were waiting for him all the time, so it didn't
really affect our play,' remembers Hoppy's laid-back
playing partner. 'So then after he got kicked off, we
had to wait for the ones in front! And that's when I
tended to play most of my bad shots. We were always
hanging about, once he'd left. I never made it to the
Open. But I can't attach any blame to him, to be fair.
My not qualifying is entirely my own fault.'

Back in the clubhouse, our unnamed official was
informed of Hoppy's true identity by Bill Johnson,
the man who had interviewed Flitcroft – and fed him
with cigars and brandies – back in 1976 at Formby.
Johnson eagerly sought out the man now known to
the world as Gerald Hoppy.

'You're Maurice Flitcroft!' he exclaimed.

'Yes,' said Maurice, gingerly.

'Don't you remember me?' asked Johnson. The
penny dropped, and the two chatted amiably for ten
minutes. Johnson's presence had ensured the cat was
out of the bag. The media might have been blissfully
unaware of the exploits of Gene Pacecki, but they
weren't going to let the story of Gerald Hoppy slip
through their fingers.

Hole 15: A Man of letters

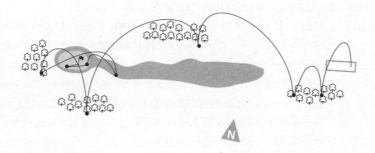

'Everything was going well and according to plan until I five-putted from eight feet at the second.' It was one of the all-time great golfing quotes. Whether Maurice Flitcroft actually said it in the immediate wake of his disastrous Open cameo as Gerald Hoppy is a moot point. He would later distance himself from the words: having seen them rendered in stark newsprint, he considered them an affront to his character, forming a self-harming statement of competitive weakness.

'I did not say that,' he insisted, two months after they were widely reported. 'The five-putts from eight feet was just one of those things which I dismissed from my mind when I got on the next tee.' But the denial smacks of revisionism: many papers and magazines carried the quip, which only a notoriously chippy man like Maurice would process as a slight anyway. Though in any case, did it really matter? Shoeless Joe Jackson was never begged by a young Chicago White Sox fan to 'say it ain't so, Joe' either; in sport, just as in *The Man Who Shot Liberty Valance*, when the legend becomes fact, print the legend.

The Man Who Shot Sixty-three Over Nine Holes was now fast becoming a legend himself. Gene Pacecki may have been utterly ignored by the national press pack, but Hoppy was an instant hit. It was the summer of 1976 all over again, the papers once more going to town: HOPPY'S SWISS MISS; FLITCROFT STRIKES AGAIN, AND AGAIN, AND AGAIN; BOGUS GOLFER'S SWISS ROLL; SUPER RABBIT DOES IT AGAIN; MAGIC TRY, OUR MAURICE; and, of course, the obligatory CRAZY GOLF.

'It's always been my ambition to qualify for the Open,' Maurice told the papers, 'but my practice was interrupted yesterday by a terrible headache. I had hoped to do better.' The *Guardian* wondered aloud whether Maurice's figures of 6-9-8-6-5-10-6-5-8 were the numbers of a Swiss bank account set up in Hoppy's name. Another reported one R&A official explaining how they had 'another Maurice Flitcroft' on their hands. 'Imagine their surprise when they discovered they had the actual Maurice Flitcroft,' deadpanned the man himself.

Despite harbouring concerns about that five-putt quote, Maurice was on the whole happy with the coverage Hoppy afforded him. 'I enjoyed reading the stories,' he said, 'which were written in a humorous tone. I realised my credibility had suffered a setback as a result of my poor performance, but that was something I was going to have to live with. I became even more determined to do better the next time, by continuing with my practice in spite of the difficulties I faced.'

Keith Mackenzie and the R&A, meanwhile, made no comment. Mackenzie had decided to retire from his post as secretary at the end of the year, and so the 1983 Open at Royal Birkdale would be his last. With this in mind, he decided to keep a dignified silence, despite telling confidants that, 'I never want to see that man on any golf course in this country ever again!' He assumed, in any case, that the latest media storm would quickly blow over, whisking the dreaded Flitcroft out of his sight once and for all.

Sadly for Mackenzie, the producers of *Good Morning Britain*, TV-AM's breakfast magazine programme, were very much taken with the Hoppy story, and asked Flitcroft if he would care to make his first appearance on national television on the morning of the 1983 Open's first round. Maurice immediately agreed. The night before the show, he was booked into a hotel in Swiss Cottage, near the TV-AM studios in Camden, North London, and told to bring along some golf clothes and his putter. Maurice spotted an opportunity to chance his arm.

'As the clothes I normally wore for golf were not new, and as I wished to look my best, I said that I would like to buy some new clothes to wear for my first appearance on television and added that as it was also in their interests, would they allow them as expenses.' Sadly, the response he received from the TV-AM staff was non-committal. In a mild huff, Maurice went out and bought some anyway. His mood lifted that evening as 'free, nicely chilled' lemonade was brought to his room, then plummeted again as he suffered yet another pre-performance migraine.

When morning came, he had regained his equilibrium. After practising his putting on the carpet of his hotel room, Maurice was picked up by a car and whisked to the studios. Having had his make-up applied by a 'quiet and efficient young woman with a soft touch, who deftly re-enforced a shadow here and a highlight there, and finished with a light dusting of powder', he waited in the green room alongside his fellow guest, the Liverpudlian club comic Tom O'Connor. The two chatted as they waited to do their turns. Maurice's nerves evaporated as he compared the experience to standing on the first tee at the Open. 'It was a piece of cake compared to waiting to tee off in a qualifying competition. I looked forward to it because, apart from doing my ego some good, it would give me the opportunity to answer my critics. I felt relaxed and at ease, but then I was appearing as myself, under my own name, so I didn't have to worry about being unmasked, or suffer the embarrassment of hitting a poor drive. If there is one thing I am more practised at than playing golf, it is talking.'

Maurice knew there was a chance he would be held up to ridicule, but he was confident of his ability to

straight-bat any hostile deliveries. What followed at
8.06 a.m. – after the programme's co-host Nick Owen
welcomed Maurice onto the set, plonked him down
on the famous TV-AM sofa, and ran through the plan
to interview him and get him to make a few putts –
should be a landmark in understated British television comedy akin to the finest of Dave Allen sketches.
Sadly it has been long forgotten – until now.

*NICK OWEN: First day of the British Open begins at Royal
Birkdale today, for those golfers who made it through the qualifying
round. But Maurice Flitcroft, from Barrow-in-Furness, is one who
didn't. Probably because he's the world's worst professional golfer.*

[An already visibly piqued Maurice, wearing a brand-new
beige diamond-patterned V-neck and out-of-the-box shiny
white peaked cap, wearily rolls his eyes skywards at the
description.]

*NICK OWEN: He was banned from the tournament after he
hacked a record 121 shots in a qualifying round for the Open
seven years ago. But golf nut Maurice didn't give up, and this
year he sneaked back under the name Gerald Hoppy of Switzerland.
But an official spotted Maurice when he'd taken sixty-three for
the first nine holes, and then he was asked to leave. Morning!*
MAURICE [atonal dead-pan delivery, so relaxed it has a
slight croak in it, a heavy Cumbrian accent]: *Ah, morning.*
NICK OWEN: I won't ask you to leave! [Owen emits Partridge-
esque guffaw at his own joke. Not one of Maurice's facial
muscles responds to the gag, forcing Nick Owen to move
quickly on.] *You're a bit of a scoundrel, aren't you?*
MAURICE [biting his tongue]: *No, not really. Just keen on*

golf. And I intend to succeed one day. Actually, it wasn't an offi-cial who recognised me, it was a member of the Associated Press.
NICK OWEN: *He'd seen you before, had he?*
MAURICE: *Yes, he said he'd interviewed me at Formby, and recognised me, so when he said 'you're Mr Flitcroft', well, I couldn't deny it.*
NICK OWEN: *What I can't understand is, if you're a profes-sional, how do you make a living as a professional golfer if you can go round nine holes in sixty-three?*
MAURICE: *Oh, that score doesn't reflect my true ability. I am prepared to prove it by taking on the likes of Peter Alliss and Lee Trevino, and all the others.*
NICK OWEN: *Professionals are scratch.*
MAURICE: *Well, that's what I play off. I play off scratch.*
NICK OWEN [trying to be as non-judgemental as possible]: *You play off scratch. But do you play to scratch?*
MAURICE [Pause]: *Well, I . . .* [Pinteresque pause, then a slight change of tack.] *I play most of my golf on playing fields.*
NICK OWEN [spluttering]: *Playing fields?*
MAURICE [matter-of-fact]: *Playing fields. School playing fields.*
NICK OWEN: *Why don't you play on a golf course?*
MAURICE: *Because I'm not a member of a club.*
NICK OWEN: *But don't you need to be a member to play on a golf course?*
MAURICE: *Well, not really. If you've got the money, et cetera, then you can go there as a visitor and* [spitting out the next word] *pay to play.*
NICK OWEN: *So let's get this straight. You're a professional golfer, but you never play on a golf course?*
MAURICE: *Oh, only once in a while. Once in a blue moon.*
TOM O'CONNOR [interjecting in the jaunty northern-

club style]: *Well, if you take sixty-three for nine holes, you're hardly on the course then, are ya?*

MAURICE [totally ignoring Tom O'Connor's light-hearted conversational gambit]: *In actual fact, at Pleasington, one of the chaps I played with hooked his first drive into the trees on the left, the next chap sliced his shot, very nearly went into a bunker, I hit a beautiful drive straight down the middle. Now that's what I can do, most of the time at home on the playing fields.* [Cranks 'rationalisation' up to 11.] *It's like somebody practising snooker on a six-foot table and hoping to beat Steve Davis and Hurricane Higgins on a twelve-foot table.*

NICK OWEN: *Isn't it all a bit pointless?*

MAURICE: *Not really, I enjoy it. I'm doing what I like doing.* [Suddenly highly irritated at the perceived slight] *What the hell else would I be doing, twiddling my thumbs?*

NICK OWEN: *Because you're an out-of-work crane driver, aren't you?*

MAURICE [without embarrassment, a true class warrior]: *Yeah, I'm unemployed.*

NICK OWEN: *Can you show us a bit of your, sort of, skills now? Because we've got a little putting green laid out for you. You've got the balls with you, perhaps we can get up and see you . . .*

[The camera pans out to reveal a three foot by ten foot stretch of green carpet laid out across the studio floor just in front of the coffee table. The machine in question is a Putt-o-matic™, a black dustpan-shaped box, a golf 'hole' at the top of a ramp. The idea is to putt a ball up into the hole, activating a device which spits the ball all the way back towards the golfer, his reward for hitting the target. The device will be very familiar to anyone whose father was a golfer, or who had their own office and little to do at work during the 1980s. As Maurice slowly goes about placing his golf balls onto the carpet, five feet or so in front of the putting machine, Nick Owen's co-host Anne Diamond opens the discussion to the floor.]

ANNE DIAMOND: Tom, you're a very keen golfer, aren't you?
TOM O'CONNOR: Yes indeed, and I was amazed because Maurice is upset with sixty-three for nine holes. I'd be thrilled! I'd have had a good day if I'd got that!

[Laughter. Maurice, knowing full well Tom O'Connor is laying on the self-deprecation a bit thick, toe-punts the putting machine in a fit of mild irritation, nudging it millimetres to the right. In doing so, he appears quite the golfing expert.]

NICK OWEN [filling in time as Maurice faffs around putting a glove on]: *Pro golfers are usually just about satisfied with sixty-three over the eighteen, innit? Just to explain to those who don't know much about golf, what you're going to do now is, you're going to putt as if you were on a green. You're gonna aim for this thing* [points to putting machine]. *Is it gonna shoot back?*
MAURICE: Yes, it shoots it back.

[Nick Owen inexplicably dances from side to side.]

NICK OWEN: Sorry, is my shadow in the way? This is quite dramatic, isn't it?

[Maurice lines up the putt, takes a few practice strokes then goes for it. It misses, hitting the left-hand rim of the machine cup.]
TOM O'CONNOR: Oh, that was a 'nearly'. That's an 'if only', that one. Better than nowt.

ANNE DIAMOND [as Maurice is lining up his second attempt]: *Another dramatic putt . . . Oh, I shouldn't speak when he's just about to putt, should I?*
NICK OWEN: No.

[Maurice's second putt sails well left of the target.]

MAURICE: I need a few practice shots to get used to the pace of the green.
NICK OWEN [the greatest study in patience since Job]: *Course you do. With all the sun we've had, I should imagine it's running quite fast down there.*

[Maurice's third putt veers left of centre, too, and hits the first ball. Tension has given way to vague embarrassment.]

TOM O'CONNOR [attempting to help Maurice, who is dying out there]: *Oh, that's an in off. He's got, what is it, 118 more shots, hasn't he?*
NICK OWEN: How do you manage for income?
MAURICE: Well, my wife is employed full time as a secretary.
ANNE DIAMOND: Poor wife, that's rotten!
NICK OWEN: I bet she really appreciates this sort of thing, doesn't she?
MAURICE [super-agitated]: *Well, she'd be doing that anyway if I was working full time as a crane driver, whatever.*

[His fourth putt misses, way to the left.]

NICK OWEN: This isn't going too well, is it?
MAURICE: Well, this floor is sloping.
NICK OWEN: But you've got to allow for that, haven't you?

[Maurice's increasingly frenzied putting mechanism is falling to pieces, shades of the second green at

Pleasington. A fifth attempt misses, again miles to the left.]

ANNE DIAMOND [audibly tiring of the segment]: *We've got to make this one our last.*
NICK OWEN [politely making excuses for Maurice]: *Sorry to talk when you're actually putting, Maurice. What I want to know is, if you try to get into the Open next year, what name will you use then?*

[A sixth putt rolls almost apologetically up to the front ramp of the machine. It so nearly goes in, but doesn't quite make it, resting just before the machine.]

ANNE DIAMOND: *Oh!*
MAURICE [almost giving the game away]: *Next year? I've got four . . .*

[He taps a loose ball into the machine. It shoots out, rolls past Maurice, and miles back down the studio carpet.]

ANNE DIAMOND [in shock, interrupting Maurice's answer]: *Oh!*
TOM O'CONNOR [slipping into wisecracking mode]: *That one went further than the ones you hit.*
NICK OWEN: *I think we ought to see that again!*

[Nick Owen drops another ball into the machine. It spits out and rolls towards Maurice, who had been preparing to putt using another ball. Maurice knocks it away in irritation.]

ANNE DIAMOND [referring to the machine]: *Tom was just saying, he's got one of these at home and the cat plays with it.*
TOM O'CONNOR [confirming the breaking news]: *Our cat plays with it.*

MAURICE [answering Nick Owen's earlier question regarding next year's Open subterfuge]*: That would be giving the game away if I told you what name I was entering with next year.*
ANNE DIAMOND: Gentlemen, we must thank you for coming in. Thanks very much to the world's worst golfer . . .

[Maurice clacks his ball. As a seventh missed putt sails wide left, he turns to face Anne Diamond and pipes up in high dudgeon.]

MAURICE: Hold on, I don't agree with that. I'm not the world's worst golfer, and I intend to prove it.
NICK OWEN: Are you the world's worst professional?
MAURICE [equally forcefully]*: No.*
NICK OWEN [reasonably, aware that Anne Diamond might have just lit a powder keg]*: OK.*
ANNE DIAMOND: And thanks very much to Tom. In fact, you're off to play golf, aren't you?
TOM O'CONNOR: Yes, indeed I am.
ANNE DIAMOND: Where you going?
TOM O'CONNOR: I'm going down to Ascot now to a big charity game.
ANNE DIAMOND: Well, good luck. Presumably if it's for charity, you'll try to raise lots of money?
TOM O'CONNOR: I'm going to start very early because I could take about 150 the way the weather is today. I'll need to get some tips from Maurice.
MAURICE [a genuine offer]*: I'll give you some tips. Any time you're near my home.*

Maurice considered the interview a qualified success. He wasn't sure how his response to Anne Diamond's jibe went down – 'I replied with some heat,' he admitted – but convinced himself his display of putting skills had been far from disastrous. 'This didn't go too badly,' he reasoned, going on to utilise fishing-tale logic to make his case. 'Not as well as I would have liked, but that was my own fault for attempting my putts from something like ten feet rather than three feet or five feet. Statistics have shown that the odds are against the most proficient of putters getting down in one from distances of five feet or more. Of course, all golfers hole long putts every now and then, but it is the golfer who does it most often who usually wins the purse.'

Nick Owen also thought the exchange went well, albeit more from a comedic viewpoint than a sporting one. 'I mostly recall how incredulous I was about it all,' laughs Owen, now a BBC presenter. 'I couldn't comprehend how he had the gall to play in one of the greatest golf tournaments in the world when he was obviously hopeless and how he managed to get into it in the first place. I didn't want to be rude but I was constantly trying to suppress a giggle. It was a bit like a comedy sketch – but it was real.'

Back at home, Maurice's twin sons Gene and James were equally amused, and the 'any time you're near my home' pay-off became something of a household catchphrase.

Just how amusing Keith Mackenzie found such an interview, transmitted at exactly the same time as the early first-round groupings were going out at Royal Birkdale, is a matter for conjecture. He kept schtum in the face of Flitcroftian provocation, although his managerial approach to the 1983 event was admittedly more laissez-faire than usual, this being his last Open, former British amateur golfing champion Michael Bonallack waiting in the wings to take over.

Mackenzie's new hands-off style was vividly illustrated in the early hours of Saturday morning, before the third round, when the sixth green was dug up by political protestors. With the rest of the tournament in the balance, attempts to inform the outgoing secretary, who had been out on the sauce that evening, were made at around 2 a.m. Upon being awoken, a tired and emotional Mackenzie argued that there was little he could do at such an early hour, and that they should bugger off and ask Bonallack what to do anyway. Mackenzie went back to sleep as the green-keeper did his level best to patch things up. The next morning, a decision was taken to allow players to place on the green and putt down two untarnished strips of turf.

With Mackenzie otherwise engaged, it would take a while longer for that particular dam to break – though with Maurice steadily chipping away at it for sport, not much longer. *Golf World* magazine gave a prominent place to a news report of Maurice's exploits at Pleasington in their Open review issue. HOPPY HOPS IN, they cried, pointing out in scrupulous detail how the R&A had 'vowed to close the loopholes' that had let Flitcroft shoot 121 in 1976, only for him to 'slip through the screening by playing under the assumed name of Gerald Hoppy of Switzerland'. The maga-

zine provided a little analysis of Maurice's development since the heady days of Formby: 'Sadly, his golf
has not improved in the intervening years. He took
sixty-three over nine holes before the R&A caught up
with him and turfed him off.'

Maurice was not about to get off the stage. 'I was
not "turfed off" but politely asked if I would consider
withdrawing because of my score and nothing else,'
he fired back in the letters column, splitting hairs with
the sort of precision that would have put Robert
Oppenheimer to shame. 'I withdrew of my own voli-
tion, on the condition my entrance fee was refunded
in full.' It was now in the public domain that the R&A
had not even profited for the privilege of their secretary having rings run round his ample girth. 'My
credibility took a knock, but it is not true to say I
have not improved since 1976. When I played at
Pleasington, it was only the second time I'd been on
a course in the past two years, and it was that which
showed up in my game.'

He then delivered the killer blow to Mackenzie's
ego: 'I shall be taking steps to remedy this before next
year's Open.' The message was unambiguous. Flitcroft
was fully intending to compete in 1984. The gauntlet
had been thrown down with a hefty clang. Just in case
Mackenzie hadn't got the message, Maurice repeated
his intentions in another letter of complaint, this time
to the local Barrow paper, the *North West Evening Mail*,
regarding a report of his recent appearance in front
of the magistrate.

Dear Sir,

You suggest that I am not really a professional golfer.
Well in 1976 when I entered the Open as a professional
I automatically forfeited my amateur status. I have been
paid for playing golf and been paid for a written
contribution to a golf magazine. So there is no way I
can be considered an amateur.

The definition of a professional golfer is not deter-
mined by the amount of money he makes or whether he
or she makes a living from it. Less than 40 per cent I
would say make a living from the game.

In my evidence I stated that my ambition was to
succeed as a professional golfer and to prove my
playing ability. That is still my ambition and I am
looking forward to next year's Open.

Maurice G. Flitcroft

This was the last straw for Mackenzie, who until now
had been keeping his powder dry. He ditched the
powder and went atomic instead. He might have been
handing over the reins to Michael Bonallack, but there
was no way he was going out before he had dealt with
Flitcroft once and for all. His obsession to crush
Flitcroft became so rabid, he made Ahab look like a
fully paid-up member of Greenpeace.

'He was a stickler for golf etiquette and stern
guardian of the Royal & Ancient clubhouse against
women,' says former *Express* golf correspondent Mark
Wilson drily. 'He could deal with both these challenges

with a sense of humour. But Flitcroft drove him mad.'
Mackenzie had tried to ban Flitcroft from every golf
course in the country, and changed the rules of entry
to ensure he would never play in the Open, and yet
here he was, the secretary of the grandest sporting
organisation on the planet, tormented by a simple
crane driver from Barrow. There was only one option
left. A legal one.

He wrote a letter to Flitcroft which spelt out his position in no uncertain terms and gave full reign to his
feelings. He chided him for his 'presumption' to appear
under the assumed name of Gerald Hoppy, and said
he had brought the matter up with the Championship
Committee, promising that every effort would be taken
to ensure that 'any such participation in 1984 or on
future occasions is pre-empted'. Then, in a final bout
of posturing intended to see off the pest for good, he
informed Flitcroft that the R&A's lawyers had been
asked for their opinion 'particularly with regard to falsi-
fying your entry this year'. Mackenzie intimated that
Flitcroft should see reason, that he had not fulfilled his
'obvious ambitions to become a first-class golfer', and
that the 'importance and significance' of the Open
should be considered above all. It was using a sledge-
hammer to crack a nut, a Big Bertha for a two-foot
putt. It was unnecessarily bellicose.

'The R&A's default mode is pomposity,' suggests
Patrick Collins, now chief sportswriter for the *Mail on
Sunday*, then following events with interest when a
journalist for the *Evening News*. 'Much of the reason
Flitcroft became such a good story was the attitude

of Mackenzie, who behaved like one of those British film characters from the 1950s. He was basically an R&A man from central casting. And in acting the way that he did, he didn't have the wit or insight to see he was building old Maurice up with his excessive reactions. He could have neutralised him in about three sentences. He could have patronised him. "Good chap, I understand perfectly, he wants a few head-lines." Instead, he behaved like a prat.'

Maurice wasn't going to take Mackenzie's threats lying down. His reply, fired immediately back to golf's HQ in Fife, was a textbook case study in standing one's ground in the face of extreme provocation. It was the literary equivalent of a flurry of rabbit punches around Mackenzie's irate jowls.

Dear Mr Mackenzie,

I do realise the importance and significance of the R&A in connection with the Open Championship. I can see the need to have a ruling body in such a popular and growing sport, to whom people can turn for help and guidance, etc. I see no need to speak of it in hushed tones. I must say I don't altogether approve of the setup, which seems to me to be too autocratic, too hide bound by customs and conventions, not to mention middle and upper class snobbery and conservatism, highlighted by the World of Golf currently being shown in seven parts on BBC television.

To me the most important thing is the game, which I consider myself to be close to mastering.

*When I attempted to qualify for the Open at
Pleasington, as it was only my second time on a course
in two years, it is no wonder that I dropped shots on
and around the green.*

*It has been suggested that my play could adversely
have affected the chances of my fellow competitors. This
is nonsense. I may have taken more strokes, but in
actual fact, I got in less trouble than my fellow competitors, one of whom did worse after I retired than before.*

*With reference to my score, I would like to correct the
impression given that I am the only person to shoot a
high score in connection with the Open. In 1935 at
Muirfield, a Scottish professional took 65 to reach the
9th hole. Neither do I hold the record for a high score
at one hole. Only last year, Greg Norman took 14 at
one hole, and higher scores than that have been
recorded.*

*The tone of your letter suggests that regardless of my
ability next year – which shouldn't be based on the
number of strokes I took at Pleasington – an entry
under my own name would not be considered. What I
did at Pleasington does not reflect my true ability.
Handicaps are not based on one round of golf, but
many.*

*Since 1976 I have dedicated myself to mastering the
game in difficult circumstances. I am not about to
throw it all away now that I am so close to succeeding.*

*I have been insulted and abused, pelted with stones,
held up to ridicule, threatened by the authorities,
manhandled by the police, prosecuted and fined, threatened with violence, and only recently actually physically*

*assaulted. In spite of this I shall continue to practise
when and where I can, with one goal in mind – to
succeed as a professional golfer, because that is what I
have chosen to do, and no amount of sabre rattling is
going to stop me from trying.*

Yours sincerely,
Maurice G. Flitcroft

Mackenzie didn't deign to respond. He merely quietly
spent the rest of the year harrumphing, ensuring that
everyone in the R&A, Michael Bonallack especially,
was aware of this man Flitcroft. Public opinion,
though, was firmly against the R&A. In the *New York
Times*, the legendary golf writer Peter Dobereiner
argued that the Open is 'golf's equal-opportunity
event', and only the presence of your Flitcrofts and
Hoppys proved that. 'In banishing Maurice from the
course, the Royal and Ancient was betraying the very
policy of free and open competition,' he wrote. 'Gerald
Hoppy could never have an opportunity to display
his skills at Augusta.' It should be asked whether
keeping the Maurice Flitcrofts of this world out of the
Masters is such a bad thing. But only if one accepts
the answer is yes it *is* a crying shame: who would not,
if they could turn back time, pay ready money to
witness the spectacle of Maurice struggling round
Amen Corner with his mail-order clubs?

Momentarily changing his tack, and taking Gene
Pacecki out of cold storage, Maurice sent in an entry
form for the 1983 European Open, held towards the

end of the season in late August. The application was successful, and Pacecki – still resident in Switzerland – was destined to embark on his greatest round.

The European Open qualifiers were to be played at Foxhills Golf Club in London, so Maurice, accompanied by caddy James, made base camp at his stepson Michael's new flat in Wandsworth. The day before the qualifier, Michael invited Maurice to join him for a round at the public course at Rickmansworth. Maurice declined the invite, on account of a pre-tournament migraine you could by now set your clock by. Come the day of the big event, Maurice whiled away the hours before his 3.12 p.m. tee time by lunching on burgers, nervously forcing them down his gizzard. He then made his way to the course and hit a few warm-up shots, where the nerves dissipated.

'I believed I presented the picture of a cool, calm professional who was no stranger to tournament golf,' he said. Given that this was Maurice's fifth entry into pro competition, that was surely no wonder.

On the first tee, Maurice's confidence took another couple of boosts before he even hit a ball. First, he tested the effectiveness of a slight change to his image – he had bought a different hat to the floppy fisherman's titfer he usually sported – by asking an official for a course planner. His request was granted without incident, or the vaguest sign of recognition.

'I didn't expect to learn a lot from it,' said Maurice, 'but thought a quick perusal of it would give me some idea of what lay ahead.'

Then he watched one of his fellow competitors send his drive, then two provisional balls, into deep woodland on the left. While sympathising, Maurice was comforted by the knowledge that, if he too made a poor shot, he wouldn't be the only one. Playing it safe, yet calm and confident, Maurice opted to take his 3-iron instead of his more errant driver. It was the sensible decision of a mature professional. He hit one straight down the middle.

Unfortunately, while the direction was A1, he had topped the ball, sending it a mere 100 yards down the fairway. 'I reflected afterwards that for all the good playing safe had done me, I might as well have gone with my driver, because I cut my second shot into the trees on the right of the fairway.' Maurice threaded the ball back out of the copse, with 'a shot Seve Ballesteros would have been proud of'. It's unlikely that the mercurial Spaniard would have felt a similar sensation after any of the other six shots Maurice played on the opening par four.

'Things began to look a little bleak when I triple-bogeyed the next two holes,' continued Maurice's report, which already had a claim to be the most understated in the history of all sports journalism. Nine over after three, Maurice looked to have steadied the ship on the par-three fourth, creaming a tee shot to 15 feet. Sadly, he three-putted to drop another stroke. A fourth triple-bogey in five holes followed, before Maurice 'put it together' in some style, only dropping one on the long par-four sixth, then securing a par on the par-five seventh after knocking a 7-iron dead from fully 30 yards. Unfortunately, he failed to keep this momentum going. In the wake of his solitary par of the day came his fifth triple-bogey, a 6 at the par-three eighth which saw him slam-dunk a looping iron from tee to the centre of a clump of thick bushes.

A workmanlike bogey 5 at the ninth ended a front nine over which Gene Pacecki took fifty-five strokes, a mere eighteen over par, thrashing his personal best by one shot. His card: 7-7-8-4-8-5-5-6-5. 'Thoughts of retiring had entered my head by this time,' said Maurice, ever the realist, 'but having showed some resilience on the ninth, I decided to wait and see how I did on the tenth.' Sure enough, Maurice sliced his drive into impenetrable shrubbery on the right and, after failing to find his ball, walked in. Almost as predictably, Pacecki's travails failed to make any impression on the national consciousness, though in truth this was something of a surprise given the furore of Hoppy's sixty-three at Pleasington. The European Open, however, was not *the* Open. And the PGA European Tour did not operate with the same pompous bluster of the R&A. A week after Pacecki's latest on-course meltdown, the Tour sent the Swiss figment of Maurice's imagination a letter politely requesting membership confirmation of his national federation. Maurice did not reply but, in what may have been a subconscious thank-you to an administration who was telling him to bugger off with a light touch, he would never seriously engage in battle with the Tour. He had different plans for the R&A, of course.

The remainder of 1983 was quiet, save a minor spat with TV-AM over unpaid expenses.

'I was given to understand that I would be reimbursed about three weeks later,' he wrote of a promise made in July. 'I am still waiting. I trust that my faith in the integrity of TV-AM when I accepted the invitation to take part will be justified by a satisfactory reply and a cheque.' The cash was duly sent to Maurice, who had kept his combat skills sharp over the winter months, like a good professional sportsman should.

He would soon require those skills, as the R&A were about to make it clear that they were upping their own game considerably. Mackenzie had by now handed over the day-to-day running of the R&A to Michael Bonallack, and had waddled off into a corner of the St Andrews clubhouse to take root. (In 1990, the US magazine *Sports Illustrated* pictured Mackenzie as 'a heavy, large-featured man with a gravel-pit voice and a Churchillian glare. Imagine a figure out of P.G. Wodehouse, a retired colonial officer with a gout-ravaged foot raised on a pillow, *The Times* in one hand, claret in the other. Except for the gout, that's Mackenzie.') But he had left his successor with strict instructions to see off Flitcroft at all costs.

'Maurice drove Keith absolutely crazy,' says Sir Michael (who was knighted in 1998) today. 'He used to bristle if things didn't go right. And Maurice Flitcroft certainly upset his Opens for him.' Back in the mid 1980s, Bonallack was merely the owner of a shiny OBE. He had earned it for his feats as an amateur golfer:

he had tied for eleventh place in the 1959 Open, six shots behind the eventual winner Gary Player, and played three times in the Masters between 1966 and 1970. He would never quite be as energised by combating Flitcroft as his predecessor was – but no matter, because for the first few years of Bonallack's reign Mackenzie was always hovering in the background, on hand to make sure his instructions were followed to the letter.

Quite literally to the letter, in the case of Bonallack's first run-in with Maurice. While sifting through the entries for the 1984 Open, the new secretary spotted a form filled out by a golfer called Gerald Thornbush. The R&A drafted in a handwriting expert, who compared the form to the earlier entry of Gerald Hoppy. A positive match was made, and a gleeful R&A press-released the news that Maurice's entry had been intercepted. The fact that the episode was like a plot from a cheap spy novel was faintly ridiculous; that it was unfolding at the height of worldwide Cold War paranoia elevated it to the realms of utter preposterousness.

Adding to the general air of other-worldliness, Maurice only found out about the interception while watching the BBC News one evening, a smiling Jan Leeming relating the tale to the nation – and to Thornbush himself.

'Who would have thought the Royal & Ancient Golf Club of St Andrews would go to such lengths, resort to such underhand tactics, to stop me from trying to qualify for the Open?' wondered Maurice, who had named his new character after the shrub on which he hung his waterproof jacket while practising at the rugby fields. 'One would expect such organisations such as MI5, MI6, the FBI, the CIA and Scotland Yard fraud squad to employ handwriting experts – but not the R&A.'

Despite the R&A's efforts – or, more likely, precisely because of them – Maurice's star continued to rise back in the real world. Ever since he'd tried to tap the magazine *Golf World* for a new set of clubs in 1980, Maurice had engaged in occasional correspondence with editor Peter Haslam. The good-natured Haslam understood Maurice, and got the joke. 'I can well understand that you are having problems in convincing the R&A that you are a golfer of sufficient ability to join the highly paid pros in the British Open,' wrote Haslam in a letter that year to Maurice. 'To be fair, I think you would have difficulty in convincing anyone of this! But I do wish you well. If you do make it to the top, who knows, I might even buy your old clubs myself for posterity!'

Haslam began sending Maurice a Christmas card every year. 'A thank-you for the card, which I rather liked,' wrote Maurice in a letter to Haslam early in 1982. 'There was a time when I considered making a living from painting, of taking over from Picasso. Then I took up golf.' ('It's nice to have a choice, isn't it?' said Haslam with a smile, years later.) Even though this relationship hadn't stopped Maurice going off half-cocked at *Golf World*'s report of Gerald Hoppy's sixty-three in 1983, the two men were on good terms.

So much so that Haslam asked Maurice if he would fancy a round with legendary golf commentator Peter Alliss. The summit meeting between two of golf's more colourful characters was on.

'I arranged for him to play at Old Thorns with myself and Peter Alliss,' says Haslam. 'Alliss was amazed. A chap came out, and he was dragging his clubs onto the first tee. And Alliss said to me: "This chap can't even carry his clubs properly!"' Which was nothing to do with golf, really, but you know what he meant.

'We had an interesting round. On one hole, where quite a sharp dog-leg goes round to the right, Flitcroft sliced his drive into heavy rough on the right-hand side. And what he was faced with was a line of tall conifer trees running in line at right angles to where he had to go. Alliss said to him: "You've got no chance there, you've only got a small gap. Hit it out to the left and you've got an easy nine iron onto the green." But Flitcroft said, "Nah, I can get through there." Alliss replied: "You cannot get through there, man!" "Oh I can get through there," insisted Flitcroft. And Alliss looked at me in absolute despair. Of course, Flitcroft promptly smacked the ball straight through that narrow gap and onto the green. We were amazed!

'But he was no good. He just wasn't any good. I suppose his average round would have been ninety-five to a hundred, minimum. I don't recall what he went round in that day. He had corned-beef sandwiches in his bag for halfway round, which he proceeded to munch away at. When he went home, he sent me a bill for everything. He even charged for the sandwiches he had bought.'

Alliss, too, was distinctly unimpressed with Maurice's on-course skills. 'He couldn't play at all,' remembers the former Ryder Cup player today. 'He really was hopeless. And of course you know he was wasting everybody's time. He was an enthusiastic eccentric who loved golf, but it's like someone who thinks they can sing opera but they can't even sing in tune. He was the golfing equivalent of caterwauling.'

Despite both Alliss and Haslam's swingeing criticisms of Flitcroft as Open hopeful, they both enjoyed his company, liking him as a man. As a result the piece – A ROUND WITH FLITCROFT – was afforded a cover line on the July 1984 issue of the magazine, Maurice sharing billing with Jack Nicklaus and Seve Ballesteros. It was a sympathetic take. 'My initial reaction was that here was a kindly man,' wrote Alliss, 'not devious, certainly not very clever or slick. Eccentric yes, but the overriding thing for me was his kindliness, his humility and, above all, his enthusiasm.

'Now the cynics might say he has plenty to be humble about . . . The plain facts are that he does not know how to play the game, how to carry a bag of clubs, how to tee up, put a head cover on, keep his clubs in proper order, and how to place them on the ground. He has no knowledge of etiquette and on the putting green he frequently walked over my line . . . At Old Thorns, on the back nine where we started, he had two pars and the rest added up to about 60. I can understand why the R&A have become paranoiac about him . . . I can see that the authorities would become cheesed off with him, particularly Keith Mackenzie who in his days as secretary of the R&A was not given to outrageous bursts of goon-like humour.

'But at the same time, I think the R&A could have had broader shoulders and might have put a smile on their austere faces, because, if I interpret the rules correctly, he was not robbing anyone else of a place.' It was a startling take from a member of the British golfing establishment, and one which showed how out-of-touch and stuffy Mackenzie and the R&A had been. Alliss went on: 'He may well have got there by deception, which is reprehensible and a bit naughty, but it does show a bit of native cunning.

'I would love to think there were a few young professionals around who shared his outlook that golf is so magical, to have the dreams that are so obviously floating through his mind. A dear friend once told me that no one should ever take anyone's dreams away. Flitcroft dreams of being the Open Champion, and what is wrong with that? Maurice Flitcroft is a one-off, a genuine chap with a kindly heart and it's no good thinking that, under different circumstances, he could have been a great golfer. I would venture to say that he would never have been. But I also said that of Gary Player in 1952 so my opinion may not really amount to much! But in his heart and in his face you could see a warmth and a smile and a thought and something that made you think that he has contributed something already to the game of golf – even if it is only a smile.'

From the voice of British golf, this was a generous

reading indeed. Never before had Maurice been so warmly embraced by a full card-carrying member of the golfing fraternity. And yet – predictably – Maurice was able to find fault with the article when he finally clapped eyes on it. 'While the story presented a complimentary picture of me as a person and would have made a very good character reference, it did nothing to enhance my reputation as an Open contender,' he decided. He phoned Haslam, a hurt voice coming down the line to declare: 'I wouldn't have come down if I knew you were going to make fun of me like that.' The editor, stunned, nevertheless apologised out of politeness. Alliss was also made aware of Maurice's ire. 'He was quite annoyed with me,' recalls the commentator. 'He thought I was being very harsh on him. He was so serious. But he couldn't play!'

Maurice sat down at his typewriter to clatter out a livid three-page diatribe to the letters page of *Golf World*, putting the piece to rights before pulling it to bits. The letter would be a sprawling epic, a vituperative classic. 'I carry my bag the way it suits me,' he blasted, 'and that goes for the way I put my clubs in the bag, and the way I put the head covers on.' Regarding any breaches of etiquette, he breathlessly explained: 'Up to now I have practised most of my golf on playing fields, and on my own, so I have not had to worry about stepping on someone's line, which doesn't mean to say when I do play with others on a course, I do not take care to avoid doing such a thing, but I am likely, on the odd occasion, when deep in concentration, to forget.' Maurice being Maurice, an abrupt 180-degree turn to justify his on-course behaviour was not slow in coming. 'Having said that, I don't know what all the fuss is about, especially when the grass is cut short and the ground firm. I wouldn't make a fuss, nor would I blame a missed putt on such an act.'

Maurice then took issue with Alliss' reference to his humility. 'As I was among strangers and had a feeling I was on trial, my quietness and reserve should not be mistaken for humbleness,' he wrote. 'I remember feeling humble once, it was when I was in the Merchant Navy and sailing on the *Empress of England*'s maiden voyage out of Liverpool to Montreal, Canada. I wasn't feeling very well, so I went up onto the deck for a breath of air. It was night and it was dark, black almost, no moon or stars were visible, the only lights the ship's lights. I stared out at that vast emptiness and thought about being thousands of miles from home, from land. I felt humble then.' As vessels of complaint go, this particular one had taken a violent steer to the port side.

Maurice returned to matters related to golf, and the playing of. 'I hit a fair number of poor shots,' he admitted, 'but then so did my fellow competitors and there isn't a player in the world, and I include the top players, who don't hit a fair number of poor shots during the course of a round . . . I took three out of a bunker on one hole, but then so did Tom Watson in the last series of *Pro-Celebrity Golf*.' As for the much-derided, if successful, tactic of firing a 3-iron straight through a clump of trees, Maurice explained his reasoning: 'The odds were on my side, the gaps being wider than the trunks. I hit the perfect shot and heard

Peter Haslam exclaim in a tone of disbelief: "You did just what you said you would!" . . . A number of shots I hit were unfortunate enough to run into the trenches that abound on Old Thorns, and under the local rules you are not allowed a free drop. But if you are not concerned with playing par golf, or breaking the course record, it doesn't matter.'

He went on to dispute his score over nine holes of 'about sixty', and accuse Alliss – who in the 1950s and 1960s finished in the top ten of the Open four times – of running up a larger one. 'I would welcome a return match with Alliss over eighteen holes or thirty-six,' he added, before blowing a small hole in his argument by asking for 'twenty strokes if we played for a small stake'.

Working himself up into a lather of a climax, Maurice applied the letter's final flourish. And it revealed who its author was really angry with. 'When I wrote to the R&A this year, requesting an entry form for the Open, M.F. Bonallack wrote back to say he regretted he was unable to send me a form because of my past perform- ances. He makes no allowance for any radical improvement in my game since last year. If I were to sit an exam for O Levels or A Levels or even a degree, should I fail I would not be barred from entering again the next year, or the next year. I don't like doors being slammed in my face, and should I obtain entrance to the Open once again, there will be no question of my withdrawing just to save someone's face. I will be going all out to win. You see, I too have got a face.'

Sadly for Maurice, despite a postscript which demanded: 'I trust you will publish my reply, and give

it the same prominence as the Alliss article', this particular holler of rage against the machine would not be
heard in public. Also ignored, possibly with good
reason after his three-page rant, was a post-postscript
fishing for free equipment: 'In case you have forgotten,
when might I expect to receive my golf umbrella,
trousers, etc.' Haslam, nevertheless, published another
reader's letter which argued that Maurice provided
'an element of light relief amidst the automatons who
dominate the game today', and continued to send
Maurice a Christmas card each and every year.

The 1984 Open at St Andrews, the home of golf and
the R&A, came and went without any input from
Maurice, save a small article in the *Daily Mail* detailing
his latest actions. Entitled HANGING IN THERE
WITH THE WASHING, it pictured Maurice sinking
a putt in his back garden while performing a small jig;
two pairs of his trousers dried on the line in the background. The paper gave him a platform to dismiss the
Alliss article as a 'hatchet job', and to ensure the R&A
were publicly informed that he did not consider his
Open dream to be over. 'My game is pretty good at
the moment,' he said, every inch the professional media
operator. 'I have worked out one or two technical faults
in my swing and I am on the right lines now.' It was
clear Maurice was not going to give up, and that at
least one application would be winging its way from
Barrow-in-Furness to St Andrews the following year.

In 1985, Maurice sent off his annual application
under his own name, but he had a new argument
with which he intended to state his case.

Dear Sir,

As a professional golfer I expect to be treated like any other professional golfer, and not discriminated against. Golf is what I have chosen to do to try to make a living, and as success in the Open would enable me to do just that, I think I am perfectly entitled to try and qualify.

The Conservative Government have spent billions the past twelve months, supposedly to protect the rights of people to do their jobs, and as members of the establishment and supporters of the Conservative Government, I would expect you to act accordingly.

With regard to my performance in the 1983 Open, I think it compares favourably with that of Zola Budd's in the Olympics, and the England cricket team's against the West Indies in 1984.

Before I close, I take this opportunity to remind you that I have not received the £15 refund to which I am entitled under the rules, when I failed to qualify under the name of G. Hoppy, in the regional competition held at Pleasington in 1983.

Yours faithfully,
M.G. Flitcroft

Once again, Flitcroft's logic was unquestionable: the much-trumpeted Budd's bid for Olympic gold in Los Angeles ended in farce as she collided with Mary Decker in the 3,000 metres, while the West Indies whitewashed their hosts England 5–0 in one of the most one-sided Test series in cricketing history. In the face of it, Bonallack was already showing mild signs of tiring of the fight a mere year into the job, not being consumed by the mania that had devoured Keith Mackenzie. For an easy life, the new secretary sent Maurice a form, which was duly filled in and dispatched straight back to HQ. However, the wily Bonallack perhaps knew Flitcroft had been cutting it fine; by the time the papers reached St Andrews, the cut-off point for entries had passed. The R&A politely wrote back to inform Maurice of this, also pointing out that they would not be returning any entrance fee, as Maurice didn't include one with the entry form in the first place. Once again, the request to replenish Hoppy's Swiss bank account was politely ignored.

Maurice also attempted to enter under the pseudonym Francis W. Monk, whose home town was given as Scottsdale, Phoenix, Arizona (though Maurice requested all of Monk's correspondence be sent to an address in Kendal, Cumbria). Bonallack, who one can picture attempting to stifle a yawn, wrote back asking for proof of playing ability, as Monk did not appear to be a member of the PGA in America. The Scottsdale sharpshooter failed to respond. After a fortnight of waiting, Bonallack simply returned Monk's entrance cheque, and the American's 'career' was stymied after the very first move.

This didn't stop Maurice putting in the hours on the local rugby field, attempting to raise his game to professional standard. It was a twenty-minute walk each way, though, time Maurice reckoned would be better spent clacking balls up and over the goalposts. This was a point he made when writing to several car manufacturers in June 1985 requesting sponsorship.

Dear Sirs,

My name is Maurice G. Flitcroft, the G is for Gerald. Since 1976 when I made my first attempt to qualify for the Open golf championship, and failed so magnificently, I have dedicated myself to mastering the game, in sometimes somewhat difficult circumstances, with the intention of one day qualifying for the Open or some other major European event.

I do not enjoy the same advantages as most other golf professionals, but I do not intend to let that stop me. It takes me 40 minutes brisk walking to get to and from the place where I practise, time and energy which I could more profitably use practising. On the other hand, it does improve my fitness.

At this juncture, Maurice decided to go well off-piste. It is worth remembering that he was asking for goods totalling around £10,000.

On reflection, being prosecuted for practising on the playing fields near my home turned out to be a blessing in disguise, because I had to look further afield for somewhere to practise and I found a place where I could practise undisturbed; as a consequence, my game has improved considerably, so much so I am quite confi-

*dent I will succeed given the right circumstances. I am
certain I would do much better than I have done in the
past if I were able to get in more course practice. This I
have not been able to do because of my particular situation. I am unemployed and do not possess a car which
makes it difficult for me to get to a course, which
brings me to the purpose of my letter. I could do with a
car, and your company manufactures cars, so perhaps
we could come to some mutually acceptable arrange-
ment, whereby you supply me with a car, and in return,
I allow you to use my name – which has become
synonymous with the Open championship – my worldwide fame, or exploits, in your advertising and
promotion in some way.*

Yours faithfully,
M.G. Flitcroft

As business pitches, or even begging letters, go, this
one broke the mould. Maurice only broached the
subject of a free car – the whole point of the letter
– midway through a sprawling third paragraph. By
which time he had already mentioned a magnificent
failure, his unemployment, and a recent prosecution
for trespassing in a local school. Many of the companies he had targeted – which included Ford, Rover,
Volkswagen, Talbot, Renault and Peugeot, as well as
the premium marques Range Rover, Jaguar and Audi
– wrote kind letters back, but none were willing to
associate their vehicles with a man whose main claim
to fame was that he had 'failed so magnificently'.

Maurice widened the net. He wanted sponsorship, and he didn't just want a free sleeve of balls from Dunlop. He drew up a list of the UK's top brands, and fired off nearly a hundred letters to manufacturers of premium product.

Dear Sirs,

The year 1985/86 marks the tenth year since I first attempted to qualify for the Open championship and failed so magnificently. It will also mark the year when I win the Open, given the opportunity and the right conditions.

To celebrate the occasion, and a decade during which my name – Maurice G. Flitcroft – has become synonymous with the Open, I am writing to a few select companies involved in golf, to share in the event by supplying me with their particular products.

I have been going it alone and doing it my way since I took up the game. I am prepared to continue in this way, but I realise if I am to compete on equal terms with all the other would-be champions, I will need to enjoy some of the advantages that they do.

At odds of 1,000,000 to 1 this year – next year it would be a shame not to take advantage of this golden opportunity to tip the scales etc.

I look forward to a positive response.

Yours faithfully,
M.G. Flitcroft

He did not get the positive response he had been looking forward to. The Rolex Watch Company Ltd, for example, sent a reply explaining that they already had a publicity tie-up with Seve Ballesteros, and also enjoyed an excellent and highly valued relationship with the R&A. Neither deal was something they wanted to put in jeopardy. It was a politic brush-off. Maurice was unimpressed. 'From the tone of their reply it was clear they were afraid any connection with me would upset the famous player,' he sniffed. 'Not the kind of reply to persuade me to buy one of their watches.'

As Rolex struggled along without the benefit of an international marketing campaign based on the face of Flitcroft, and without a gratis executive saloon to transport him around Cumbria's finest courses, Maurice was forced to continue practising at the local rugby field. He did however get eighteen holes in when his stepson Michael visited and took him to Furness Golf Club. But with grim inevitability, the day was destined to turn sour.

Upon arrival, Maurice and Michael found the clubhouse empty, and with nobody authorised to take their green fees, they filled out tickets left for the convenience of visitors and put their £2.50 fees in envelopes left for that purpose. After the round, it was put to Maurice by a member that the green fee was, in fact, £5 each, and that the 'likes of him' were not welcome on the course anyway. Maurice replied that it was only the second time he had played Furness since taking up the game, and if he never played it again, he wouldn't miss it as he had played on better courses. The incident thankfully passed without the dusting of cheeks with knuckles, but Maurice was soon the recipient of a letter from the Furness secretary asking for the club's missing fiver or 'appropriate action' would be taken. Maurice didn't bother to reply. No punitive measures were forthcoming, though it was assumed he had been banned from the course for life. Having already been expelled from Barrow Golf Club *sine die*, now only Dunnerholme was open to him. Even though, of course, thanks to the efforts of Keith Mackenzie, as a professional without a PGA card even Dunnerholme technically was not.

As the 1986 Open loomed, and he approached his fifty-sixth birthday, Maurice's passion for entering the Open finally began to fade. He was practising more than ever, his game improving with every session. But the will wasn't quite there. Even Beau was getting slower at catching the balls, as the long walk to Walney Beach knackered the pair of them before they'd even started training, and the traipse back tested the knee sockets of human and canine alike. Maurice decided he would try one last time. He took pen to paper and scrawled a letter to the R&A. But gone were the blatant pisstakes of earlier years. No entries under pseudonyms were sent. Now he had a deadly serious proposition for Michael Bonallack, R&A secretary, and five-time British and English amateur champion. There was nothing else for it, argued Maurice: the two men would have to face off on the golf course, *mano a mano*.

Dear Sir,

*One last time I am writing to request that you send me
an entry form for this year's Open championship.*

  *As I anticipate that it will be accompanied by a letter
directing my attention to Condition of Entry 3(h), and
as I would much prefer to play under my own name, I
have a suggestion which, because of my particular
circumstances, seems to me to be a simple way of
proving my ability at the present time.*

  *My suggestion is that I play a round of golf with, or
in the presence of, anyone you care to nominate on any
course that you consider fair, any time between the 21st
May 1986 and the closing date for entries.*

Yours faithfully,
M.G. Flitcroft

Bonallack refused to bow to sentimentality and
volleyed an instant reply straight past Flitcroft's lugs.
Within the week, a letter dropped on Maurice's
doormat which insisted: 'Proof of playing ability
required by the Championship Committee does not
include playing a round of golf with a representative
of the Committee but requires records of performances in actual competitive play.'

  There would be no duel. Maurice was crestfallen.
'You could accuse the R&A of a lot of things,' he philo-
sophically sighed, the last gasp of wind in his sails,
'but you couldn't accuse them of being sporting.' The
final battle looked over, the war won. The pompous

despot Mackenzie and his petty minions at the R&A had routed Maurice G. Flitcroft. They had thrashed Gene Pacecki, belaboured Gerald Hoppy, hung, drawn and quartered Gerald Thornbush. They had even drowned Francis W. Monk at birth, like a blind puppy in a sack. It was carnage. But it was perhaps with some relief that Maurice admitted defeat. He had 'tryed' – but now he was done.

Little did Maurice know that round the corner lay redemption, justification – and the sweetest of final flings.

Hole 16: Vindication from a kindred nation

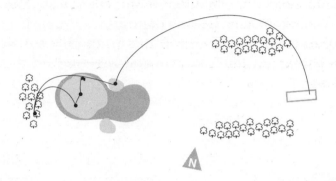

B Y THE time 1987 had come round, a telephone had been installed *chez* Flitcroft. It barely rang. It had been three years since Gerald Thornbush's handwriting had been decoded by the Cold War spies at the R&A, four years since Gerald Hoppy had romped all over the first nine at Pleasington, and a massive eleven years since Maurice himself had made all the papers with his life-defining jaunt at Formby. Every year, without fail, at least one journalist would contact him just before the Open; every year, without fail, Maurice would give the journalist what they wanted, to wit, a promise that he'd 'be back next year' because his 'game is good enough now' to win the Open. Everyone knew they were just going through the motions, but they danced all the same.

In September 1987, Maurice received a call from one such journalist, Richard Dodd, the golf correspondent for the *Yorkshire Post*. Maurice thought this would be an opportunity to announce his retirement to the world, but instead he was knocked off his feet with a blow not felt since his boxing days. The journalist told Maurice that he'd just had a phone call from the United States of America. A chap called Terry Moore, from the Blythefield Golf and Country Club, Michigan, was trying to get in touch with him. He'd chanced his arm by ringing Barrow Golf Club, but whoever had answered told him in no uncertain terms to bugger off. So instead he called what he assumed was the local Barrow paper. (The *Post*, based in Leeds, was just under 100 miles away down the A65, a mere walk to the shop in American terms, no doubt.) Moore had requested Maurice's address, and hit paydirt: Dodd had written a piece about him years before, so passed the information on to Moore. Now he was warning Maurice to expect a letter.

'This Moore chap says that when they read about your round at Formby back in 1976, him and his mates at the club named a trophy after you,' explained Dodd.

'Where is this again?'

'Grand Rapids, Michigan.'

'What, do they want a signed photo or something?' Maurice asked, by now familiar with overtures from the States.

'No. He wants to fly you and your wife out there, first class, put you up in a hotel, and for you to play in a tournament, The Maurice Flitcroft Trophy.'

There was a long pause. This was not so familiar. 'Is this a joke?'

Maurice telephoned Jean at work immediately, the couple confused but excited. Over supper that evening, they vowed not to expect too much, just to get on with their lives. If you don't count his stint in the Army in Trieste, which he had basically treated as a jaunt at a spa hotel, Maurice had never been on holiday outside the UK before. Never mind to America. Neither had Jean. They had never been on an aeroplane, they didn't even have passports, so the prospect of flying to America was barely conceivable.

It became even less so over the months that followed. 1987 turned into 1988, and Richard Dodd's phone call seemed to be the last, distant word spoken of The Maurice Flitcroft Trophy. Maurice simply assumed this Terry Moore chap was a hoaxer – and nobody likes being messed around by one of those! Maurice and Jean had been victims of a sick trick, their hopes raised and dashed by . . . well, who, exactly? Probably someone who had decided golf's good name had been sullied, and fancied teaching him a lesson. There were plenty of nutjobs in America, reasoned Maurice, who had read enough papers and watched enough television to know that when they weren't going round shooting their presidents or members of The Beatles, they would meticulously dye the grass on their golf courses to make it even greener, then sweep up all the leaves with a special outdoor Hoover. He'd seen the Masters. Madmen one and all.

He consigned The Maurice Flitcroft Trophy to the past, putting it down as some sort of prank. Until, on 24 February 1988, buried among the usual depressing spread of bills and arrears papers on his doormat, he found an envelope with an Airmail stamp on it. Maurice tore it open without hesitation.

Dear Maurice,

As you may have learned from talking to Richard Dodd, golf writer from the Yorkshire Post, *there is a golf tournament held in your honor in Grand Rapids, Michigan, USA. This year as a special celebration we'd like to invite you and a guest to attend the tournament. British Airways had agreed to two (2) round trip tickets for you to arrive in the US on May 18 and to return to England by May 23. Your accommodations will also be complimentary. The tournament itself takes place on Friday, May 20. Obviously you are most welcomed and encouraged to play in the event, which is a four man scramble. It's a fun tournament ending with an ample cocktail hour and dinner banquet.*

Your presence will be a highlight for the event. Golfers at our club are aware of your dauntless and pluckish attempts to qualify for the British Open and consider you quite a golf folk hero. British Airways feel the same and that is why they're willing to donate the tickets. I hope you're able to attend.

Please let me know as soon as possible on your interest in the self addressed envelope included. I'm looking forward to hearing from you.

Sincerely,
Terry Moore

Moore was the editor of *The Michigan Golfer*, a magazine which served a state with the highest amount of public courses in the US, providing enough of a readership to keep the small publication going. He had recently played in The Maurice Flitcroft Trophy at Blythefield Golf and Country Club – officially known as The Maurice G. Flitcroft Spring Stag – and had decided the man whose name graced the competition since its inception in 1978 should also grace the event itself.

'Blythefield held a Spring Stag every year in May,' he explains. 'It's a social day where members bring guests and compete in a Texas Scramble, which is where teams of four all take a shot, choose the best one, then all take their next shot from there, and so on. Anyway, my brother Tim was a member of Blythefield back then. He has a lively sense of humour and always looks for the quirky things in life and golf. So he was quite taken with the Flitcroft story after discovering his feat while flicking through the *Guinness Book of World Records* in 1978. It was his idea to name the trophy the Maurice G. Flitcroft Spring Stag, and it stuck over the years. It's still being played now.'

Renaming the trophy gave the tournament an identity over and above all the other member–guest tournaments at the club. As participants and organisers embraced the Flitcroft ethos, the competition became less about winning and more about just having unpretentious fun, a philosophy shift which led to the event becoming one of the most popular in the members' calendar. Special features included Mulligans for sale, a green with two flags, a hole with a two-foot wide cup and – surreally – prizes of goldfish bowls and bowling balls for the team with the *highest* score.

Terry Moore had been invited by his brother to partake in the Flitcroft on numerous occasions. Ironically, however, it was a golf shot of pure golfing bliss that set the wheels in motion to bring Flitcroft to Michigan. 'I was playing with Tim in the Flitcroft in 1987 when I had a hole in one on the fifteenth,' explains Terry, with great pride. It was his first hole in one, and like all golfers, the recounting of the tale will never lose its lustre. 'It was two hundred yards and I aced it with a one-iron. Beautiful. It helped the team to a fifty-nine, the lowest winning score ever. We were all on a high afterwards, celebrating in the bar, when I thought we should do something special next year for the ten-year anniversary. We should track this guy Maurice down and get him over here. So that's what we did.'

That moment of inspired inception – doffing the cap to an everyday hero and showing an understanding of grassroots golfers that put the R&A to shame – led to Maurice standing in the corridor of his modest council house, staring in disbelief at the letter in front of him. 'Was he interested in coming over?' He read and reread the line. 'I thought to myself, I'm more than interested!' recalled Maurice. 'I was absolutely beside myself and wrote back immediately!'

Dear Terry,

I received your letter Monday morning. I am delighted to hear you hold a tournament in my honour, and I gladly accept your invitation to attend and play in the event.

I will be bringing my wife Jean, who over the years has been most supportive in my attempts to play in the Open, etc.

With regard to the cocktail hour and the banquet, will it be formal or informal? My wife is concerned that I make a good impression. Do I need to bring my own clubs? Or should I hire a set?

And the travel arrangements, have they been finalised? Given the choice we would like to fly from Manchester.

My wife and I are looking forward to the occasion, which we are sure will be a memorable one.

Sincerely,
Maurice G. Flitcroft

There must have been something peculiar in the air that day, because no sooner had he signed his name on the letter and posted it off, than the telephone, so long silent, rang again. It was Brian Dempster, a journalist from BBC Belfast, who was working on a series about famous eccentrics in sport. Would Maurice like to talk him through his life and achievements so far? All of a sudden, Maurice was famous again! Of course he would.

Maurice held court on his favourite subject, chatting away breezily about how he had foxed the automatons of the R&A again and again, though he felt an instinct not to mention the good news he'd received that morning. That had nothing to do with modesty, more a concern that if the news found its way to the press, it might jeopardise the invite in some way. That plan was swiftly jettisoned, however, when Maurice lost his temper at something Brian mentioned during the conversation.

He was not directing his anger at Brian himself, rather at the secretary of Furness Golf Club. In his bid to track Maurice down, Brian had – like Terry Moore before him – tried to contact him through one of the local golfing establishments. It made perfect sense: where else would a journalist start his research? He was trying to track down a man famous for his golfing exploits, after all. What made less sense, to Maurice at least, was that for a second time, a gentleman of the press had been showered with opprobrious language after asking politely for Maurice Flitcroft's whereabouts.

'Brian said that the secretary of Furness Golf Club replied, somewhat heatedly, that the mere mention of my name made his blood boil,' remembered

Maurice. 'Well, I was so incensed by that, I told him that not everybody felt that way, and although I didn't intend to, I told him of my invite I had received that very morning. The cat was out of the bag.' Not only that, it was running around the place, tearing strips off all the furniture. Sure enough, the national news-papers were soon carrying headlines such as US JUST LOVES FLITCROFT DRIVE and OPEN JOKER BOUND FOR USA. And it turned out Maurice's instinct had yet again been absolutely spot on: the press interest did backfire, and very nearly jeopard-ised the whole trip.

When the Moore brothers had recovered from their historic 1987 win in the Flitcroft, they started making enquiries into potential sponsors for the 'Bring Maurice to Blythefield' campaign. After all, it would not be a cheap job. They would have to cover flights and accommodation, as well as keeping Maurice and his companion fed and entertained. It would be of a cost well beyond the usual clubhouse whip-round. Eventually they found someone who could see the stunt's potential for publicity, a marketing man for a regional office of British Airways USA by the name of (no, not that one) Mike Myers.

'We were very fortunate really,' says Terry. 'It's like a lot of these things, you have to hit the right people with the right idea at the right time. Mike thought it would be a nice platform to launch British Airways in the minds of the Michigan golfer with this kind of publicity vehicle.'

Myers offered to pay for two first-class return tickets

for Maurice and Jean, plus a further two first-class tickets that would form the jackpot in the evening prize draw. It was a great deal for Maurice, and for Blythefield Golf and Country Club, as well as being great publicity for British Airways. Or was it? 'I remember everything was going fine until I got this phone call at three in the morning from a British journalist saying, "Hey, what's the deal with Flitcroft?"' recalls Moore. 'And I said, "Look, do you know what time it is?" And he said, "Yeah, but I got a deadline to hit." I said, "So what? What's your circulation?" He said, "1.3 million." So I said, "OK gimme a minute!"' Moore told his side of the story, putting flesh on the bare bones.

When the story broke, questions were asked about British Airways' involvement in the scheme. 'That's when the corporate wheels fell off,' sighs Moore. 'I guess Maurice was coming over here with a lot of baggage – no pun intended – with British Airways. I guess people felt it would be embarrassing for the R&A, which is a true-blue starched-shirt kind of organisation. I think maybe some shareholder called British Airways and said, "Hey, what are we doing giving first-class tickets to Maurice Flitcroft? This guy's an imposter, a rogue. Why are we doing that?"' Exactly whose cage had been rattled has never been ascertained, but in the resulting internal inquiry Maurice and Jean's first-class tickets were knocked down to coach. Yet in a move some might interpret as laughably cynical, the prize draw tickets on offer from British Airways remained first class. It appeared nobody wanted to upset any 'real' golfers. It was also clear that the R&A's insidious influence stretched further than even a naturally chippy working-class warrior like Maurice had anticipated.

As a postscript to the inquiry, Gene and James Flitcroft strenuously denied that the downgrade ever happened. 'They definitely flew first class,' insisted James, delving into a drawer and digging out a perfectly preserved first-class menu from the flight, complete with champagne truffle stains. It was a genuine article, sure enough, although it's not hard to imagine Maurice bagging one for himself on his way back from the toilet. When this was put to the twins, a bit of the infamous Flitcroft heat was emitted by Gene. 'I'm telling you, mate, they went first class! Maybe there was a cover-up by British Airways to try and save face, but when they got on that fucking plane, that's where they were.' A suspicious tale of corporate machinations, it would flummox Michael Moore, never mind his namesake Terry.

First class or coach, in the weeks that led up to the trip, Maurice and Jean busied themselves acquiring passports and US visas. Then there was the little matter of 'making a good impression'. Maurice desperately needed golf clothes and a new suit, while Jean required a new dress. Money was tight in the Flitcroft household: Maurice had been unemployed for some time and had lost the right to unemployment benefit. The job market in Barrow during the height of the Thatcher economic miracle was nothing short of diabolical – Maurice claimed that upon applying for the job of street cleaner he was stunned to find himself up against 1,600 others. Even if that figure had been bolstered by some Flitcroftian exaggeration, it is not a leap to assume that times were grim. It was good timing, then, for one of Jean's famous bingo wins. A whopping £300 booty was more than enough to kit them both out for their once-in-a-lifetime trip around the world.

Flight 95 took off from Manchester Airport to Detroit City via Montreal. Although Maurice had been around the world during his days in the Army and Merchant Navy, as well as his ill-fated period on the ferries, this was the first time he'd been on an aeroplane. He was fifty-eight years old, but would always remember feeling the excitement of a small child upon experiencing new things. He felt exhilarated as the plane took off, marvelling at the mechanics required to get such a beast off the ground. He felt a little travel sickness, but on the whole the journey went well. Except, that is, for the nuisance caused by 'a rather large party of noisy, restless young men, until the huge amounts of drink they imbibed induced a state of torpor in them, much to everyone's relief'.

Maurice and Jean were met at Detroit by Terry Moore and Mike Myers. Terry had borrowed his wife's car, as it had a bigger boot to accommodate the Flitcroft luggage. As it turns out, he needn't have bothered. 'It was amazing,' recalls Terry. 'After all the fuss that had been made about the seats, British Airways lost their luggage! It was truly comical. No one knew where it went. I think they got it back eventually but

that was right at the end of their trip. On the first
day I had to lend Maurice some of my own duds.
Then the next day we took them out and bought
them both outfits to wear. You shouldn't laugh but it
was quite funny.'

During the two-hour journey from the airport to
Grand Rapids, Terry gained his first impressions of
Maurice. 'The first thing I noticed was that he didn't
seem to have any teeth in his head at all. He seemed
to need false teeth but I never saw him with any. It
added to his comical look and made him stand out
amongst the rest of us even more.' He asked Maurice
about his record-breaking 121. What he got in response
was a list of excuses that went on for the entire journey:
he didn't have time to practise, the balls were the
wrong size, he didn't have certain clubs, the wind was
wrong. 'This is when I knew he was actually a real
golfer,' says Terry, 'because we all make excuses like
that. Mind you, you gotta have a lot of excuses to
shoot a 121.'

For the duration of their stay in Grand Rapids,
Maurice and Jean were guests of the Marriott Hotel.
Maurice had never seen such luxuriousness, and was
a little confused by some of the excesses, such as their
suite having *two* king-size double beds when they only
really needed one. They spent the Thursday before
the tournament looking for somewhere to have some
nice fish and chips and a pot of tea. Maurice spent
the evening talking to the local Grand Rapids press,
who were to run a front-page story on him.

On the day of the tournament, Maurice and Jean

were chauffeured to the Blythefield Country Club and greeted by Tom Wurst, the club president, and Bill Brown, the club manager. They were presented with gifts from the club membership, including three silk ties, in navy, red and green embossed with the club emblem: a leaping stag over the initials B.G.C.C. They hadn't forgotten Jean, either, presenting her with six lead crystal tumblers, engraved with the same emblem. This was a momentous occasion, unthinkable, even. Maurice Flitcroft, the scourge of the British golfing establishment, was being presented with gifts by blazer-wearing dignitaries. The drinking receptacles, gripped tightly by a beaming Jean, weren't quite the Auld Claret Jug. But to Maurice, it damn well felt near enough.

They were also presented with the keys to a beautiful white Buick Park Avenue; the gleaming luxury limo was theirs for the week. And then the *coup de grâce*, an envelope containing $600, donated by the members for the purchase of food and drink throughout their stay. Maurice received the envelope with proud tears welling up in his grateful eyes.

It was time, as guest of honour, to take the opening drive of the tournament itself. Here he was, Maurice G. Flitcroft, an unemployed crane driver from Barrow, walking to the first tee to drive off in a tournament bearing his name, a tournament held on a slightly more picturesque peninsula than the one he hailed from, thousands of miles back across the sea. He made sure to immerse himself in the moment and soak up the atmosphere. After all, this time he didn't have to worry about being rumbled, or getting chased off the course.

He cast his mind back to that moment in 1974 when he saw the opening credits of the World Matchplay at Wentworth, and caught the golf bug. Boom ba de boom, ba de boom, went the theme tune. He let it play again in his head, there and then. He glanced at the TV cameras from local station WGVU-TV-35 and national sports channel ESPN. He waved to the crowd of hundreds, who had been inspired by the articles in the Grand Rapids papers to come down and experience this 'golfing phenomenon' for themselves. Who would have thought he'd end up here?

'It was a huge moment for him,' says Terry, who understood totally what the moment meant to Maurice, both literally and symbolically. 'Everyone was there wondering what sort of shot he would hit off the first tee. With the cameras rolling and the crowds he could have been forgiven for topping it twenty yards. But he didn't.'

Maurice would always recall what happened next, the aural nectar of finding the sweet spot on the club-face: 'I got set, swung my driver and hit a super tee shot straight down the middle of the fairway, approximately 225 yards it was reported.'

What did Terry make of his swing? 'His swing was decent. It was a good swing. He didn't have much power, but it was pretty much on plane. He stood up to the ball well. He had good posture. There wasn't anything embarrassing involved. And when he holed a long putt on the first, we wondered whether the Brits had sent a ringer!'

Terry wasn't the only one who wondered if this was the real Maurice Flitcroft. It seemed that wherever he went, suspicions would always be raised. 'That first hole made some onlookers suspicious,' corroborates Maurice, 'and made them wonder if it really was me. But if any suspicions had been held they were quickly dispelled when I settled down and topped a few fairway woods, thinned a few long irons and shanked one or two chips early on in the round.'

'Yup, that's him all right,' sighed club president Tom Wurst, with a satisfied smile. The large crowd relaxed, relieved that they were going to be treated to the full gamut of dreadful golf shots. Even so, despite the odd comic miss-hit, Maurice made a decent contribution to his team's score, finishing with a creditable mid-ranking score of 66. Among the highlights was a shot he played to the 145-yard par-three eleventh. There was a prize of $50 for the tee shot closest to the pin on this tiny green surrounded by bunkers. Maurice gave it his best heave with a 6-iron, but saw his effort land short right and perch miraculously in a narrow strip of grass in between two bunkers. To his surprise, he received a $10 voucher for the shot anyway. He presumed it was because he was guest of honour.

Maurice had also filled his boots at the halfway house, where refreshments were laid on for the competitors. A common sight for club members in America and the UK, this was a first for the little man from Barrow. He could barely believe his eyes as tables groaned under the weight of hot dogs, burgers, turkey sandwiches, pineapples, water melons, bananas, strawberries and a variety of nuts, biscuits, confectionery, soft drinks and beer kept in ice-filled containers. It was, as Maurice put it, a 'veritable cornucopia of good things'. His fellow players and spectators watched in wonder as Maurice stuffed his pockets, golf bag and buggy with the goodies, so as not to miss out on a scrap of it.

After the round, the local station WGVU-TV-35 wanted a chat. His interview, conducted by an amiable cove called Dick Nelson, would prove a less combative affair than his electric spat with Nick Owen and Anne Diamond on the TV-AM sofa, but it was similarly revealing, nonetheless.

DICK NELSON: Maurice let's go back to 1976, what happened?
MAURICE: In 1976 I entered the British Open Championship as a professional. I couldn't enter as an amateur because I wasn't a member of a club. I didn't have a handicap certificate but I could enter as a professional. I didn't need those things as a professional. So I entered, my entry was accepted and that was it.
DICK NELSON: Why did you enter?
MAURICE: Well, I took up the game in the autumn of 1974. I was working full time as a crane driver or crane operator as you call them. I didn't have time to practise in the autumn and the winter, but in the following summer, I did. In the meantime I read up on the game. I got books out on it, on instruction and, well, autobiographical books. Anyway I read about the Open and thought

it would be a good tournament to play in. I thought it would be nice to reach a standard necessary to play in the Open. And that's why I entered.

DICK NELSON: *Now when you shot 121, you set an all-time high record. Were you embarrassed?*

MAURICE: *Yes, I wasn't at all pleased because I felt that score didn't reflect my true ability even then.*

DICK NELSON: *What score would have reflected your true ability back then?*

MAURICE [squirming]: *Back then? A better score than that. I mean, erm, I didn't play as well as I thought I could play.*

DICK NELSON [momentarily switching his attention to Terry Moore, who is standing alongside Maurice]: *Now, the truth: what kind of golfer is Maurice Flitcroft?*

TERRY MOORE: *He is a good golfer. He'd be described in our country as a sandbagger because he isn't someone who's going to shoot another 121. He doesn't play that regularly any more, so he doesn't get the rounds to become consistent. But he did himself proud on the first tee at Blythefield. The first drive of the day, with a lot of people watching him and the cameras rolling, he hit it right down the middle two hundred yards. It was an excellent drive. I think the Royal and Ancient would have been proud of him.*

DICK NELSON [switching back to Maurice]: *Now, you were banned . . .*

MAURICE [happily offering the information]: *Oh I was banned from two local clubs.*

DICK NELSON: *Why did they ban you?*

MAURICE [obfuscating slightly, failing to mention for example his blazer-baiting Bruce Forsyth victory pose and subsequent cry of 'bullshit' at Barrow]: *For entering the British Open.*

DICK NELSON: Now you tried again, didn't you? You changed your name.

MAURICE: They wouldn't accept my entry. I tried before under my own name but they wouldn't accept me. So I thought what I'd do is enter under an assumed name and, erm, that is what I did.

DICK NELSON: What assumed name did you use?

MAURICE: Gerald Hoppy.

DICK NELSON: How did you come up with that?

MAURICE: Well, Gerald is my middle name, that's what the G stands for. Now Hoppy was a nickname my mother used to call me when I was a youngster. I used to go along when I was very young a-hopping and skipping, and they used to call me Hoppy Johnny. And that's how, you know, I came by the name.

DICK NELSON: Any more goals as far as golf is concerned? Are you looking at the hall of fame?

MAURICE: The hall of fame? Well, back home maybe, Sportsman of the Year. I'm surprised I haven't been invited or nominated for that. Sports Personality of the Year. You know, there's something going on there, there's a conspiracy being waged against me.

DICK NELSON: It kind of isn't fair, is it?

MAURICE: It isn't. [Pause] It's sport, you know, it's all about sport, isn't it? I mean, erm, for every winner of a tournament there's a hundred and forty-nine losers.

DICK NELSON: Now, having a man of your stature here before me, I can't let you go without asking if you have any tips for duffers like myself. Someone picking up a club for the first time. What would your advice be?

MAURICE: My advice? Well . . . [A look of panicked confusion sweeps across his face.] *Erm . . . practice. That is the road to perfection! Regular practice. And a good coach. A good coach would come in very handy.*

DICK NELSON: Well, are you available?
MAURICE: Yes, I'm available, er, for a fee, for a price. You know
what I mean?

[Dick Nelson is in hysterics. Maurice is stony-faced]

That evening over dinner, after changing into his borrowed evening wear, Maurice made a speech to the assembled Blythefield members. 'It brought the house down,' recalls Terry Moore. It elicited an unprecedented five-minute standing ovation from those lucky enough to hear it, and has gone down in legend at the Michigan club – and beyond. The oft-quoted address began when the guest of honour was welcomed with a thunderous round of applause.

'Thank you, thank you,' he began. 'First of all, I'd like to thank Terry and Tim Moore for cooking up the plan to bring myself and Jean over here. We don't get to go on holiday very often these days. In fact, it's the first time we've been out of the house since the gas oven exploded.' Maurice met the huge bellows of laughter with a slightly pained but-it's-true grimace.

'I was pleased with the way I played, especially my opening drive. It's even made me think twice about my plans to retire from professional golf. Although a slight kink did develop in my swing during the middle of the round, I hope to sort it out when I do have another crack at the Open. And I shall do it without the help of David Leadbetter, believe you me.' The mention of Nick Faldo's groundbreaking coach earned another blast of laughter. Once again, Maurice looked slightly confused. That one, he thought, was true too.

'I was pleased to win the ten-dollar voucher for my shot on the eleventh, which I thought at the time was accorded to me because I was the guest of honour,' he continued. 'But on reflection it may have been for landing my ball on the small strip of grass between the right-hand bunkers, which was no mean achievement in itself, this being a much smaller target than the green and therefore a great shot.' Peals of laughter rang around the room. Maurice was used to this by now and just carried on.

'I'd like to toast absent friends. Our sons Gene and James, our budgerigar Boo-Boo, and my practice partner and coach, my dog Beau.' There was more warm laughter, before Maurice brought his speech to a heartfelt – even idiosyncratically romantic – climax. 'But most of all I'd like to thank my wife Jean. I hope this little trip has gone some way to repaying the tremendous belief you've shown me over the years. Seriously, she's a magician my wife, a magician I tell you.' The room fell silent. 'Just the other day I got a takeaway coffee but forgot to get some sugar. I thought, Well, that's that, then. I may as well chuck it away. And then Jean just reached into her bag and pulled out two sachets. A magician, I tell you. And that's Jean: whenever I've needed sugar for me tea, she's been there for me. To Jean, the sugar in me tea!'

As glasses were raised, clinked and divested of their contents, Maurice reflected on Jean's patience over the years. She had, after all, been the main breadwinner since Maurice lost his job at the shipyard in the aftermath of the 1976 Open.

Terry Moore noted the couple's harmonious relationship. 'She was very shy at first but warmed up throughout their stay,' he recalls. 'She always seemed pleasantly amused by Maurice and his antics. In fact, Jean reminded me of the actress Brenda Fricker in the movie *My Left Foot*. Very warm and motherly.'

The three days after the tournament were spent basking in fame and glory. One of Maurice's playing partners on the day, Greg Johnson, wrote another front-page article in the *Grand Rapids News*. Maurice was stopped several times to sign a copy, including one for the Chief of Police, who had been hooked by the Mauricemania sweeping the nation.

On the final full day of Maurice's stay, Terry Moore and his family hosted a farewell barbeque for the Flitcrofts. Terry's father took Jean and Maurice for a boat trip on the famous Lake Michigan. Having regaled Moore Snr with stories of his seafaring days on the way to the boat, Maurice neglected to mention the frequency with which he suffered from sea-sickness, an affliction which often lost him his job. He was not ten minutes into the trip across the 'inland sea' – as he called the lake, much to the amusement of Moore Snr – when he was struck down by the old curse and had to be helped ashore.

That was the only hiccup during the entire visit. After spending their final morning Stateside buying hats, visors and jumpers covered in Michigan logos for Gene and James, they were ready to go. It was a wrench for Maurice to leave the splendour of the hotel behind, but he had to check out. Even handing

Terry Moore his 'duds' back was a painful moment. But nothing compared to handing back the keys to the giant Buick. Tom Wurst, the club president, literally had to prise them from Maurice's clenched fist. Terry drove them to the airport, where they all said a tearful goodbye.

As the Flitcrofts flew back to their own peninsula, Terry ran his personal highlight of Maurice's trip through his head. 'I'd have to say the thing that made me laugh most was on about the fourteenth hole of the tournament,' he recalls. 'The TV stations had set the cameras up on the tee, and Maurice wanted to play up to them. So he went through this elaborate fastidious pre-shot routine, lining up his shot and posing – when he suddenly struck the visor of his cap with his club. It was a very Chaplinesque moment.' And how does he feel about Maurice's visit now, after all these years? 'You know what? It was one of those things you do in life that you look back on and think: Wow, I'm really glad I did that.'

Maurice and Jean returned to the less palatial surrounds of Laurence Avenue, Barrow-in-Furness, and were greeted by the open arms of Gene and James. Beau and Boo-Boo barked and chirped their welcome too, unaware of the small part they'd played in Maurice's odyssey.

The next day, Jean would be back in her role as a secretary at Vickers, while Maurice would find himself wandering back from another unsuccessful trip to the Job Centre. Only days earlier, he'd swanned around in a giant Buick, been showered with gifts and cash, starred on television, and participated in his very own golf tournament. And now here he couldn't even get an interview for a job in a shoe factory. Maurice opened the front door with heavy heart, walked into the lounge and slumped into his red leather chair. There he would have stayed with a black cloud over his head until Jean got home, if he hadn't felt a familiar cold moist nose nuzzling the knuckles of his right hand. He glanced up to see the ever-cheery face of Beau, eyes sparkling, golf ball in mouth, wagging his tail and nodding his head towards the old rusty seven-iron that sat propped in the hallway. Maurice sighed and smiled. 'Aye, come on then, lad,' he said, rising out of his chair and his melancholy. 'Let's away and iron out this kink.'

Hole 17: At Last, the Home of Golf conquered!

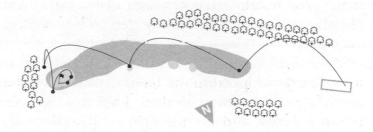

Hᴉs sᴘɪʀɪᴛs buoyed by his American adventure, Maurice decided to re-engage in battle back on the home front with the golfing authorities. He had a new – or rather nouveau – soldier in his ranks: James Beau Jolley. Named after his favourite grape-based tipple, as well as a nod to his faithful dog, Maurice's new creation attempted to gain entrance to the 1987, 1988 and 1989 Opens. The 1987 entry was unsuccessful – as was a pointless one-off attempt to get in as R.W. Street – but the R&A accepted Beau Jolley's forms in both 1988 and 1989. Not one shot was swung in anger, though: in 1988, yet another thundering migraine on the morning of the event forced Maurice to pull out. In 1989, meanwhile, his game fell apart after his four-legged friend Beau, now about

200 dog-years old, lost the ability to stick with the unique ball-gathering system they'd developed over the years, and was staggering dangerously into the ball flight during practice, a confused shadow of his former self. The sadness Maurice felt at seeing his practice partner losing his mind forced him to cut sessions short or stay at home and nurse poor old Beau, until the canine trooper eventually gave up the fight and scampered off to chase golf balls in the sky that winter.

Beau's death made Maurice question whether he still had any fight left in him too. It certainly wasn't quite what it used to be in the days of Keith Mackenzie. Michael Bonallack, Mackenzie's successor, was equally determined to keep Maurice out of the Open, but only because he had a duty to do so as secretary of the R&A. There was no personal animosity driving Bonallack – and so Maurice had less to feed off himself. His desire to play in the Open burned as fiercely as ever – he still loved the game, still needed to compete, still dreamed of becoming a top-class professional – but his beatification in the USA had robbed him of that extra bit of drive that comes with utter desperation. Maurice was no longer consumed by a need for official recognition: while the R&A might still have failed to appreciate his singular talents, it was crystal clear that the worldwide public did. To rabble-rousers and barrack-room lawyers like Maurice, the love of the people was just as vitally important as opprobrium from The Man.

Beau Jolley attempted to gain entry to the European

Open in 1987, while Maurice G. Flitcroft enquired about a sponsor's invite to the same event. Neither application was successful, but the attempts were a bit half-arsed anyway. Meanwhile other Open chancers were stealing a bit of Maurice's thunder.

In the 1988 pre-qualifiers, a forty-six-year-old American 'professional' called Bo Britt strode onto the first tee at Fairhaven Golf Club wearing a cowboy hat, black jeans and a style of boot not seen since John Ford stopped directing movies. His first drive flew all of 150 yards. 'I couldn't believe it,' said Tony Mahoney, one of Britt's playing partners that day. 'I thought he must have a physical disorder.' Britt scrambled a face-saving bogey on the first, and parred the second with two putts from off the green, forcing Mahoney to re-evaluate: 'I thought perhaps I'd misjudged him, and he was just a great putter.'

But Mahoney's first instincts were proved spot on as Britt imploded on the third hole, following up a drive of just over 100 yards with two duck hooks. Britt ended up in a greenside bunker, and was still in it three attempts later. He successfully escaped with his fourth – but unfortunately thinned the shot through the green and into a bush at the back. The lie was unplayable, and Britt was asked to leave the course. 'I don't understand it, I was only one over par yesterday,' he insisted. His other playing partner, Keith MacDonald, wasn't so confused. 'My mother has a better swing than Britt,' he said, 'and she doesn't even play golf.'

A year later, another wannabe-Maurice turned up

from overseas. Clemens Bayer, a twenty-nine-year-old German upholsterer, went round the prequalifying Kentish course of Langley Park in 105 shots. He had only taken seven clubs along with him, not a sand iron amongst them. 'It's very difficult to join a club at home,' explained Bayer, as if he was reading from an instruction book written by Maurice. 'I use the local park in the evenings and we have no bunkers in our parks.' He even managed to get under the authorities' skin with a wanton dig: 'Frankly, I was astonished the R&A accepted my entry.'

Even Maurice's unofficial tag as the 'world's worst golfer' was coming under threat. In 1986, the US magazine *Golf Digest* held a competition at Sawgrass to find the most inept player in the country. After sixteen holes over one of the world's hardest courses, hacker Angelo Spagnolo was tied for the 'lead' on a risible 104 over par. The score didn't bode well for the test that followed. The seventeenth at Sawgrass is one of the most famous holes in golf, a par three with an island green. A player must send their tee shot high into the air, landing their ball onto a precise target. Spagnolo, however, had proved himself totally incapable of getting any loft whatsoever in his shots, and found it impossible to send the ball sailing anywhere near the green, his flat approaches glugging immediately into the drink. Eventually he was persuaded to putt down the walkway linking the water-bound green with the rest of the course. All in all, he took sixty-three shots to reach the green – and even then he three-putted. Spagnolo eventually carded 257 for his round, though unlike Maurice's 121, the whole affair had the strong cheesy whiff of pantomime. The *Golf Digest* competition was ersatz, arch, knowing – and, in the final analysis, effectively a staged celebration of mediocrity, with everyone in on the joke. Maurice's record was made in proper competition – and in the game's oldest major to boot.

The slapstick Open performances of Bo Britt and Clemens Bayer caused the R&A to stage another rethink. In an excruciating solo on their own trumpet, they announced a clever new rule sure to bar hackers from ever again desecrating the Open: even overseas professionals would now have to offer proof of their playing ability. 'This rule is designed to stop players entering merely by claiming they are professionals,' read the organisation's proud statement. 'It will help us to prevent a repetition of the situation which has cropped up very occasionally where one or two entries clearly did not have the ability to take part in the Open Championship.' The door, for so long left carelessly ajar by the good men and true of the Royal & Ancient Golf Club, had been firmly slammed shut.

The announcement was a red rag to a bull. And while every weekend hacker will no doubt tip their caps to the Bo Britts, Clemens Bayers and Angelo Spagnolos of this world, there really was only one Maurice Flitcroft. His edge might have been ever-so-slightly blunted by his new-found popularity in the US, and subsequent acceptance, but his anti-authoritarian streak remained. If the R&A had slammed the door shut, Maurice Flitcroft would simply have to prise it open again.

Maurice kept calm and thought things through rationally. It was never his strong suit, but the situation demanded precise thinking. When the solution came, it was simple. James Beau Jolley had been accepted in 1988 and 1989 – so there was no reason to think he wouldn't be accepted in 1990. After all, just because the R&A had brought in a new rule, it wouldn't necessarily mean they would retrospectively harangue professionals who had previously applied to play for proof of playing ability. James Beau Jolley wrote to the R&A for an entry form, filled one in – and was accepted to play at Ormskirk, Lancashire. Simple. So simple, it was almost as simple as the R&A. Maurice Flitcroft's last hurrah was on.

Even though his brother Roy still lived in Skelmersdale, which was only a few minutes drive from Ormskirk, Maurice opted to travel down from Barrow on the morning of the qualifier. His tee time was at 2.20 p.m., which gave him plenty of time to play with. Gene was at the wheel of the brand-new Flitmobile. 'He came to pick me up in the white Maestro van my wife had bought at my suggestion from the auctions,' remembered Maurice. 'Not for me your Ferrari T, your Porsche or your Rolls-Royce. I like cars that are not only handsome but practical as well.' The Open hopeful relaxed in the passenger seat of the British Leyland Austin wagon, his caddy alongside him, a set of clubs rattling around in the back.

In scenes reminiscent of Formby in 1976, Maurice

arrived at the course with minutes to spare, just after 2.10 p.m. He gathered his clubs from the boot of the van, hoping not to be recognised. With this in mind, his wife Jean had altered the shade of his hair and moustache with food colouring. His hair – on both his head and top lip – was now a strange and sickly brown, as though he had soaked it in tobacco juice for a week. Even though his hair was all his own, he appeared to be sporting an ill-fitting toupee and comedy moustache. It was not a flattering look.

The starter called out for 'James B. Jolley'. Nobody replied. The name was called out again.

'Here I am!' shouted Maurice, running out of the clubhouse towards the tee, Gene a step or two behind him.

The starter gave the out-of-breath player a long look up and down, then shot a disapproving glance at his caddy's unruly pony-tail, anathema to golfing types. Maurice took a deep gulp, and only released his breath when the starter issued him with his score-card, a pencil and a metallic blue pitch-mark repairer with the R&A logo emblazoned on it. His young playing partners, nineteen-year-old professional Gary Dermot and amateur entrant Neil Self, took their turns to drive off. Then it was Maurice's turn to step up.

'Conscious that everyone's eyes were on me, I steeled myself to stay calm as I bent and teed up my ball.' Maurice had finally figured that getting down on all fours to balance his ball on a tee-peg was a bit of a giveaway. 'Straightening, I picked a spot in the distance to aim at, addressed my ball, got set, then swung my driver. It worked a treat, much to my relief, and I hit a good drive which was heading straight for the area of fairway I had targeted – until a sudden gust of wind pushed it slightly off line to the right.'

Despite Maurice's upbeat record, the ball had barely travelled 80 yards. Still, there was time on the short walk between shots to introduce himself to his partners. They were both already suspicious. 'When I got the draw sheet – it was the first time I'd entered – I thought, I don't know this guy,' recalls Neil Self. 'And I know most of the others, cos I'm involved in the golf trade. And the first thing that came into my mind was, I hope this isn't a wind-up. Honestly. I thought, I've not heard of this guy, so I hope it's not some guy entering who can't play. I sort of suspected who it could be, from his swing and his appearance. And there were murmurings around the first tee, who it could be. He just didn't look like a golfer, you could tell the moment he swung that he was not a pro.'

As Self wondered if he had just become another supporting character in the Flitcroft story, Gary Dermot confirmed his suspicion. 'I shook his hand when he came off the tee, cos he had been late and I couldn't do it beforehand,' he remembers. 'I knew who he was. I knew he wasn't James Beau Jolley! I knew he was Flitcroft. Me and Neil knew. Cos I said to him: "You know who this is, don't you?" And Neil said: "Yeah, of course!" as we were walking off the first tee.'

Maurice's play did not impress his partners. 'His swing was poor, a twenty-handicap-plus effort,' says Self. 'He was taking two shots to get past our drives.

I think he started six–five, which was quite good for him, but looking at his game I don't think he'd have broke one hundred that day. He'd have shot just over a hundred, something like that.'

On the par-four second hole, Maurice came close to his first – and what would have been his only – birdie in tournament play. Reaching the apron of the green in two, he used his 9-iron to bounce a chip up towards the hole. Allowing for a left-to-right break, he aimed just to the left of the pin. Gauging the strength to perfection, Maurice watched in impotent frustration as the ball held its line, refusing to break right towards the cup and staying high of the hole, three feet away. To cap a minor tragedy, Maurice then missed his easy par putt, and was forced to settle for a bogey.

By the time he had reached the third tee, Maurice had stopped worrying about being recognised. The usual stress-induced migraine wasn't in evidence. Having started with confidence – even though it had yet to manifest itself in his shotmaking or on his score-card – he was looking forward to playing the sixteen remaining holes. He hit a decent drive – it only just missed the fairway on the right, creeping into semi-rough, and had travelled fully 150 yards – and began to swagger big-leggy down the fairway. But the bounce was about to be taken out of his step. As Maurice reached his ball, and looked down to ascertain its lie, he saw the tyres of a golf cart screech to a halt in front of it. Two blazered gentlemen stepped from the vehicle.

'Mr Flitcroft?'

'You mean Mr Jolley.'

'Come on, Maurice. You're going to have to go off, old boy.'

Amazingly, unbelievably, it was the same official who had thrown Gerald Hoppy off the course at Pleasington! If that unfortunate coincidence wasn't painful enough, the official's suspicion hadn't been piqued by Maurice's play – which hadn't been bad enough, yet – or even his looks – the food dye in the moustache appeared to have done the trick, if only from a distance. No, his attention was caught by the pony-tail of Maurice's caddy: Gene had also carried Hoppy's clubs in 1983, when trading under the name of Troy Atlantis, and the metronomic swish of his trendy pony-tail had rung a bell in the official's head.

Maurice wasn't going to go down without at least attempting resistance, although he knew in his heart the jig was up.

'Maurice? My name is James—'

'Look, Maurice . . .'

'Who?'

'Maurice, come on. I was at Pleasington in 1983. I'm the guy who got you off there, so I know who you are. I'm sorry, but you have to go.'

Maurice's shoulders slumped, his crest fallen. He was defeated. A demand was made for a refund, Maurice refusing to shift unless it was granted. 'As things stood,' recalled Maurice, 'there was little else I could do, short of carrying on regardless and blasting them out of the way. The thought did occur to me, but I discarded it in the interests of safety.'

The official promised to try his best to sort it out. Maurice and Gene stood on the back of the cart and, meekly, allowed themselves to be driven back to the clubhouse. 'He was disgruntled, probably at being caught, but he went quietly,' the official (who kindly contributed an interview to this book but wishes to remain anonymous) remembers today. 'At that point, I don't think he had yet to hit his peak of rubbish form. He'd only played three holes! Nobody was complaining about him, but we knew what he was capable of, and he shouldn't have been there anyway.' It is hard not to conclude that this particular official harbours some affection and perhaps even a little respect for Maurice, despite it all.

The delay in hauling Maurice off the course arguably cost Neil Self his place in final qualifying. He only missed out by one shot, and double-bogeyed the third, after being forced to stand around as Maurice argued his case with the R&A blazers. Not that the player is making any excuses. 'I was in a good position,' explains Self, who now runs Northern Golf, a golf supplies business, 'and we had to wait about five minutes while they had a chat with him, and asked him to leave. And I hit a poor shot for my second, and double bogeyed. It certainly disrupted my rhythm on that hole, but I can't say categorically that I would have qualified. I wouldn't like to say it cost me a place. It's debatable, that one. It's easy to blame other people.'

In any case, with an attitude that, given the facts, can only be described as deeply philosophical, Self remembers the experience with affection. 'A lot of people have a laugh about it,' he says. 'It's just one of those things that happen. I've played with plenty of people who are bad golfers! And anyway, he's probably the most famous player I've played with, he's probably the most well known! And he was the worst!'

Gary Dermot was equally sanguine. As Maurice was whisked away, he turned to Self and raised one eyebrow: 'Well, that's one for the grandchildren.'

It was one for the papers as well. But though James Beau Jolley's twelve-shot salvo around Ormskirk would be recorded in journals of the press, the story was treated very much as an aside. Maurice's real media splash in 1990 would be made at the home of golf. That year, the Open would be held on the R&A's front lawn: the Old Course at St Andrews.

For the first time since the *Sunday People* took him to Royal Birkdale in 1976, Maurice G. Flitcroft made it to the Open proper. This time it was at the behest of *Today* newspaper, who paid him a whopping £600 for an alternative hole-by-hole guide of the Old Course. Maurice boasted impeccable credentials as a tutor. 'I know I am good enough to play in this tournament,' he insisted, 'but my clubs are ten years old and they've got metal fatigue.' Golf's most iconic venue was about to be deconstructed by the sport's greatest iconoclast in a comic tour de force.

HOLE 1 (370 yards, par 4)
Maurice's 7-iron would have necessitated using a driver for the second shot. 'I couldn't go wrong here, this fairway is so huge an idiot could hit it. The Swilcan

Burn in front of the green isn't a problem either. If I went in it, I'd drop out.'

HOLE 2 (411 yards, par 4)
'There's a toilet on every hole with all those gorse bushes. If I went in them that would be that. But the way I hit my driver, a shot 25 yards off line would be a bad one. Mind you, I often wondered if I should work on a fade or a draw. I reckon I could get up with a driver and 4 wood here.'

HOLE 3 (371 yards, par 4)
Three Open contenders were on the third tee with Maurice's Cumbrian accent battering their ears. The resulting 'sssh' was almost as loud. 'They have it too easy. When I practise I have my Alsatian Beau dancing round me, panting and barking. Maybe that's why I am not so good at chipping. I aim for the target but he jumps up and catches the ball. I could get my drive over that gorse, I am used to hitting over rubbish. Then it would be two good shots to the green.'

HOLE 4 (463 yards, par 4)
'I would play this as a par five. A driver and a 4-iron – I haven't got a 5-iron. Then it's a long pitch and I would hope to get up and down in two. I could putt well on these greens, although sometimes I don't have a clue how hard to hit them.'

HOLE 5 (564 yards, par 5)
Although all the trouble at St Andrews is on the right,

it was here that Maurice declared: 'This is a slicer's course. I'd take driver, 3-wood, 4-wood. I've never seen such hellish bunkers as these but if you go into them you must pay the penalty. The secret is not to be too ambitious.'

HOLE 6 (416 yards, par 4)
'A 4-wood from the tee to get over those bushes. I practise on Berkeley Common, where I have to hit over a road teeming with cars. This wouldn't worry me, you can't hurt a bush! Then it would probably be another 4-wood.'

HOLE 7 (372 yards, par 4)
'I've got something in common with Ian Woosnam – we both have a bad back. Why does Nick Faldo have a coach? I sort my own problems out. When I get home, I'll write a book with a few tips and pointers. Oh, this hole? A driver, 4-wood, 4-wood. Have I got that right?'

HOLE 8 (178, par 3)
'This green is so big, I might need a 4-wood instead of a putter. It would be a 3-iron from the tee, my 4-wood would go into the grandstand at the back.'

HOLE 9 (356 yards, par 4)
Disco-dancing son Gene departed for a beer. Maurice got out the Golden Virginia and Rizlas. 'Not bad, this one. But the third hole at Ormskirk is worse than this. Just think positive. A driver and a 6-iron. I haven't got a 5 and that is the Prince of Clubs.'

HOLE 10 (342 yards, par 4)
'The bunkers are no problem, I couldn't reach them. Then I would aim at the next set of bunkers and fade the ball into the green.'

HOLE 11 (172 yards, par 3)
'My 8-iron has got a rattle in it, so I don't use that one. With a following wind, this would be a 3-iron. Look at that green, perfect surfaces are foreign to me.'

HOLE 12 (316 yards, par 4)
We are spotted by two R&A officials. 'That's Flitcroft!' is the hushed response. 'They have no sense of humour,' says Maurice. 'I'm like Clint Eastwood, recognised wherever I go. Us stars like to stand out. Greg Norman is quite good but he hits wayward shots as well. I know what he goes through. I've been under that pressure myself. A driver and 4-wood at this one.'

HOLE 13 (425 yards, par 4)
'I'll play safe and go with the 4-wood. Then another 4-wood, dropping it short of the green and just let it run down into the hole for an eagle two.'

HOLE 14 (567 yards, par 5)
One of the classic par fives in Championship golf. 'It's only frightening if you want to get on in three.' Mark Roe and US star Mark McCumber invite Maurice under the ropes. 'At last I am on the fairways of St Andrews.' He turns to McCumber: 'I've seen you on the telly. I've been on too.' McCumber looks hard at

Maurice. 'What, in cartoons?' Mark Roe fills Maurice's mouth with toffee before a muffled: 'Driver, 4-wood, 4-iron, taking care to avoid Hell Bunker.'

HOLE 15 (413 yards, par 4)
'I think in terms of flying my 4-wood 200 yards, so I should clear the bunkers. Then I'll go for the green with my 4-wood. After watching Roe and McCumber, I'll go for it.'

HOLE 16 (382 yards, par 4)
The R&A clubhouse comes into view. 'It looks unbalanced to me, a bit like its occupants. I'd be annoyed if I went out of bounds here, so I'll go to the left, followed by a low fade with the 4-wood. I've practised hitting those shots like Lee Trevino. But I prefer my own technique.'

HOLE 17 (461 yards, par 4)
Maurice clambers up a grandstand to get a better view of the most famous tee shot in golf. 'I would take the direct line over the hotel on the right. Don't steer it, hit it. The Road Hole bunker? The answer is not to go in it. I'll lay up short with a 4-wood and run the ball onto the green. It's a tricky shot, but I've practised similar ones.'

HOLE 18 (354 yards, par 4)
'An easy tee shot. I'd hit a soft drive left and soft 4-iron to run onto the green.' What about the Valley of Sin in front of the green on that side? 'I would put an

*extra bit of top spin on the second shot. That would
solve the problem. Next year? Yes, I'll be back. I've
already started growing a beard.'*

Having compared himself favourably with other
world-famous celebrities such as Greg Norman, Nick
Faldo, Ian Woosnam and Clint Eastwood, it could be
argued that Maurice had totally lost the run of
himself. Then again, it was simply inarguable that he
did possess star quality: when he turned up to meet
journalist Bill Blighton to write the piece, the
announcement of his arrival emptied the press tent in
seconds, as every single hack raced to meet the famous
Flitcroft.

Jock Howard, writing for *Golf World* magazine,
watched on in awe: 'Every big-name golfer was at St
Andrews that year, from the best players of the time
in Faldo and Norman, to the legends like Jack Nicklaus
and Arnold Palmer. But Maurice Flitcroft was the only
man to completely empty the press room. It was unbe-
lievable.' Howard would later report that Maurice was
'accompanied by a man masquerading as his agent'.
The man – Troy Atlantis, aka Gene Flitcroft –
demanded 'a couple of notes' from every journalist
who wanted to talk to Maurice. Sometimes he got his
money; sometimes he didn't, and Maurice talked
anyway. 'It slightly tarnished my whole image of him,'
remembers Howard, 'because he was a bit of a hero,
and the fact that he was now asking for readies to
open his mouth, it slightly got to me. But I suppose
he had to earn some money somehow.'

One person Troy Atlantis didn't demand money from for services rendered was Lee Trevino. The 1971 and 1972 Open Champion was waiting for his caddy to join him for an informal practice round, when Gene brazenly asked him if he could carry his clubs. 'Sure thing,' the irrepressibly cheery Trevino smiled, allowing Gene to caddy for him for nine holes while his usual bagman put his feet up. Whether Trevino took any advice from Troy Atlantis on matters such as club selection, line, yardage or strategy is unknown – but it is worth pointing out that he ended the tournament tied for twenty-fifth place, no mean feat for a fifty-year-old player. 'Coincidence?' asks Gene. 'I think not.'

For Maurice, however, the curtain was coming down on a brave golfing career. He had hoodwinked the R&A one final time at Ormskirk as James Beau Jolley, but despite his public insistence that he'd be back the following year, everyone secretly knew the chances of him getting another tee time were practically non-existent. By running circles round the R&A for fourteen years, he'd alerted them to every possible route into the Open, and enabled them to close all the loopholes.

'He did us a favour in the end,' admits Sir Michael Bonallack today. 'As a result of him in particular we tightened the conditions of entry. I think it was a good thing in a way because it made us look at the conditions of entry and make sure that it didn't happen again.' It was an admission of past failings – and, therefore, extrapolating with the cold logic much favoured by our hero, effectively an official R&A admission of defeat. Defeat at the hands of Maurice Gerald Flitcroft.

Hole 18: Maurice G. Flitcroft: the real Car Park Champion

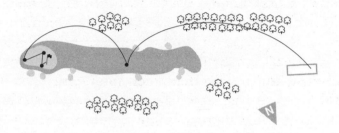

MICHIGAN HAD festooned Maurice with some overdue plaudits from the golfing establishment, but Ormskirk brought him some much-needed closure with it. Not only had he bodyswerved the R&A one last glorious time, he'd also – in his own mind, at least – finally proven his sporting ability to the world on the big stage. He had, after all, nearly eagled the second, even if he did end up carding a bogey on the hole. 'I think I can hold my own with any of them now,' the sixty-one-year-old told the *North West Evening Mail*, days after being bundled off the course. 'If I was paired with someone like Seve Ballesteros, I wouldn't be over-awed.'

His work was, to all intents and purposes, complete. The Open was now closed to the likes of him, almost single-handedly as a result of his relentless fourteen-year campaign, which had pulverised the R&A's old defences and forced the implementation of entry mechanisms so complicated, they'd have flummoxed the scientists constructing the nuclear submarines in the shipyards where Maurice used to work. He'd become infamous in British establishment circles, but a folk hero to common hackers worldwide. A much-loved figure, he was indelibly linked to the Open story, his record score of 121 unlikely ever to be matched. He was certain to be remembered years after Keith Mackenzie and the like had been forgotten.

But Maurice was never likely to go gently into that good night while there was still a little raging to be done. It was almost as though a higher being, some mischievous golfing deity, was aware of one last loose end to be knotted, one piece of unfinished business for Maurice to attend to before he could enjoy his retirement.

Over the course of his professional golfing career, Maurice had managed to get himself banned from both Barrow and Furness golf clubs. They were absolute no-go areas, Maurice having enjoyed blistering arguments with blazered gents frequenting both establishments. It gave him an impressive 66.6667 per cent strike rate of local clubs, albeit one that had arguably hindered his progress as a touring professional over the years. Only Dunnerholme remained open to him in the locale.

It was April 1992, and the Flitcroft household was bursting at the seams. Michael, Jean's son and

Maurice's stepson, was up from London for the Easter break. Maurice's nephew Alex, a corporal in the paratroopers, was also visiting for a few days. Michael had taken up golf in the early eighties, becoming a more-than-competent player, and had put his clubs in the back of his MG sports car in the hope of getting a game with the auld legend.

Maurice and Michael decided they would visit Dunnerholme on Maundy Thursday, with the weather forecast to be good. Maurice asked his nephew if he'd like to join them. Alex replied that he'd be glad to, but as he'd never played the game before, perhaps caddying may be the best way to join in. Gene and James also expressed their wish to play, so with a four-ball complete, a tee-off time was booked. And so was a date with destiny.

It was the perfect morning for golf. The sun was shining, the sky was a brilliant blue, there was a slight nip in the air to keep you on your toes, and the dew promised not to outstay its welcome. The stage was set. All four players hit good opening drives, Maurice's nearly reaching 200 yards, an unprecedented clack for a man used to seeing his opening stroke fizz into thickets 80 yards up the track. As they walked up the fairway, Maurice began to ruminate on the beauty of the game, riding the serotonin rush caused by his good opening drive. '*This* is what the game is all about,' he mused, observing his sons and stepson heaving at their second shots. (And before Maurice had hit his, too, which was even sweeter!) For perhaps the first time in his life, he was playing golf, on a golf course – totally stress-free! There was no crowd to follow the

freak show, no need to hot-tail it from R&A blazers
determined to chase him away, no hectically accu-
mulating score to worry about, no headlines to fret
over, and no migraine making the inside of his skull
feel like a collapsed supernova. It was idyllic: just
Maurice and his boys, the sun warming his cheeks,
the scent of freshly cut grass filling his nostrils, and
the mellifluous sound of the waves lapping the beach
nearby. It was as close to heaven as a man could get.
What could possibly go wrong?

Maurice eyed up his second shot. 'Seven-iron,
please, Alex.' He took aim. Perhaps without the pressure, I will finally show my promise, he thought. He
swung the club through the spring air in a smooth
arc – and shanked the ball into a caravan site separ-
ating the first fairway and the beach. He heaved that
special sigh he knew all too well – the sigh all amateur
golfers emit when they realise that today won't be the
day of their miracle round. Maurice let out that sigh
good and loud before thrashing the hosel of the club
deep into the ground, like a demented axeman, to
disperse the anger like earthed electricity.

That ritual over, Maurice began to laugh. Michael,
Gene and James giggled, too, taking turns to nudge
their balls haphazardly up the fairway. 'I have always
believed that fun is what the game is all about,'
observed Maurice. 'Away from the professional tour,
that is,' he added, reminding us of his credentials.
The five all laughed and giggled, this group of men,
this family of golfers laughed and laughed and slapped
each other on the back.

But back on the first tee, an ominous cloud was gathering. Seeing a five-ball wandering down the first fairway is the one sight guaranteed to send your average club member into paroxysms of rage and fury. Observations in the mild golf-humour style – 'It's like a chimpanzees' tea party!'; 'Is the circus in town?'; 'I thought the Marx Brothers were dead!' – soon give way to darker rumblings – 'Christ, this'll be a five-hour job'; 'Are they members? I bet they haven't paid a green fee'; 'Someone should inform the secretary' – as each member hurls a log onto the communal fire of discontent. It would be considered acceptable if the team of five were visiting dignitaries: the Duke of Edinburgh, perhaps, or Terry Wogan. Or possibly, at a push, a visiting low-ranking pro enjoying a little swing-loosener with friends. But this group clearly contained no such exalted figures. They were unkempt, not a Pringle jumper or pair of Farah slacks between them, and they hit the ball like . . . well, like Maurice Flitcroft. Word soon got back to the corridors of power within the clubhouse: something had to be done.

A member was sent on reconnaissance with a remit to encourage the Flitcroft party to hurry themselves along. When he reached the second tee, he found the group enjoying an early rest. Scarcely believing his eyes at the sight of a picnicking fivesome, he asked if he could play through, informing them that there were a number of two-balls coming up behind. 'I'm pretty sure they'll need to play through, too, seeing as how you have such a large group,' he blustered.

All of the group smiled, nodded and waved the fellow through politely. All, that is, apart from Maurice.

'When my companions waved him through I remarked, in a spirit of mischievousness, and to show off my intimate knowledge of the rules of etiquette, that single players had no standing,' recalled Maurice. 'It was not meant to be taken seriously, but my companions, taken in by the seriousness of my acting, began to remonstrate with me. I had to assure everyone that I was only joking. I don't know what the single player thought as he teed off.' We will never know for sure, though it is not difficult to speculate.

Team Flitcroft ambled around the next few holes incident-free until the seventh, when Maurice remarked that the two-ball behind them seemed to be 'more interested in catching us up than playing golf'. With not a jot of reluctance, they let those two players play through, then another duo at the eighth, 'as we stopped for a break and a flask of tea'. Yet another two-ball was waved through at the ninth. So far, so good, even though Maurice had noted his party being shot some familiar looks, ones not a million miles from the dismissive up-and-down glances he received when playing at Formby. But he had been suffering those slights for well over a decade, and by now it was water off a duck's back. He resolved to enjoy the rest of the round, and to hell with the attitudes of others.

Sadly, the climate was closing in on Maurice, and the heavens would open on the tenth tee, where a heinous crime was committed. A good drive is required on the hole to clear a large marshy ditch running across the front of the tee. Maurice and his playing partners all sent their tee shots soaring over the valley and onto the fairway. It was at this point that Alex asked if he could try a shot; he had been carting Maurice's bag around the course, after all. Maurice was quick to agree to his request, teed Alex up a ball, and gave him a quick tutorial on the art of creaming a good drive. Alex seized the driver and let fly, only to miss the ball entirely, as newcomers to the game are apt to do. But after several more swipes, swishes and wild fresh-air misses, Alex finally connected with the ball, sending it fizzing low into the ditch, out of sight. He gave the driver back to Maurice with a smile, and picked up his bag to resume his caddying duties.

A split second after the ball disappeared from view, however, a sound pierced the morning air, a sound that Maurice could only describe as 'a bull bellowing in pain'. What was the source of this guttural bovine holler? The mystery was soon solved.

'Oi, you there! Get off the course!' There, behind them, on the top of the steep bank that separated the ninth green and tenth tee, was the source of the brouhaha. It was a superannuated club member, provoked into action after seeing Alex's errant drive. The man had clearly been keeping an eye on the Flitcrofts, waiting for any old excuse to intervene. Seeing the caddy striking a shot gave him exactly that: in the eyes of the law, the group had officially become a five-ball, and therefore in breach of the rules of golf. Finally, the puffed-up pedant had irrefutable proof that these men were louts, and hopping around wildly on one foot in the cartoon style, all the while throwing his arms around in semaphore shapes, the irate member yelled at the top of his voice: 'Get off the course! Five-balls are not allowed!'

'The man must be out of his tiny mind,' Maurice remarked to his companions. 'Ignore him.' Which is exactly what they did as they began to search the ditch for the offending lost ball. Maurice nevertheless furtively glanced up, expecting to have to wave the bellowing bull through once he'd reached the tee, but to his surprise he found that he, along with his playing companion, were suddenly nowhere to be seen. They had obviously given up shouting, and walked in. Maurice thought nothing more of them.

The rest of the round was played without incident or distraction. The good humour returned, as balls soared into the wide blue skies, left, right and sometimes even down the centre. Tea was drunk, soup and sandwiches were devoured, and on the eighteenth green, after the final putt had hit the back of the cup, the five members of the Flitcroft group shook hands and hugged, as only folk who've just enjoyed an eventful eighteen holes can.

But Bellowing Bull and his companion did not share the *joie de vivre* that had enveloped the Flitcroft clan. They had been so infuriated at the sight of five men slowly shuffling around the course that they had walked in after nine holes in a mad funk, and had spent the last two hours working each other into an etiquette-defying frenzy in the men-only bar. Seeing

Maurice and his merry men heading from the eighteenth green towards the car park, they scuttled out of the bar, leaving their warm gin and tonics behind, to instigate a confrontation.

'They thought we were playing in a five-ball,' recalls James, 'which we weren't. Alex was just caddying. Yeah, he'd had a shot, but so what? We would have let them through but they just stormed off.'

A heated exchange kicked off between the parked cars. 'The irascible duo,' as Maurice called them in his memoir, 'came out of the clubhouse, ignored my companions, and headed straight for me.'

EXT. CAR PARK, DUNNERHOLME GOLF CLUB
BELLOWING BULL: Hold on there! You lot! Hold on!
MAURICE: Can I help you?
BULL: You certainly can.

[The Bull pushes Maurice in the chest with his hand.]

BULL: What did I say to you? Five-balls are not allowed! I said, leave the course. Why didn't you leave the course?

[Maurice's left eye begins to twitch involuntarily. He decides to ignore the physical discourtesy he has just suffered, in favour of a peaceful resolution.]

MAURICE: We weren't a five-ball. The lad was caddying, he hit one shot, no need to get your knickers in a twist.

[Gene, James, Michael and Alex have assembled behind Maurice.]

MAURICE: It's OK, lads, let's just go home, eh?

[Maurice turns to close the boot of his car but the Bull 'dances' in front of him and places his hand on Maurice's chest once again.]

BULL: *Not before we've finished with you, you won't.*

[Maurice's patience snaps and he swishes the arm away.]

MAURICE: *All right pal, that'll do!*
BULL'S COMPANION [stepping into the fray]: *Hey! We'll have none of that!*
MAURICE: *You'd be better to address that remark to your friend here.*
BULL'S COMPANION: *Don't think we don't know who you are.*
MAURICE: *And who am I?*
BULL: *Maurice Flitcroft. The Open joke.*
BULL'S COMPANION: *The hacker. The bloody idiot.*
MAURICE [puffing up his chest]: *That is correct, I am he. I am the Open joke, as you say. But by the looks of your swings, you're hardly a pair of Severiano Ballesteroses yourselves. If you want any tips, you know where to find me.*

[With a showbiz flourish, having ended on a high note, Maurice signals to the boys that it's time to go. He opens the door to his car.]

BULL: *Now it's my turn to tell you who I am! I'm on the committee of this golf club and if I were you I'd watch what you say to me!*

[The Bull places his palm on Maurice's car door, stopping the owner opening it. Maurice slaps the hand out of the way and spins around. He blocks another attempted push on his chest with a right forehand parry, before delivering a sharp open left-handed slap to the cheek. It is a dignified sally, especially considering it's the first time he's laid a hand on a member of the golfing establishment, despite being goaded by them for fourteen years.]

MAURICE: *If you're on the committee, you'd do well to mind your manners.*
BULL: *I'll show you manners!*

[An untidy scuffle ensues, described by Gene as 'nothing too serious, handbags at ten paces really'. The two are eventually pulled apart.]

MAURICE: *I don't mind telling you, sir, that I'm not a fan of your attitude. I'm not being taken in by this humbug. Take yourselves off!*

[Maurice opens his car door once again, this time unencumbered by the Bull, who is being escorted back to the clubhouse by his companion.]

BULL [turning to have the last word]: *And I don't mind telling you, sir, that you will not be welcome at this club in the future.*
MAURICE [a wry smile playing across his face]: *You do surprise me.*

And so Maurice had finally succeeded in being banned from all three of his local courses. Yet it's hard not to sympathise with him on this occasion. It's all very well for golf commentators to bemoan the epidemic of slow play at club level, but for some who love the game – and for those who can't afford to play that often – it's a chance to spend some time with family and friends. So why not spread it out over an extra hour or two?

After all, it wasn't a Saturday or Sunday, they weren't holding up a competition, and there wasn't a moment during the round where they didn't wave players through as soon as they could. As for Alex taking a shot, what junior hasn't started the game by caddying for his dad, mum, aunt or uncle, and being allowed the odd shot now and again?

'The problem was that Dad was very recognisable and club golfers didn't want him at their club,' offers James. 'Like that fella in the car park. He knew who Dad was and that's why he picked a fight with him. He probably wanted to go back in the bar and say he's just kicked Maurice Flitcroft out of the club. It's a good story, innit?'

Michael, too, recalls the scene with some amazement. 'They were quite drunk, those guys, and they were goading him, prodding him in the chest, looking for a reaction. He would have been well within his rights to snap. I'm amazed that he didn't, in a way. Remember, he used to be a boxer; he could have sparked them out in two seconds without batting an eyelid. But he didn't. He knew there was a crowd of people watching from the bar, and he didn't want to rise to the bait.'

Nobody knew it at the time, but on that holy Thursday, Maurice Gerald Flitcroft had played his last-ever eighteen holes of golf. It was a sad end to a career, but then Maurice had spent his entire golfing life taking on the system, a one-man class war waged in the sporting arena. So it was somehow apt that a journey started in August 1974 ended there, eighteen years later, in a club car park, doing battle with those who would rather walk the corridors of power than walk the golf course.

Epilogue: The Nineteenth Hole

Sensing an air of *fin de siècle* after James Beau Jolley's performance at Ormskirk in 1990, followed by his barnstorming appearance at St Andrews the following week, when he sashayed into the Home of Golf and mobilised the press tent like a star of silver-screen-era Hollywood, Maurice eased off the gas and started to go through the motions. Requests for entry forms were regularly dispatched to R&A HQ, but not with much conviction, a fact betrayed by the signal lack of any innovative psuedonyms; signing the letters off in his own name, or that of James Beau Jolley, was the combative equivalent of sawing halfway through his 4-wood before he walked onto the first tee, or rubbing sandpaper all over his Titelists. Attempts were made to enter the European Open again, but never followed up with any gusto. Demands for sponsorship were put in to blue-chip companies, but for what reason even Maurice didn't know any more. He had a new perspective on life, and simply could no longer be bothered. Like many a big-name sportsman before him, Maurice decided it was time, after a long career devoted to the pursuit of excellence, to relax with his family, and in particular a new addition: James's daughter, his granddaugher.

'Bianca Rose captured my heart from the moment I set eyes on her sweet adorable face, cradled her in my arms and marvelled at the perfection of her tiny hands and feet,' he wrote. 'Her beautiful red hair, blue eyes and peach complexion led me to refer to her as "my Technicolored dream". (Bianca is now an actress, following Maurice into the Barrow newspapers recently for her starring role in a local theatre production.) He was clearly enjoying his new role of grandfather but, like many ageing sporting legends before him, he was about to experience something of an unexpected Indian summer.

In the spring of 1993, Lewine Mair, the golf correspondent of the *Daily Telegraph*, called out of the blue and invited Maurice for a round of golf, at a local course of his choosing. 'Having pointed out that I was persona non grata at the main local courses in my area,' recalled Maurice, 'it was arranged that we played at Windermere, where I was given to understand they would be pleased to accommodate us.'

The rest of the negotiations had, however, not gone without hitches, Maurice demanding 'appearance money' the *Telegraph* were not keen to pay. 'I thought the *Telegraph*'s attitude rather stingy,' Maurice would say. 'I didn't think much of their argument that they didn't pay such luminaries of the golfing world as Jack Nicklaus and Nick Faldo for interviews, because while on the one hand being millionaires they didn't really need the money, on the other they did have some obligations to their agents, sponsors and tournament organisers to fulfil; whereas I, with no such obligations but struggling to get by on Income Support, welcomed the opportunity to make a bit of extra money in order to ease the burden of paying our bills.' Proving that even though Maurice had taken his foot off the pedal, the pipe dream never quite died, he added: 'Should there be any money left over, then I might use it to cover my Open expenses.' The *Telegraph* offered to cover his basic expenses for the Windermere jaunt, plus pay for his lunch. Maurice officially accepted the invitation. It was on.

Maurice took Gene along with him to caddy. Lewine Mair was quite taken with the pair's entrance. 'As soon as they got to the club,' she says, 'they took one look at Gene and said he couldn't go out on the course dressed like that. Then he went and put on this awful England shellsuit from the football World Cup, and I personally thought it looked a lot worse. But it had the right degree of collar, or whatever you're meant to have, and so apparently that made it OK.' For his part, Maurice was sporting an ensemble of lightweight mulberry-coloured designer slacks and toning polo shirt, topped off with an eye-catching red peaked cap patterned with green stars, a present from James. He had, it is almost totally unnecessary to report, left no time to warm up and very little to compose himself.

Even so, Maurice was quite pleased with his opening drive, which Mair would describe in her eventual article, GATECRASHER STILL SETS SIGHTS ON BEING INVITED TO THE PARTY, as being 'unexpectedly

good, a little high and a little left, but entirely
respectable'. Mair recalls today that he 'never looked
like a golfer, oh no. He wore a very odd hat. It had
sort of earflaps hanging down the side. He looked very
odd. But his opening drive wasn't nearly as bad as I
thought it would be. That surprised me.' Had there
been a bit of distance on it? 'Oh no! I think it had
gone about 140 or something. It was downhill, I think.'

Maurice would soon career out of control, the
wheels clanking off. On the second hole, a par three,
he pulled out his driver. 'There was a notice warning
of vehicles on the adjacent road,' Mair would report.
'By the time Gene had finished drawing our attention to it, there was no question as to where his father
would hit.'

Mair picks up the reminiscence. 'Gene had said,
"Dad, you need to read this". And the dad read it.
So the ball went careering down the road, and it
finished at the bottom of the road, parallel to the hole,
out of bounds. And the son consoled the father by
saying: "You're all right, Dad, you're pin high!"'

'They had a row about two holes later. Maurice hit
his first into a bush, and had taken about eight shots
to get to the edge of the green. He pulled out his
wedge, but Gene argued that he couldn't use his
wedge, and wanted him to putt instead. After a lot of
shouting at each other, the father finally said: "I know
what I'm doing!" And the son said, "No, you don't,
Dad."'

After nine holes, Mair was nine up. ('I never
mentioned that in my piece, but I think enough water

has now passed under the bridge,' she quips.) Having got all she needed for her article, Mair suggested the pair go in at the turn. Maurice, for whom opportunities to play on a proper course were limited, was initially eager to continue, but quickly changed his mind when he was informed that the clubhouse would no longer be serving lunch by the time they had played eighteen holes.

Maurice had enjoyed the experience, though predictably there would be tremors of aftershock. Mair's *Telegraph* piece, published just before the 1993 Open, carried the sub-heading LEWINE MAIR SEES 12 BALLS DISAPPEAR IN A ROUND WITH THE SCOURGE OF THE R&A. While precedent suggests the lost-ball count was surely accurate, or at least in the right ballpark – Mair 'distinctly remembers one disappearing into a bush, another down a road' on the opening two holes alone – Maurice took umbrage at the slight.

'The implication was obvious,' he said, 'but the truth of the matter was that anyone, regardless of ability, playing golf on the beautiful and challenging Windermere course with its humps and its hollows, its hills and its mounds, its trees and its valleys, its blind tee shots on some holes and blind second shots on others, would see as many if not more balls disappear from sight. Members of a three- or four-ball match, as opposed to a twosome, would see a proportionately larger number of balls disappear from sight.'

Maurice was also unhappy that his expenses – a claim for three new grips, a glove, a fee for Gene and, coincidentally, a dozen golf balls – were not met by the *Telegraph*, who simply ignored his claim form. Little did Maurice know, however, that he was up on the deal in terms of karma: Michael Bonallack and the R&A were disgruntled at seeing their 'scourge' in the papers yet again, the sports desk at the *Telegraph* taking receipt of a long whine via telephone from Fife which the subject of the piece would have considered music to his ears.

The attention in the *Telegraph* rekindled Maurice's spirits. He began to apply for the Open again with some of his old verve, asking for entry forms under the ostentatiously ludicrous name of Count Manfred von Hoffmenstal, and the equally ridiculous but entirely delicious Arnold Palmtree. Neither application was successful, but then that really wasn't the point: Maurice had convinced himself that the requests would have rattled some cages at the R&A, a conclusion it is hard to argue with. He was rarely happier than when teasing The Man.

He wasn't so happy, however, when his perfectly serious request to play in the 1995 Seniors Open was flatly refused. While his Open entries were now played solely for laughs, Maurice was deadly serious about the Seniors Open, having decided that winning the title was within his scope, reasoning that as he had come to the game late, he might be somewhat 'fresher' than the old pros who'd worn themselves out trudging the fairways since they were eight. He wrote to Michael Bonallack requesting entry forms for both the 1995 Open and the Seniors pot. Bonallack responded with a letter explaining that the R&A saw no point in sending him any forms, as he did not meet the qualification criteria.

'Well, that is not my view,' began Maurice, his heckles raised, in a breathless letter sent to several Barrow solicitors.

What I do believe is that his refusal to send me the entry forms I requested is because of a grudge that the R&A have borne towards me since 1976, when I entered the Open as a professional and shot the highest recorded score in Open history, and the press had a field day and, though it wasn't my wish, I got a great deal of publicity, much to the chagrin of the R&A.

Since then because it was made clear that an entry from me was unlikely to be accepted, I have had to resort to the use of a variety of pseudonyms in order to try and gain entrance to the Open.

I am clearly being denied the opportunity to qualify and would like to do something about it, such as sue them for discriminating against me.

If I could get legal aid, would you be interested in taking up my case?

It was the equivalent of a last token haymaker sent swinging through fresh air in vain at the tail end of a pub brawl already lost. None of the solicitors Maurice contacted were energised to take up his cause. Maurice's abortive attempt to get into the 1995 Open and Seniors Open would be the final rockets of a two-decade battle with the R&A.

The date provided Maurice with a pleasing symmetry to his career, one that would tickle him in his dotage. He was born in 1929, the same year as Arnold Palmer. Both men would go on to have a profound influence on the history of the Open: Arnie ensured it would always be recognised as one of the world's four major events, while Maurice gave the tournament a human face, adding splashes of colour, character and humour to a sport saddled with an elitist, stuffy reputation. He'd also proved to the world that anyone could reach the Open if they really wanted it enough, a call to arms to grass-roots players seemingly beyond the R&A's ken. So it was a cute coincidence that both men effectively took their final Open bows at the same tournament, the sixty-five-year-old Palmer pictured waving goodbye to the Open crowds as he stood on the tiny stone bridge over the Swilcan Burn, the creek that runs across the eighteenth hole of the Old Course at St Andrews.

Maurice went to ground for nearly a decade, though he continued to be mentioned in dispatches every year at the Open, whenever the latest poor soul had run up a high score in qualifying, or if some disaster had befallen a hapless professional. Perhaps the most traumatic – and therefore bleakly amusing – example came in 2000, when the 'notorious spectre of Maurice Flitcroft' was raised by Essex professional David Salisbury, who opened his qualifying round at Ladybank with a first-hole 7, followed it with an 11 on the second, then took himself into the trees on the third to cry before walking in.

Meanwhile over in the USA, Maurice's memory lingered on. The Maurice G. Flitcroft Spring Stag was still being played annually at Blythefield Country Club – as it is to this day – and the regard in which he was held had been illustrated when Bill Browne, the general manager, signed off a letter to Maurice: 'Remember, you and Jean will always have friends in Grand Rapids, Michigan, and I think I have a friend in England.'

'The Flitcroft' was also the name of a trophy regularly awarded to the winner of an annual tournament, the 'Schmidt', held at the Big Oak Golf Course in Geneva, New York State. The event was true to Maurice's philosophies. 'It's no big-time event, no charity named, nothing more than a reason to play golf together and perhaps relieve some friends of their extra cash in an honourable fashion,' explains one of the organisers, Herb Cooley, who along with friend Ben Gavitt had also once bottled a home-brewed wine commemorating their hero, a 1987 vintage called Chateau Maurice.

A legend running along the bottom of the Chateau Maurice label read: 'Means a quality product every time.' One was dispatched to Maurice, although a bottle was not attached to it. 'The US and English customs prohibit the transport of alcohol without special papers,' an apologetic missive from Ben and Herb explained. 'We hope you at least enjoy the label. Every participant in the Schmidt received one. Many haven't drunk it yet. Of course we had several extra bottles that were drank the night of the award ceremony.' Maurice appreciated the gesture greatly. His knowledge of export– import legislation sketchy, he assumed the pair had simply concocted an excuse not to send the booze over, and instead kept it to neck themselves. It was what he would have done, after all; the idea of the two half-cut as they posted the label Airmail kept him highly amused for weeks. He was touched, too, that Cooley and Gavitt had informed him how a 'large gallery in Geneva' vowed to support him always, whatever punishments the R&A meted on him.

The most bizarre tribute to the little man from Barrow is described with great pride by his sons. 'You know he had a club named after him in the basement of the World Trade Center,' James enthused. Some kind of golf society, one would presume? Gene delivers the sucker punch: 'No, it was a racquetball club, weirdly. The founder member was a fan of Dad's, so he called it the Maurice Flitcroft Racquetball Club. They got in touch, actually, and Dad was gonna go over there, but Bin Lid knocked it down, didn't he, the bastard. The club's no longer going.' So Osama Bin Laden's rap sheet grows apace: as well as causing the root-and-branch restructuring of the USA's post-millennium foreign policy, he is also responsible for the demise of surely the most egalitarian sports club in the history of racquet-based sports.

In 2000, Jean joined her husband in contented retirement. Being more used to public performance, Maurice kindly offered to pen his wife's leaving speech from Vickers, where she had worked as a secretary for so long. The short address was a typical comedy classic,

proving that even late-period Flitcroft possessed a heady
mix of pure romance and chippy pugnaciousness.

> *There are quite a few things I shall miss – the happy
> smiling faces that greet me first thing of a morning,
> the good-natured banter, and my lovely typewriter.
> When I told John* [her boss] *that I would like to take
> it with me when I retired, I hoped he would say, like
> the genie in Aladdin's lamp, 'your wish is my
> command', or being John, 'Jean, we will come to some
> arrangement', but he let me down. Perhaps I rubbed
> him up the wrong way.*
>
> *Joanne* [her successor], *a word of advice, keep your
> eye on the stationery cupboard, especially when Bob
> Taylor is about.*
>
> *I am looking forward to not having to get up early
> in a morning, but I am determined to make the most
> of the abundance of time that I may do with as I please.
> I shall be retiring from work but not from life. In fact,
> I see my new state as being a voyage of discovery of
> happiness and tranquillity, adventure and romance,
> peace and prosperity. I must say the thought leaves me
> a little bit shaken but I am sure I shall get used to it.*

Maurice and Jean's journey never took them far out
of Barrow. The money wasn't there. But they enjoyed
a retirement of cosy contentment on the insular peninsula nonetheless. It snoozed on until 2002, when Jean,
the sugar in Maurice's tea, dissolved away. Her last
stirring hit Maurice, James and Gene hard, as his
stepson Michael notes. 'Mum held that whole family

together,' he says. 'She was the rock, the matriarch. When she died, the three of them went to pieces. The twins were always a bit wild, but they really hit the booze after that. And Maurice fell to bits too.'

'He were never a big drinker, my dad,' adds James, 'but he started to enjoy the odd glass or two after that. I think, to be honest, he thought, What the hell? Something in him died too.'

A couple of years had passed when Jock Howard, the deputy editor of *Golf World*, who had witnessed Maurice in his pomp, holding court outside the press tent at St Andrews in 1990, arrived in Barrow. He had travelled north to interview Maurice, and saw the emptiness in his eyes. 'You could see he was still quite hurt about his wife,' says Howard. 'I sold the idea to my editor to do something on him, because I knew he was getting old and I'd heard some stories that he was quite ill. I just wanted to meet the guy before he died. So I went up there, and it's in the middle of nowhere, it's a very poor area. It's a very dark, dingy place. And he was ill. He had a few fags, despite the fact he had emphysema, and God knows what else. I was struck by how frail and ill he looked. But there was still that spark there of mischievousness. He was a very funny guy, obviously a very witty man.'

Maurice was afforded two spreads in the magazine, four pages, in a colour feature headlined, I COULD HAVE WON THE OPEN. He was pictured standing under industrial-grey skies outside his house, in a shapeless beige cardigan, slippers and socks, propped up against his bright red golf bag and clubs. 'Those were the things he'd used in 1983 and 1990, and they had shiny grips, just awful things,' says Howard. Maurice did indeed cut a fragile figure, a shadow of the man who once leapt from the top of diving boards, trees and shipyard cranes. But somewhere within the septuagenarian, the passion still burned.

'He said that if he got his game together, he might have a chance for next year's Open,' recalls Howard. 'But it was, "Well, actually, Maurice" . . . he was a funny man. He was very media savvy, is what I'm trying to say. He knew why we were there. He knew what was funny, which was that he reckoned he could win the Open, and that's why we came up, so he would tell us again. He knew what the papers wanted.'

Which didn't mean he was content to simply trot out the same old lines. The two highlights of the piece were inadvertent asides. Philosophising on instant celebrity in the modern age, he mused: 'I watch the TV a lot. But it pisses me off when you see people who have absolutely no skills or ability, making loads of money.' With no attempt made to conceal the fit of bitter pique, it was impossible not to feel sorry for a man who would have become a worldwide star, and made a fortune, had celebrity magazines and the internet been around in 1976.

Maurice was also asked why he had a pair of binoculars on the window. 'I've just been watching a woodpecker go down that tree,' he said, 'which is unusual for them, because they usually go up.' Howard spent the interview in a state of high amusement.

'He was obviously proud of what he had done,' says Howard, 'though I do wonder if he hammed up the crap golf thing a bit. Because that was the one thing that made him famous. He definitely would have got that message. He was very media savvy.'

Another two years passed, and with his health failing further, the seventy-five-year-old golfing legend archly announced his retirement from the sport. Lawrence Donegan – who, as the *Guardian*'s golf correspondent and former bass player for Lloyd Cole and the Commotions, was the sort of sport/music polymath Maurice had always dreamed of becoming – visited Maurice's Barrow home to record the end of a glorious era. He met a man finally at ease with the world, and with his own golfing ability.

'I was good, you know,' Maurice told Donegan, in his article FLITCROFT RUNS OUT OF STEAM. 'Much better than anyone would think. I had the ability but I was never on the golf course enough times to really give myself a chance. The other problem was I used to try too hard. Golf isn't like any other sports, where strength is the most important thing. In golf the club should do all the work but I didn't work that out until it was too late.' It was an achingly bitter-sweet revelation, albeit one his interviewer took with a pinch of salt.

'When he said to me, "I only just realised you don't have to hit the ball as hard as possible", well, he'd been doing it for thirty years, of course he'd worked it out a long time ago,' opines Donegan. 'What you've got to understand about him was, he was like a comic, he was one of those northern comics, everything was said with a glint.

'People say he was mad. He was not mad. He was a bright, bright guy. He was one of those people, they're so clever they appear mad. That's what I thought, really. I think he was a very ambitious guy. You don't stay committed to it for thirty years if you're not. I mean, when I went to the house, the golf clubs were still in the hallway. So it obviously wasn't some fad that had passed twenty years ago. He'd obviously been out there, doing something with them.'

But it was about that time. Eight months after that final interview, on 24 March 2007, Maurice Gerald Flitcroft died as a result of a lung infection. Like sacrificed slaves at a Norse funeral, Gene Pacecki, Gerald Hoppy and James Beau Jolley sailed away with him.

The R&A met the news of Maurice's passing with one long sniff, refusing to comment on the grounds that he had 'only played in qualifiers'. In death, as in life, they were determined to snub him. And in death, as in life, they had catastrophically misjudged the public mood. As befits the death of a major sporting figure – whether the R&A liked it or not, that's what Maurice was – the news broke big. Obituaries were published in *The Times*, the *Daily Telegraph* and the *Guardian*. The national press had signally failed to mobilise at the passing of Keith Mackenzie.

The news quickly winged its way around the world, and the tributes soon pinged back, like a Flitcroftian duck hook flying into a thicket then back out onto the fairway via a friendly branch. It was clear Maurice had struck a chord. 'He was a lovable rogue and his transgressions were small and inconsequential,' says Terry Moore, whose Michigan club to this day honour Maurice's memory. 'Admittedly, if I were in charge of one of those R&A Open qualifiers maybe I wouldn't have found his antics so amusing. But seen from afar, Maurice represented a bit of whimsy surrounding a game that can take itself far too seriously at times.'

'He just grabs the public spirit, and their dreams,' adds Jock Howard, 'and that's what the Open is all about, the fact that anyone playing golf supposedly who has a good enough handicap can win the thing.' Mark Wilson, the former *Express* golf scribe who covered Maurice's big break in 1976, bemoans the passing of a more innocent age. 'Tiger Woods may be a fantastic player,' he says, 'but golf today could do with an occasional Flitcroft to ease the boredom of reading about the millions being won.' Peter Haslam, who played with Maurice on his round with Peter Alliss back in 1984, agrees with the sentiment. 'Heaven forbid the time that people like Flitcroft are not around,' he suggests. 'It would be a shame. He was a character, he made a lot of people smile.'

Bill Elliott, the golf correspondent for the *Observer*, notes how 'Maurice's name has certainly gone down in history. He's remembered more than a lot of people who have finished second in the Open Championship, that's for sure.' Or even those who have finished first, and not just in the distant past either. Who can remember the name of the generic American who won the championship in 2009? (It was Steve Stricker . . . Oh no, sorry . . . Stewart Cink.)

Lawrence Donegan was impressed with how Maurice 'took on the R&A, this incredibly pompous organisation, and did it with a delightful light touch. Just beautiful, just great stuff.' Patrick Collins of the *Mail on Sunday* adds that, because of the R&A's actions, 'instead of being thought of as some sort of saboteur, he was suddenly regarded as a little man doing his best for us. God help us!'

Indeed it is difficult to work out what the hell the R&A, and especially Keith Mackenzie, thought they were playing at. As Maurice said himself, in his final interview, 'despite what the R&A thought, I never set out to belittle them. Golf's just a game and I tried my best. What did they need to get so uptight about?'

Well, they were understandably embarrassed about their vetting procedures being shown up again and again, from the mid 1970s right up until the computerised age of the 1990s. But did they really think an army of Flitcroft copycats were going to attempt to breach the Open's walls? In the final analysis, *not many people would want to do what Maurice did.* If you're not a good enough player, and you play off a handicap of twenty-eight, it's the stuff of nightmares to be suddenly thrust into the Open, with the world watching! No one is queuing up to emulate him.

The R&A's other main argument, that Maurice's hacking adversely affected his playing partners, does hold water – his presence arguably ruined the chances of Jim Howard and Dave Roberts at Formby – yet only one man who played with him in five qualifying rounds between 1976 and 1990 insists he was affected adversely. ('It's sad, maybe, but it still cuts deep,' says the player, who wishes to remain anonymous.) To this there is no answer except the following: American comedian Carol Burnett once said that 'comedy is tragedy plus time'. When it came to Flitcroft, that could be amended to 'comedy is tragedy plus distance'. As long as you were safely out of the way from Maurice's flaying, hacking swings, you could easily find his exploits amusing; if you were playing with him or behind him, you could understandably find them anything but.

But it's not much evidence with which to damn a man.

What the R&A, and other golfing conservatives, can't take away from Maurice was his ability to strike a chord with the ordinary golfer. For him, Maurice was a folk hero. He was doing what every amateur merely dreamed of doing. Not only that, Maurice was doing *worse* than the average club golfer would dare to imagine.

Or was he? More than one school of thought suggests Maurice wasn't too bad after all. Terry Moore, ex-editor of *Michigan Golfer* and architect of The Blythefield Mission, argues: 'He was never going to shoot in the seventies but, on an average course, certainly wasn't going to shoot a 121. That 121 might not be a bad score for someone playing a course for the first time, especially when you play from the back tees and the pins are tough. We have a tournament for journalists in the States at Pebble Beach where they put the tees and pins in US Open positions and there wouldn't be one of them break a hundred.'

Michael Harris, editor of *Golf Monthly*, agrees with this analysis. 'Do you know what,' he begins, 'a lot of category one and two, scratch-to-twelve golfers, might have got a bit caught out that day at Formby. I went to play Albridge, which is a course over in Essex that hosted local qualifying in 2009, and the greenkeepers set it up as they had it for the Open. And it was ridiculously difficult. And it was possible to rack up nines and tens easily on some holes. And I think there were some people who did shoot in the high nineties there. And that's with modern technology, and professionals right on top of their game. So looking back on it, shooting 121 in local qualifying is not beyond the bounds of possibility. Having said that, what would probably happen these days is that people would simply no return, just not hand in their card.'

Even so, for many, Maurice represented the hapless hacker. And the public loved him for taking a tilt at the prize with an unadulterated lust for life. 'Just looking at Mr Flitcroft's face makes my day,' a letter in the *Chicago Tribune* had read. Can any golf fan say that looking at Tiger Woods' face made their day? Especially after he'd just heard a photographer's shutter in the crowd? 'I would love to think there were a few young professionals around who shared his outlook that golf is so magical,' Peter Alliss said of Maurice in 1984, a point that stands today. Where are the players with smiles on their faces? Sergio Garcia wore a dazzling one – until he became spoiled by the riches bestowed upon him and treated every bad shot with a disdain borne of false entitlement. Tom Watson, on the other hand, smiled through his triumphs and disasters at Turnberry in the 2009 Open, an example to all young pros. 'Win or lose, it's important to remember it's only a game,' was his philosophy. It is one he shared with Maurice Flitcroft.

In the final analysis, Maurice's relationship with golf was unrequited. In 1974, he fell in love with a beautiful game. She made his heart beat, she was colourful, and she loved fresh air too. They shared the same taste in music, and she made his heart go 'boom ba de boom ba de boom, and so on'. But Maurice was from the wrong side of the tracks. He was shipyard fodder – and gals like golf aren't meant for shipyard fodder. To labour the *Romeo and Juliet* analogy, he didn't get on with her parents: the committee. Every time he went to call for her, they turned him away. None of his friends knew her, no one could introduce him to her, and so he never learned how to speak her language. They remained apart, he loving her, and her pushing him in the chest in a car park.

Maurice's main fault was that he was not Golfing Class, and never would be. Neither could he afford to play the game. But it never stopped him trying. How many times would Maurice have been told at school: 'If at first you fail, try and try again.' Or, more tellingly: 'It's not the winning that counts, it's the taking part.' At what age does it become wrong to keep trying? When should he have stopped reaching out for his dream? When he left school? When he turned twenty? Thirty? Forty-six? Seventy-five?

But it is one of many points seemingly lost for eternity to the miserable mandarins of the R&A. In 2008, a forty-four-year-old amateur called John Spreadborough carded a 99 in an Open regional qualifier at Musselburgh. His entry was above board, and neither of his playing partners complained, both assuming the poor man was simply suffering the mother of all bad days at the office. Yet an R&A apparatchik phoned around the news agencies asking them to play it down. Happily, just like Keith Mackenzie's frenzied call to Formby in 1976, the blazers were too late. Much to the R&A's chagrin, Spreadborough's pain had already been wired around the world. It was impossible not to conclude that, from beyond the grave, Maurice Flitcroft plans to haunt the golfing establishment for ever.

But fittingly, the last word should be left to old Maurice, who wouldn't have had it any other way. He would be delighted to see his name adorning the cover of a book, and cock-a-hoop that at least some of the words he painstakingly penned with his arthritic hand have finally made it into print. But no doubt the old fire would still burn in his belly, and soon enough we'd all end up facing each other in court. The reason? The sub-heading: 'The world's worst golfer.'

'Newspapers, books and magazines are wont to describe me as the world's worst golfer,' he wrote. 'But what other golfer in the world, given such a short amount of time and the circumstances in which I had to practise, would have done any better? Would Arnold Palmer, Seve or Jack Nicklaus or Nick Faldo or any of that lot have done any better? I don't know if they would.'

God's mercy
On the wild
Golfing Man

Postscript

In memory of Maurice Gerald Flitcroft, Jean Flitcroft and, sadly, Gene Van Flitcroft, who danced the last dance in January 2010. Like his dad, he lived life to the full and will be greatly missed.

Acknowledgements

Not a single word of this book could have been written without the invaluable assistance of Karen Storr and Trevor Kirkwood, family friends of the Flitcrofts who went way above and beyond the call of duty to ensure Maurice's amazing story was told. We owe them both a huge debt of gratitude.

James Harlequin Flitcroft and Gene Van Flitcroft (RIP) spoke warmly of their dad, and gave us a night out on the Gaza Strip we're unlikely to forget in a hurry. Heartfelt thanks to them – and the people of Barrow-in-Furness, a singular but strangely beautiful place – for that one.

Rowan Yapp, our editor at Yellow Jersey, was a bottomless pit of patience, especially in the face of loose interpretations of deadlines which bordered on freestyle jazz. Thanks also to her colleagues Matt Phillips, Louise Rhind-Tutt and Tom Drake-Lee, and Tristan Jones, who was so energised by our project that upon commissioning it he immediately left the publishing industry. Our agents at PFD – Annabel Murello, Tom Williams and Jessica Cooper – also did the patience thing in spades, while Alastair O'Neill, course designer extraordinaire, kindly kept his counsel despite being asked to redraw Maurice's 121 shots 121 times.

Tom Miller helped us get the ball rolling back in 2008, since when we've also received more than our fair share of encouragement and succour from Tom Cox, Kate Farnaby, Kerry Gilbert, Paul Farnaby, Isaac May, Alan McArthur, Rob Smyth, Arnold Widdowson, JJ Feild, Julian Barratt, Tom Meeten and Rowan Walker. Thanks also to Maurice's stepson Michael Flitcroft, everyone at guardian.co.uk, and the members of the Stage Golf Society.

Chris Barker, secretary of Formby Golf Club, treated our many enquiries with good humour and equanimity. Sands Johnson, club historian and the man who officially rubberstamped Maurice's record-breaking scorecard in 1976, helped us fill in at least as many gaps as Maurice took strokes, a truly Homeric effort.

Terry Moore, erstwhile editor of the Michigan Golfer, did likewise for Maurice's American adventures. Thanks across the pond also go to Dick Nelson of WGVU-TV, and Herb Cooley, Ben Gavitt and Russ Simon, the vintners responsible for Chateau Maurice.

Jock Howard at Golf World and Michael Harris at Golf Monthly were always on hand to help, as were many other top sportswriters and broadcasters, all of whom were equally generous with their time and advice: Lawrence Donegan, Bill Elliott, Marina Hyde, Patrick Collins, Peter Alliss, Leo Clarke, Tom Clarke, Jeff Connor, Peter Haslam, Bob Herbert, Lewine Mair,

Michael McDonnell, Malcolm Campbell, Nick Owen and Mark Wilson.

And in the world of golf (playing it, that is, and playing it properly) we must thank Gary Dermot, Jim Howard, Michael More, Mark Sharman, Ken Schofield, Neil Self – and Sir Michael Bonallack, former secretary of the R&A, who would have been well within his rights to tell us to bugger off at the mere mention of Maurice's name, but ever so kindly didn't.

Text and picture credits

Hot breakfast-based golf chat comes to you thanks to Moving Image Communications Ltd / TV-am. Maurice's guide to getting safely round Fife's finest comes courtesy of © *Today* 1990 / nisyndication.com.

Pictures are courtesy of *The North-West Evening Mail*, Getty Images, Bauer, Phil Sheldon Golf Picture Library, Northpix and MGN.

We have genuinely tried our best, really hard just like Maurice, to ascertain clearance for everything we have used. We think we have done that, but if anyone feels differently, please get in touch with us, as we'd love to sort it out. 'Us' being not *us*, technically, but Yellow Jersey. But they'll pass it on, and send their henchmen round to hoof us about the shop so we get the message.